W9-BIY-192

LOCAL AND REGIONAL ECONOMIC DEVELOPMENT: RENEGOTIATING POWER UNDER LABOUR

Local and Regional Economic Development: Renegotiating Power Under Labour

ROBERT J. BENNETT
University of Cambridge

DIANE PAYNE
University College Dublin

Aldershot • Burlington USA • Singapore • Sydney

HC
266.7
·B46
2000

Published by
Ashgate Publishing Limited
Gower House
Croft Road
Aldershot
Hampshire GU11 3HR
England

Ashgate Publishing Company
131 Main Street
Burlington VT 05401-5600 USA

Ashgate website: http://www.ashgate.com

British Library Cataloguing in Publication Data
Bennett, R.J. (Robert John), 1948-
    Local and regional economic development : renegotiating
    power under Labour
    1. Economic development projects - Government policy - Great
    Britain 2. Great Britain - Economic conditions - 1997-
    3. Great Britain - Economic conditions - Regional
    disparities 4. Great Britain - Economic policy - 1997-
    I. Title II. Payne, Diane
    330.9'41'0859

Library of Congress Control Number: 00-109123

ISBN 0 7546 1553 7

Printed in Great Britain by
Antony Rowe Ltd, Chippenham, Wiltshire.

Contents

List of Figures

List of Tables

List of Abbreviations and Acronynms

BCC	British Chambers of Commerce
BGT	Business Growth Training
BiTC	Business in the Community
BL	Business Link
BLNC	Business Link Network Company
BPIF	British Printing Industry Federation
BOTB	British Overseas Trade Board
BSI	British Standards Institute
CBI	Confederation of British Industry
CCTE	Chamber of Commerce Training and Enterprise
CNT	Commission for New Towns
DCMS	Department of Culture, Media and Sports
DE	Department of Employment (up to 1995)
DETR	Department of Environment, Transport and the Regions (from June 1997)
DES	Department of Education and Science (up to May 1992)
DFE	Department of Education (May 1992–95)
DfEE	Department of Education and Employment (from 1995)
DoE	Department of Environment
DoH	Department of Health
DSS	Department of Social Security
DTI	Department of Trade and Industry
EAS	Enterprise Allowance Scheme
EP	English Partnerships
ES	Employment Service
ETB	English Tourist Board
FE	Further Education
FEFC	Further Education Funding Council (for England)
FPB	Forum of Private Business
FSB	Federation of Small Businesses

GOR	Government Office of the Regions
HE	Higher Education
HEFCE	Higher Education Funding Council for England
HIDB	Highlands and Islands Development Board
HIE	Highlands and Islands Enterprise
HO	Home Office
HoC	House of Commons
IBA	Institute of Business Advisers
IBB	Invest in Britain Bureau
IiP	Investors in People
IoD	Institute of Directors
ISG	Implementation Strategy Group (for Business Link)
ITO	Industrial Training Organisation
LEA	Local Education Authority
LEC	Local Enterprise Company
LEN	Local Employer Network
LGA	Local Government Association
LLP	Local Learning Partnership
LLSC	Local Learning and Skills Council
LSC	Learning and Skills Council
MSC	Manpower Services Commission
NACETT	National Advisory Council for Education and Training Targets
NACRO	National Association for the Care and Rehabitation of Offenders
NAO	National Audit Office
NCVO	National Council for Voluntary Organisations
NDPB	Non-Departmental Public Body
NEDC	National Economic Development Council
NETT	National Education and Training Target
ND	New Deal
NDTF	New Deal Task Force
NFEA	National Federation of Enterprise Agencies
NHSE	National Health Service Executive
NLT	National Learning Target
NSTO	Non-statutory Training Organisation
NTO	National Training Organisation
NTTF	National Training Task Force
NVQ	National Vocational Qualification
OECD	Organisation for Economic Cooperation and Development
OFSTED	Office for Standards in Education

PBA	Personal Business Advisor
PYBT	Prince's Youth Business Trust
RDA	Regional Development Agency
RDC	Regional Development Commission
RDO	Regional Development Organisation
RPC	Regional Policy Commission
RSA	Regional Selective Assistance
SBS	Small Business Service
SDA	Scottish Development Agency
SE	Scottish Enterprise
SFS	Small Firms Service
SME	Small and Medium Sized Enterprise
SO	Scottish Office
SRB	Single Regeneration Budget
SSA	Standard Spending Assessment
TA	Trade Association
TEC	Training and Enterprise Council
TFW	Training for Work
TQM	Total Quality Management
TTWA	Travel to Work Area
TUC	Trade Union Congress
UDC	Urban Development Corporation
WBTA	Work-based Training for Adults
WDA	Welsh Development Agency

Executive Summary and Foreword

This book assesses the impact of change in local and regional economic development policy under Labour. It is based on extensive interviews with key decision makers in four areas of government policy:

- Regional Development Agencies (RDAs);
- New Deal local partnerships;
- Local Learning and Skills Councils (LLSCs) that replace TECs;
- Small Business Service (SBS) and Business Link (BL).

The book analyses the negotiation process that has developed in these four areas. It shows how different interests have combined or conflicted and who the final winners and losers have been. A resulting 'barometer' of change under Labour (Figure 9.1) displays a systematic shift against allowing economic interests to have key executive positions for economic development policy in favour of public sector control.

The research findings suggest that there are gaps in present policies that need to be tackled (chapter 9). From these the book identifies a way forward to unblock change and increase economic growth in the future (chapter 10). A summary of the key challenges for Labour policy is as follows:

- successful local and regional economic development needs improved integration between agents – what we term acting in 'concert' to develop a local economic capacity;
- local economic capacity needs greater emphasis on the endogenous capacity to respond to globalisation: what Michael Porter has argued are the institutional underpinnings of competitiveness; or what Rosbeth Moss Kanter calls the 'skills of collaborative advantage';
- despite the need for concerted action, local economic development policy continues to be fragmented with conflicting priorities between government programmes. This was recognised as 'a patchwork quilt of complexity

and idiosyncrasy' by an Audit Commission Report in 1989. Evaluation of policies 10 years later, by the Cabinet Office in 2000 and the Audit Commission in 1999, still finds a 'Labyrinth of programmes ... with fragmentation, duplication and a maze of strategies';

- Labour's approach has sought to change the 'governance regime', from which there have been some important benefits:
  - the potential for improved strategic focus at regional level through RDAs with business-led boards;
  - considerable volumes of previously unemployed participants in New Deal attached to the labour force;
  - a strong potential to overcome tensions between incentives for the unemployed by creating the single gateway for benefits, job centres and training through the ONE Service;
  - an important potential for economic benefits from drawing together of college-based training with the structures of work-based training in the new LLSCs;
  - improved focus of small business support policy within the Small Business Service.
- But there are considerable challenges still remaining:
  - more pluralism has increased the need for government to exercise strategic leadership;
  - the government's emphasis on 'what matters is what works' varies between different programmes;
  - an increased emphasis on 'accountability' has increased the public sector dominance in most policy areas;
  - the focus on individual government departmental performance has increased local fragmentation which is resulting in greater difficulties of joining-up between projects and initiatives;
  - this has been exacerbated by departments inventing a plethora of initiatives, local 'action zones'; and developing separation of training policy under LLSCs and the DfEE, from business support policy under SBS and the DTI, and from RDAs under the DETR.
- Our analysis of policy negotiations between agents shows a strong exchange process to have occurred in the setting up of RDAs, but a largely conflictual process imposed on local development agents and businesses in the case of New Deal, LLSCs and SBS. We conclude that these areas evidence attempts by government to exert a new form of state-led corporatism. We do not see these developments as a well-defined 'third way'.

- The chief changes of power under Labour have been between government departments. There is a strong impression that what has been chiefly achieved is a 'reshuffling of the furniture' of central government departmental power and responsibilities, largely in favour of Treasury, the DfEE, the Employment Service, and to a lesser extent DTI, at the expense of DETR. The overall pattern of utility change has been modest (Table 9.2).
- Where other agents have gained or lost, the changes have done little for economic improvement or increased endogenous growth, which appear relatively remote from most of what has happened under Labour. We demonstrate the truth of the statement by Douglass North, that 'political efficiency is not economic efficiency'.
- The Comprehensive Spending Review of July 2000 does little to overcome these deficiencies, and its renewed emphasis on targets will still further reduce local flexibility.
- We propose that economic development criteria can be met by government only by improving on present methods. We propose four main directions of change (chapter 10):
  1 further improving information exchange;
  2 improving the credibility of government commitments;
  3 offering still stronger government leadership and focus to strengthen business inputs; and
  4 filling gaps more effectively.
- Specific improvements suggested in local and regional economic development policy are listed fully in chapter 10. In summary they are:
  1 increase openness and consultation *before* as well as after the announcement of policy initiatives;
  2 recognise defects in structures to strengthen the economic view: increase further the proportion of business members on LLSCs; strengthen their quality on RDAs; embed the Better Regulation Task Force; maintain the strength of business leadership on the New Deal Task Force and improve it in local New Deal partnerships; and give all of these bodies greater financial flexibility;
  3 improve civil service private sector skills, align civil service training more closely with the general market for skills, radically reduce the need for specialist 'public sector' skills that are low in tradability and isolate government from the economy;
  4 develop credible commitment. Match rhetoric to reality in resourcing. Align objectives, guidance and targets with the resources available. Offer sustained commitment. Focus on the public purpose of

government initiatives, and leave the rest to the economic agents. Do not attempt to claim indirect effects of government on increasing GNP when the contributions cannot be measured and chiefly depend on business not government. Adjust the framework and targets of the Treasury's public service agreements for departments to focus on managerial effectiveness not unmeasurable impacts;

5   improve the opportunities for specialist exchange of economic information and give it greater weight. Ensure that consultations on design of policy involve a strong presence of economic and other interests, not merely departmental representatives. Be led by 'what really matters' outside of Whitehall in the economy and society. Key elements of this are the development of improved information gateways through enhanced intermediaries.

- Develop further the DTI's sectoral sponsorship model. Give it greater independence, higher profile staff and status, greater private sector leadership and stronger access to senior level government policy making.
- Develop sponsorship into a standing brief independent of ministerial initiatives.
- Apply the sponsorship model across *all* departments.
- Resource, staff and support the SBS as a strong independent intermediary. This requires urgent simplification of the role of SBS: *not* to 'represent SME interests at the heart of government', but to ensure that the most accurate information on SME issues is provided at the heart of government and that it is fully weighed.
- Give all of these intermediaries full access, across government, to the policy development stage as well as consulting on implementation;

6   realign the needs of 'accountability' with stronger representation of economic needs;

7   provide more flexibility in funding streams to allow greater flexibility on the ground, at the level of the individual initiative or project. Encourage the agents at the grass roots to identify and respond, not command or constrain what they can do;

8   recognise RDAs for what they are and align the 'spin' accordingly. They have the capacity to offer business leadership and partnership working at the regional level that can give a broad context and can shape strategic priorities at the local level. But their scope for specific action should not be exaggerated. Also clarify the issue of 'accountability' at regional level: recognise that the modest role of RDAs

does not need a complex architecture of elected assemblies, streamline existing regional Chambers;

9 clarify the trails of responsibility at regional level by abolishing the functions of Government Regional Offices. Rely on the strength of the local agents to respond to endogenous requirements, remove all the residual architecture that seeks to 'direct' change.

- The key changes we advocate are: (i) to give the agents supporting endogenous growth greater freedom to act: placing responsibility in the hands of those that are closest to the problem, backing them with resources and support, offering guidance and leadership, but accepting that the best outcomes will derive from flexibility case-by-case, project-by-project, place-by-place; and (ii) to develop new information gateways based on an enhanced structure of intermediaries, building on a sustainable and standing structure for bodies such as the Better Regulation Task Force.

In writing this book we have an enormous debt to many people. We would particularly like to acknowledge the time and input received from our many interviewees, most of whom have had to remain as confidential. Without these key informants our work would have been impossible. The software for calculation of the various policy negotiation gains and losses was licensed to us by the University of Groningen, Inter-University Social Science Centre. The work has received financial support through a Leverhulme Trust Personal Research Professorship. We are also grateful for the comments from Cambridge colleagues Paul Robson and Sian Bowen, for graphics by Phil Stickler and secretarial support from Virginia Mullins.

1 Renegotiating Local and Regional Economic Development

1.1 Introduction

This book focuses on the renegotiation of power in Britain between the agents that are concerned with local and regional economic development in the period since the election of the Labour government in May 1997. Local and regional economic development has been a long-running concern of both central and local government. The period covered by the Conservative governments from 1979 until 1997 saw many of the former economic development powers of the different agents abolished or modified. Labour was elected with a new agenda which emphasised a re-invigoration of the regional level, a stronger role for local government, greater emphasis on social objectives, a higher degree of consultation with key agents, and an emphasis on partnership between public and private interests. Nowhere more than in the fields of local and regional economic development has this agenda been as fully tested.

The book disentangles how the renegotiations between agents have operated. The interaction of agents has depended on their predisposition to influence government, their power to do so, and on their relative power to influence other interests and agents. We develop an approach that allows the process and outcomes of the negotiations between the agents to be examined. The methods used have been applied extensively in previous studies outside of Britain, for example to assess European Commission decision making,[1] government decision in a variety of countries,[2] and a variety of other areas. One of our main aims is to apply these negotiation models for the first time to a broad range of UK policy discussions. In the book we assess in detail how negotiations have developed in four case studies that cover the main areas of

---

1   Bueno de Mesquita and Stokman, 1994; Payne, 1999.
2   Stokman et al.,1985; Stokman and Van den Bos,1992, Payne et al., 1997.

1

policy change affecting local and regional economic development in the first three years of Labour's new agenda, up to mid-2000.

These case studies focus on:

- the establishment of Regional Development Agencies (RDAs);
- the development of the New Deal for the long term unemployed through local delivery partnerships;
- the replacement of Training and Enterprise Councils (TECs) by local Learning and Skills Councils (LLSCs); and
- the establishment of the Small Business Service (SBS) structure for local business supports delivered through Business Link (BL).

These policy developments focus on the key dimensions of local and regional development, respectively: physical regeneration infrastructure and inward investment (RDAs); labour market social inclusion and skills development (New Deal and LLSCs); small business startups and endogenous growth (SBS and BL).

The analysis we develop demonstrates how the policy objectives of each agent feed into the policy process that leads to the final outcomes for each of the case studies. We assess winners and loses. We demonstrate the extent of improvement achieved for economic development. And we also assess how alternative scenarios might develop in future negotiations. Because Labour's agenda is not fixed, but is conceived of more as an ongoing project,[3] understanding the shape of possible future developments is a crucial part of assessing how the local and regional economy will be influenced by public policy in the future. Each case study assesses in turn:

- the match of actual outcomes with each agent's preferred outcome;
- the winners and losers in each case;
- the extent to which the outcomes of Labour's changes have actually improved the economy;
- how alternative scenarios which gave more power to different interests might have improved the outcomes.

Our chief conclusions, developed in chapters 9 and 10, but presented in the executive summary at the start of this book, indicate that whilst considerable contributions to local and regional development are likely to be achieved as a

---

3 See Philip Gould, 1998, *Unfinished Revolution*.

result of the reforms developed under Labour, there has been a loss of strategic vision, increased fragmentation, and an erosion of economic focus. There is thus still a long way to go before a fully effective institutional structure will be in place that gives a greater assurance that long term economic and social objectives will be secure. In chapter 10 we indicate the key improvements needed.

1.2 Local and Regional Economic Development

Local and regional economic development concerns the development of resources and wealth, employment, and social opportunities at the sub-national level. Generally the *local level* is associated with local labour markets and/or local networks of inter-business relations. This is also the level at which operate the key agents of local government and many social and voluntary sector bodies, as well as many small business support organizations. The *regional level* is usually interpreted in the UK as consisting of Scotland, Wales, Northern Ireland and the regions of England. However, the English regions have no fixed or easily definable boundaries. We use for our purposes the nine government statistical regions in England utilized for government purposes. At this scale economic development is chiefly focused on inward investment, major infrastructure, and development of a strategic interface between central government funding priorities and specific regional or local objectives.

Local and regional economic development is concerned with improving each of the five key elements of:

- human resources, workforce skills and social opportunities;
- land, infrastructure and site provision;
- capital formation and investment;
- innovation, entrepreneurship and technological change;
- a supportive institutional context.

Each of these elements constitutes a factor of production necessary for the successful functioning of the economy and the social structures that this supports in any locality or region. Each factor separately contributes to economic development. But its supply depends on different and overlapping agents which have to cooperate with each other if the full potential of economic development is to be achieved. This process of cooperation is central to the analysis in this book. Cooperation has to be an ongoing 'negotiation process'.

To achieve cooperation requires a willingness to exchange information, to develop joint policy positions between agents, and to back those positions with commitment and resources. Successful local and regional economies will have successfully built that process of cooperation founded on commitment. Less successful economies usually have gaps in exchange or commitment between agents. This process of exchange and development of commitment we refer to as capacity building.[4]

Capacity building is a concept used to define the development of the potential to influence economic development positively. A strong capacity indicates that the agents that control each factor of production undertake exchanges that ensure a full development of policy commitments, so that each agent is pointing in similar directions and mutually supports the local or regional economy. This does not necessarily imply that all agents agree on all matters, or that all are equally important to the economic development process, or that there is some command and control coordination process. But it does require each agent to fulfil its responsibility in the economic development process. Hence our emphasis on capacity building is one which focuses particular concern on agent objectives, institutional power, agent commitment, and inter-agent exchange of information and adaptation.

1.3   Capacity Building and Endogenous Growth

Our emphasis on the inter-agent exchanges required to assure economic growth draws heavily on the concepts underlying endogenous growth theory. Gordon Brown, when Shadow Chancellor in 1994, drew attention to Labour's interest in 'post-neo-classical endogenous growth theory'. He subsequently continued to develop this framework by focusing on 'the productivity gap' of British businesses with those of other OECD economies.[5] However, Gordon Brown has tended to interpret endogenous growth and productivity in a narrow sense as recognising the importance of technological change to endogenous growth. Indeed, the DTI has placed considerable emphasis on this since its 1998 Competitiveness White Paper.[6] However, we emphasise that endogenous growth is not just derived from technological change, but also incorporates *institutional* development that increases the productive capacity of the economy.

---

4   The capacity building concept used here is developed at greater length in Bennett and Krebs 1991; Bennett and McCoshan, 1993.

5   *Budget 2000: Prudent for Purpose*, HM Treasury March Statement.

6   DTI, 1998.

This wider interpretation of endogenous growth theory has been given considerable attention following the publication of a McKinsey report in 1998.[7] This report emphasised the importance of improving productivity in the UK through reforms to the way in which business and government interface; particularly, to improve the regulatory process. This is an aspect largely ignored by Labour and much criticized by business.[8] We take this argument further by highlighting the need for a much broader base of inter-agent cooperation to be in place; not only between central government and businesses, but between all the agents that influence the development of the economy; at central/national level, and also at regional and local level.

Endogenous growth theory in part stimulates and in part derives from recognising the importance of technical drivers of change in modern economies. These changes all emphasise the increasing importance of adaptive efficiency within companies, and within those government and other agents and personnel that deal with companies and operate policies that influence the economy. Adaptive efficiency has been given increasing emphasis by almost all commentators as a result of the need to adjust to e-commerce and the 'new economy'.[9] Mokyr[10] and others have demonstrated through detailed historical analysis that the ability of a society to absorb and benefit from technological change results for the complex interplay of many different agents, all of which are mutually critical. Many of these are influenced by government policy: through the structure of institutions and property rights, through smoothing the hardships created by technological change for its victims, through encouraging a climate of priorities, and by stimulating supportive educational and training attitudes. As Crafts argues, institutions are seen to be 'at the heart of the growth process' in endogenous growth theory.[11] It is these institutional structures which Labour could do most to change to encourage local and regional economic development.

A key aspect of the developments required is improvement of the interface between elements of government (departments, agencies, regulatory regimes) and economic agents. Our chief focus in this book is on how this interface

---

7   McKinsey Global Institute, 1998.
8   See *Financial Times* 29 March 2000 'Honeymoon over, business leaders warn Labour'. *Financial Times* 23 March 2000 'Little air behind the smokescreen: budget personal view, Chris Humphries'.
9   E.g. John Philpott, 'The New Economy', Employment Policy Institute, *Economic Report*, 14 (8), February 2000.
10 See Mokyr, 1990, 1992; Atkinson and Coleman, 1992; Aghiou and Howitt, 1998; Nelson and Winter, 1982; Audretsch, 1989; Nickell et al., 1997.
11 Crafts, 1997, p. 68.

operates and can be improved. One aspect of this exchange, that has been developed in the DTI through its 1998 Competitiveness White Paper[12] and subsequent reports, is a focus on encouraging local business clusters. This has drawn from the arguments of Michael Porter,[13] who emphasises that the competitive underpinnings of nations, regions and localities derives from four mutually reinforcing components:

- *factor conditions*: the availability of skilled labour, capital, infrastructure and technology;
- *demand conditions:* the availability of 'local' demand that allows the accumulation of information, assets, skills and inter-agent experiences, that stimulate learning, quality and performance;
- *related and supporting industries:* the presence of suppliers and customers that are major leaders and form the basis of 'clusters' of development;
- *business strategy and competition:* the conditions governing how firms are created, merged, compete or cooperate with each other.

Competitive success occurs when each of these components is jointly present in a locality or region. In a similar vein, Rosbeth Moss Kanter has enlarged on the role of local conditions in contributing to the global competitiveness of companies and economies. She focuses especially on the role of: (1) local 'thinkers', as magnets of brainpower channelled into knowledge industries; (2) local 'makers', who specialize in executional competence affecting quality standards, value added and cost effectiveness; and (3) local 'traders' who specialize in connections, networking, overcoming local divergences and grasping global opportunities. In addition, she emphasises the role of minimum standards of support institutions, infrastructure, amenities, diversity of employment, and a positive business climate. She categorizes the two key ingredients as first, the complementary aspects of 'magnets' – to attract a flow of external resources; and second, 'glue' which provides means to hold local communities together and provide appropriate local conditions. This is very close to our arguments developed here. She sees the final outcome as the development of 'skills for collaborative advantage'.[14] Collaboration skills are essentially those of exchange, negotiation and partnership. These are the concepts we develop further in later chapters by focusing on agent exchanges.

---

12 DTI, 1998.
13 Porter, 1990, 1998.
14 Kanter, 1995, p. 334.

1.4   Recognizing the Multi-agent Environment

Local and regional economic development involves a wide range of different agents. These are the individuals, agents and institutions responsible for allocating resources or making the decisions that influence the elements of economic development with which we are concerned. Their relations are political and social, as well as economic. Hence endogenous growth depends on their inter-relations and how government deals with each agent. Government, at both local and national level, is a key agent in economic development decisions. We are concerned in this book with the negotiations that influence government in its attempts to improve the application of different public policies and initiatives to economic development.

Government is, however, only one of many agents is a complex scene. There are also the businesses and economic agents that are directly responsible for the decisions that make investments, generate wealth and innovate technological change. In negotiations on public policy business may act directly, but often the business interest is also represented by associations or other representative bodies. These may be national, sectoral or regional/local. There is also a range of social and other agents concerned with how public policy is implemented at the community level on how it influences the rights or interests of specific groups. Thus, local and regional economic development is a multi-agent process within which government has to develop exchanges. To be effective these exchanges should carry information both ways so that public policy initiatives that are initiated are appropriate and are supported by the commitment of the agents that have to be involved in their implementation. We outline the chief agents and their power in the local and regional economy in chapter 2.

But government is itself a complex multi-agent entity. Government is not a single, monolithic department. It is subdivided between ministers, administrative departments and agencies, and other special purpose bodies. There is also the influence of European Commission programmes of funding streams. At the local and regional level the picture is often confusing. The negotiation process is made more complex because of these subdivisions. And the implementation process is made more difficult. Attempts to reduce this complexity and confusion have been made by Labour through improved inter-departmental liaison and the establishment of Regional Development Agencies. The aim has been to produce a 'joined-up government' approach.

Despite attempts to join up government, economic development at local and regional level remains a multi-agent process. Co-working, partnership and cooperation have to be key elements for policy development to be successful. The need to cooperate, share and exchange information are pervasive aspects of the policy process. Attempts to understand this process in the academic literature have tended to emphasise simplistic single interpretations. In chapter 3 we give a brief overview of the main academic interpretations: pluralism; corporatism; the resource-dependence model; the social class model; and the institutional model. Instead of these individual isolated interpretations we adopt a broader more encompassing approach focused on the power relations that determine the outcome of the exchange process that occurs during policy negotiations. Our approach uses a *negotiation model*. This in turn draws on the power, commitment and policy objectives of each agent and how they are combined. This approach is discussed in detail in chapter 4.

1.5   Plan of the Book

Our presentation is based on extensive primary interviews and policy analysis as well as synthesis of the secondary literature and policy documents. Our primary analysis derives chiefly from a set of structured interviews with each of the key agents that have been involved in local and regional economic development policy discussions. This approach is applied in depth to each of four case studies of: RDAs, New Deal, Local Learning and Skills Councils, and Business Link. These case studies cover the main regional and local initiatives of Labour since 1997.

The book first outlines the structure of the agents involved (in chapter 2). These cover central government, local government, business agents and social agents. The change in governance regime sought by Labour and the interpretations that have been developed to explain how agents influence the policy process are reviewed in chapter 3. We find the main previous interpretations unsatisfactory because of the emphasis on single sources or processes of influence. We develop a more encompassing approach which we term a *negotiation model*. This is outlined in chapter 4 together with details of how each area of policy can be assessed through structured interviews and analysis of relevant practitioner policy statements.

The analysis we develop contexts the *negotiation process* between agents within the set of *policy issues* relevant to each given policy intervention. The interventions themselves are contexted within the *governance regime* sought by the government of the day, and the environment of other influences. The overall structure nests each element within the others, as shown in Figure 1.1. This structure forms the framework for Part 2 of the book, which is devoted to four case studies of Labour's key local and regional development policy initiatives.

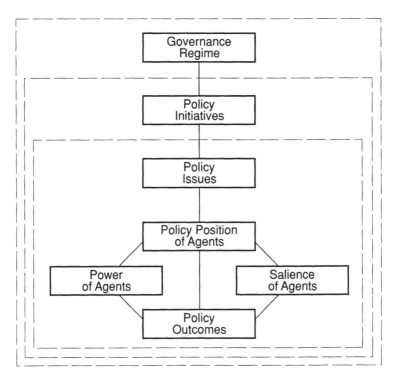

Figure 1.1 **The negotiation process, as a nested structure within which each agent operates**

The case studies occupy chapters 5–8. Each case study is structured in the same way. First, a brief history of the development of the initiative under Labour is given which focuses on its objectives and the agents affected. Second, the perspectives of each stakeholder with respect to the chief policy issues is analysed, together with an assessment of their commitment to the policy objectives and an analysis of their power to influence events. Third, we use our negotiation model to assess to what extent agents engaged in an exchange of information and policy positions during the negotiation process. This leads to an assessment of how far each agent gained or lost during negotiations and whether the outcome is improved or worse than previously. Fourth, a series of scenarios is assessed which seeks to demonstrate how the policy outcomes would have changed if the power of various key agents had been assigned differently. We assess four scenarios: a greater influence of national business objectives (as represented by the CBI); a greater influence of local business objectives (as represented by the chambers of commerce); a greater emphasis on integrated public-private partnerships (as represented by the TECs); and a greater emphasis on local government's objectives.

The final chapters of the book summarise the implications of our case studies for Labour's policies of regional and local economic development (chapter 9). We develop in chapter 10 proposals for a number of further reforms that are required.

PART I
POWER RELATIONS

2 Agents and Power in the Local and Regional Economy

2.1 The Complex Map

Local and regional economic development is not the monopoly of any one agent. It involves many agents of which government and its departments are an important but by no means dominant set of forces. As recognised by many in the Labour government, it is businesses that create economic growth not government.[1] But government is a key support to economic development through its interface with and support for the many interests that develop initiatives for local and regional economic development. Similarly, other agents have also to develop complex networks of exchange. The resulting map of agencies and their interactions is complex. It involves both a complex institutional map of inter-agent relations, but also a complex geographical map of how these agents interface at the local and regional level. Negotiating and aligning interests at both levels, institutional and geographical, is often very difficult.

In this chapter we introduce the institutional structure that defines the key agents and their power relations. We discuss in turn central government; local government; business and economic agents; and social and other agents.

2.2 Central Government

Central government in Britain, as in most countries, is organized with strong vertical divisions of functions between ministers and their departmental administrations. This leads to a situation in which many different government departments and ministers have an important role in economic development. But it is quite possible for these roles to be developed independently of each other. This can result in conflicts, overlaps and certainly a loss of synergies.

---

1   E.g. speech by Tony Blair to 25th Socialist International, 8 November 1999; Stephen Byers speech at CBI Conference,November 1999.

On the ground, at the local and regional level, it can result in a bewildering array of different initiatives. The Audit Commission in 1989 commented that local economic development activity was *'a patchwork quilt'* of complexity and idiosyncrasy. '[Government programmes] ... baffle local authorities and businesses alike. The rules of the games seem over-complex and sometimes capricious. They encourage compartmentalised policy approaches rather than a coherent strategy'.[2] These comments are echoed in the Audit Commission's follow-up report 10 years later. Although quoting Tony Blair, that 'government had to work more coherently' recognising the 'importance of integrated approaches', the Commission's conclusion is clear:[3]

> fragmentation and duplication on the ground persists, underpinned by a maze of strategies, partnerships and organizational configurations. Government and European regeneration programmes extol the virtues of long-term, comprehensive strategies, but many of the funding systems involved promote the opposite ... [There is a] Labyrinth of programmes ... The current system mirrors the 'patchwork quilt' described in the Audit Commission 1990 report.

Thus, although Labour has recognised the need for greater coordination, or what the government has sometimes termed 'joined-up government', it has yet to deliver it. And this has been strongly recognised in a Cabinet Office report of February 2000 that criticised proliferation of initiatives by individual Whitehall departments.[4]

Hence, despite recognising difficulties of fragmentation, it is still the case that economic development responsibility within central government falls between three main department (DETR, DTI and DfEE), as well as touching to a greater or less extent on many other departments. By its very nature, as we have argued, economic development is multifaceted and hence involves a wide range of agents. It is hardly surprising, therefore, that many government departments are involved. The full range of the main economic development and regeneration institutions and initiatives in existence in 2000/2001 is shown in Table 2.1. This list is not exhaustive. It is also a major expansion of that under the previous government.

From among the main departments relevant to economic development in England, the Department of Trade and Industry (DTI) is responsible for regional industrial policy, chiefly involving Regional Selective Assistance

---

2   Audit Commission, 1989, p. 1.
3   Audit Commission, 1999, pp. 74, 84.
4   Cabinet Office Performance and Innovation Unit, February 2000.

and incentives to inward investment promoted through the Invest in Britain Bureau, most aspects of small business supports, and the structure of the competition regime. The Department of Environment, Transport and the Regions (DETR) is responsible for regional and local planning policy, the allocation of grants to support local government expenditure through the mechanism of the standard spending assessment (SSA), specific regeneration funds allocated through a bidding process for area regeneration schemes and the Single Regeneration Budget (SRB), environment and sustainability policy, transport, and urban regeneration including housing. The Department for Education and Employment (DfEE) is responsible for education and vocational training, unemployment and manpower policy, the funding of further and higher education and local job centres. Since April 2000 the Learning and Skills Council (LSC) has been the main channel for vocational education and work-based training funding operating through local Learning and Skills Councils (LLSCs), which replaced the TECs, across England.

There are also major European aspects of economic development funding for each of the main central government departments. The DETR is primarily responsible for the European Regional Development Fund, the DTI is responsible for industrial assistance, and the DfEE is solely responsible for the European Social Fund. The chief elements of EU funding are shown in Table 2.2. In total, EU funds contributed nearly £10 billion over 1994/5–1998/9. Funds are allocated following the drawing up of Single Programming Documents agreed between the European Commission and the member states. Over 1994–98 there were 30 such documents related to regional and local economic and social objectives.

The EU funding streams are an important aspect of regional and local economic development. However, within the negotiations we examine, the Commission and other European bodies are not agents whose policy objectives, salience or power directly influence outcomes. Hence, the EU and Commission programmes do not figure directly in our analysis of agents within our case studies. Rather, European bodies form a major element of the governance regime within which negotiations take place. They have chief influence on the way in which government departments construct programmes and draw down resources.

The three chief departments of the DETR, DTI and DfEE, as well as interrelating to each other through RDAs, are also subject to coordination at regional level through the Government Offices for the Regions (GORs). These were created in 1994 as an earlier attempt to coordinate Whitehall activity at regional level. Only the three chief departments are included in GORs. The

Table 2.1   Economic and regeneration schemes 1998/99 (developed from Audit Commission, 1999, exhibit 26)

Scheme	Purpose	Coverage	Resources	Selection and administration	Dept.
Single Regeneration Budget	"to help to improve local areas and enhance the quality of life"	England	£564 million (1998/99)	Allocation to local partnership by mixture of competition and need	DETR/ RDAs
New Deal for Communities	Tackling social exclusion	17 pathfinders in England and Wales	£12.5m in 1998/9 (£800 m in total) £370m for 8 areas in 2000/1	Partnerships (including community-led) in most needy areas	DETR/ GORs
National Lottery	Six fields, including millennium projects	33,000 projects across UK	£5.7 billion (total in 1998/ 99)	Bidding	DCMS
Coalfields Initiative	Regeneration of coalfield communities	Former coalfield areas	£354 million over 3 years	National partnership bringing together existing funds	DETR
New Commitment to Regeneration	Better coordination of regeneration and mainstream spending	22 main pathfinders in England	Existing resources with flexibility	Pathfinders selected on basis of innovative strategies and partnerships	LGA/ DETR
Regional Selective Assistance	Attracting investment and creating/ safeguarding jobs in Assisted Areas	Assisted Areas cover 34% of British working population but under review	£110 million in 1998/99 £785m proposed for 2000– 03	Grants cover up to 40% of investment	DTI/GORs
Employment Zones	Tailored support for long-term unemployed	5 prototypes 1998–2000; 13 fully-fledged 2000– (across UK)	Primary legislation will enable budget pooling	Prototypes led by Local Authorities and LLSCs, in partnership with ES	DfEE/ES
Education Action Zones	Improving educational performance	25 in UK	£1 million per zone per year for three years	Targeted on areas of need disadvantage via partnerships	DfEE
Health Action Zones	Address health inequalities, improve services and develop partnerships	11 from April 1998, 15 more from April 1999	Flexibilities and £110 million 1998–2002	Partnerships including NHS, local authorities, third and private sectors	DoH/ NHSE

New Deal for 18–24 Year Olds	Personal assistance and four options, including subsidised employment	UK	Windfall Tax	Local delivery partnerships led by Employment Service	DfEE
New Deal for the Long Term Unemployed	Welfare to work for over 25s	28 pilots for 12–18 months unemployed; 28 pilots for 2 years unemployed	£129 million for 12–18 months; £350 million for 2 years	Local delivery partnerships led Employment Service	DfEE/ES
New Deal for Lone Parents	Providing support to enable lone parents to enter employment	8 pilots around UK	£200 million in this parliament	Contracts for delivery from Employment Service	DSS/DfEE
New Deal for Disabled People	Allowing people claiming incapacity benefit to work for trial period without losing benefit	13 areas in two tranches (UK)	£12 million for 1999/2000	First tranche led by Employment Service; second tranche through bidding process	DfEE/DSS
New Start	Re-engaging 14–17 year olds who drop out of education	18 in round 1	£4m in round 1	Partnerships of local authorities, FE, schools and LLSCs	DfEE
Sure Start	Helping parents and children in disadvantaged areas	250 planned 1999–2002	£452m over 3 years	Partnerships with voluntary sector	DoH, DfEE, DETR
Gateway to Work 'ONE' service	Single point of access and support for benefit and employment	12 pilots started in 1999 (UK)	£112 million including existing resources	Employment Service, Benefits Agency and Local Authorities	DfEE/DSS

Table 2.2   Structural Fund allocations to the UK 1994–99 (£million)

Objective	Coverage	European Social Fund	European Regional Development Fund	European Agricultural Guidance and Guarantee Fund	Financial Instrument for Fisheries Guidance
Objective 1	Targeted on lagging regions (Merseyside, Highlands and Islands, N. Ireland)	578	1,031	190	27
Objective 2	Targeted on declining industrial areas (13 in UK)	925	2,797	–	–
Objective 3	Nationwide to combat unemployment, social exclusion and promote equal opps.	2,442	–	–	–
Objective 4	Nationwide to facilitate adaptation of workers to industrial change	188	–	–	–
Objective 5a	Nationwide to facilitate structural adaptation of agriculture and fisheries	–	–	144	69
Objective 5b	Targeted on vulnerable rural areas (11 in UK)	104	412	117	–
Community Initiatives	Various (usually targeted)	394	509	24	7
Total		**4,816**	**4,749**	**475**	**103**

Source: European Commission, reported in Audit Commission, 1999.

Note: eligible areas have been redefined from 2000 with transition arrangements

result is some confusion at regional level since there now exist three bodies, RDAs, GORs and Regional Chambers (composed of indirectly elected local government representatives), which each have a formal responsibility to coordinate local and regional economic development policy of the three departments. This is a confusion that has led to calls for the abolition of the GORs.[5] This has so far been formally resisted but an important de facto change

---

5   E.g. by the House of Commons Employment Sub-Committee, and Environment, Transport and Regional Affairs Committee; HoC, 1997, 1998a.

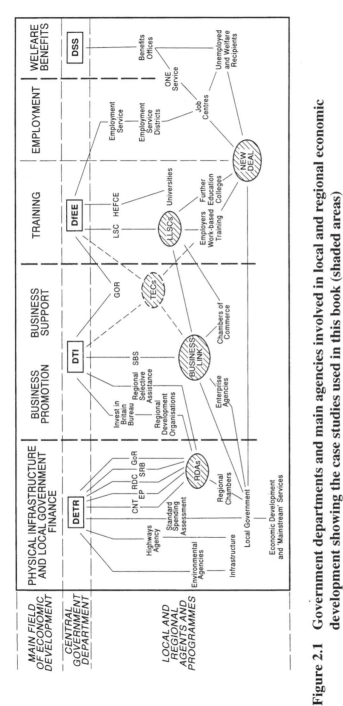

Figure 2.1   Government departments and main agencies involved in local and regional economic development showing the case studies used in this book (shaded areas)

Note: the TECs, which were superseded by the LLSCs in a transition period from April 2000 – April 2001 are shown dotted. The GOR links are shown bracketed for DfEE and DTI because of the partial withdrawal of these two departments from regional coordination with DETR in late 1999. For definition of acronyms see text and list at the start of this book.

occurred in September 1999 when the DfEE and DTI were withdrawn from key elements of the GORs, leaving them responsible chiefly only for DETR regional activities. In effect, therefore, the GORs have tended to become merely an element of one department.

The relations between these department responsibilities and the key dimensions of local and regional economic development are shown in Figure 2.1. This figure, which is a simplification of only the main interlinkages and chief departmental programmes, demonstrates the complexity of the structures. For most observers this still presents a pattern of 'confusion' or a 'patchwork quilt', as argued by the Audit Commission,[6] despite Labour's attempt to develop a more joined-up approach.

A key element of Labour's attempt to join up government has been through Regional Development Agencies (RDAs). These are the responsibility of the DETR, but the two other departments of DTI and DfEE have 'to take account' of RDA regional strategies in their decisions. However, since June 1999, the DTI and DfEE have developed their own sub-regional agencies, respectively, of the Small Business Service Business Link (BL), and the Local Learning and Skills Councils (LLSCs) which replaced the Training and Enterprise Councils (TECs). Although these two agencies have to coordinate with RDAs within each region, as we shall see, much doubt remains about the effectiveness of the coordination process.

The four case studies which we examine in depth in later chapters (the RDAs, New Deal, LLSCs and BL) are the key parts of the new local and regional economic development structure established by Labour. Our framework of analysis, which emphasises inter-agent negotiation is thus highly appropriate to help disentangle the power relations between the government departments and other agents depicted in Figure 2.1.

In addition to the DETR, DTI, and DfEE, many other government departments also influence the local and regional economy. Chief among these are: (i) the Home Office (HO) (which is responsible for voluntary sector involvement and is relevant to many aspects of social inclusion, particularly relating to ex-offenders); (ii) the Department of Health (DoH) (which is responsible with the National Health Service Executive (NHSE) for health and hence many social and care issues); (iii) the Department of Culture, Media and Sport (DCMS) (which is responsible for many areas influencing heritage and leisure that can contribute to economic development, but also is responsible for National Lottery Funds which contribute to many local regeneration

---

6   See also Mawson and Hall, 2000; Hall and Martin, 1999.

projects); and (iv) the Department of Social Security (DSS) (which is responsible for the welfare and benefits regime).

In addition to the departmental structures there is also a range of executive agencies, and non-departmental public bodies (NDPBs) that are of significance. The chief of these, shown in Figure 2.1, are the Employment Service (ES) (responsible for administering the local job centres and contracting for New Deal and other training for the unemployed); the Benefits Agency (responsible for administering the welfare benefits system through local benefits offices); the Learning and Skills Council (which has sub-regional bodies responsible for contracting for work-based training and allocating funds to FE colleges); and the Small Business Service (SBS). The benefits offices and job centres are moving towards merger in the 'ONE service' initiative, hailed as a single gateway.[7] There is also growing integration between Inland Revenue administration (under the Treasury) and the local benefits office system. However, as full integration between these offices is not likely to be achieved before 2001, if at all, the structure of inter-agency relations shown in Figure 2.1 accurately covers the period of Labour development we assess.

In addition there is the Higher Education Funding Council (HEFC) which is responsible for universities and colleges of higher education, and the Further Education Funding Council (FEFC) which was responsible for further education funding until its absorption into the Learning and Skills Council after April 2000. Before April 1999 there were also, under the DETR, the Rural Development Commission (RDC), English Partnerships (EP), and the Commission for New Towns (CNT). Since 1999 these bodies have been merged into the RDAs.

2.3 Local Government

Local government is an important agent of development in the local and regional economy. Local authorities have formal economic development powers, as well as more general powers deriving from their main services which can be important influences on economic development. They also can contribute leadership and participation in projects by working with others.

(i) Formal economic development powers Until 1989 there were only limited permissive powers of economic development under Section 137 of the Local

---

7   DSS/DfEE, 1998; HoC, 1999b.

Government Act 1972 in England and Wales, and its equivalent Section 83 of the Local Government (Scotland) Act 1973. Under these Section 137/83 powers, local authorities were able to incur expenditures for local economic development (as well as other purposes) up to a maximum of a 2p product of their local property tax, the rates. Most authorities used at least a 1.5p power, and the general level of use increased rapidly after 1981.[8] The Section 137/83 powers allowed local authorities to develop a wide range of local economic initiatives with almost all authorities involved in at least some activities by 1989, a significant increase from 1981. Mean economic expenditure by 1989 was about £2.2 per head of local population, accounting for about 0.2 per cent of local expenditure.[9]

A major change occurred with the Local Government and Housing Act of 1989. This aimed to regularize the Section 137/83 powers and to emphasise a greater centralisation of control of economic development policy within local government corporate strategy. The Act was followed up by Audit Commission guidance which advocated locating the economic function in the Chief Executive's Department of a local authority 'especially if it is small, since it should ensure that it receives top level support'.[10] The 1989 Act gave local authorities the power to take 'such steps as they may from time to time consider appropriate for promoting the economic development of their area' subject to the annual preparation of an economics development plan which has to be subject to consultation with business and other local interests.

The general power given in the 1989 Act has resulted in a further marked increase in local authority economic development activity. The Audit Commission in a 1998 survey reported that economic development expenditures had risen to £4.4 per head. A wider survey undertaken in conjunction with the analysis in this book demonstrates that local authority economic development expenditure in 1998 was about 2.4 per cent of local expenditure and had pervaded 100 per cent of local authorities, with the most widespread activities being: preparing economic strategies, promoting inward investment, publishing a site or premises directory, promoting or advertising local businesses, and provision of business startup advice.[11] However, there is a wide range of spending and types of initiatives between areas, with only a loose relation between level of spend or type of activity and the type of problem an area faces.[12]

---

8   See Ramsdale and Capon, 1986.
9   See Sellgren 1987, 1989; Mills and Young, 1986; Bennett and McCoshan, 1993.
10 Audit Commission, 1990, p. 126.
11 Bennett and LGA, 1998, *Survey of Local Economic Development*.
12 Audit Commission, 1999.

Labour has developed the 1989 framework further, giving local authorities from April 2001 a 'new duty' for local economic development. This requires councils to develop a comprehensive strategy for promoting the well-being of their area, integrated with the objectives and strategy of the RDAs and other stakeholders. This duty does not go as far as many local authorities would wish, particularly in not giving them the formal freedom or expenditure support they have sought for more ambitious investment programmes. However, it thrusts the attention of local authorities not just on their specific economic development activities, but also on their wider range of services and their cooperation with other agents. As commented by the Audit Commission in 1999, the new duty sends 'a clear message that regeneration is not so much the activity of a certain department, but an objective that is pivotal to local government'.[13]

(ii) Mainstream services As recognised in the preceding discussion, specific economic development expenditures are only a relatively small part of the mechanisms which local authorities can use to influence their local economy. Indeed the rest of their activities, their 'mainstream', accounts for 97.6 per cent of their expenditure[14] and hence usually has a much greater potential for influencing the economy and social change. The local authority mainstream includes a number of services that have important influences on the local economy, the perception of it by its resident population and businesses, and its attractiveness to outsiders interested in investment or residence in the area. Key local services are housing, education, transport, planning, and environmental services etc. Of these services, the most significant, in terms of the negotiations we examine, are planning and the Local Education Authority (LEA). The LEA is the formal administration and council committee structure responsible for schools in Britain. It is the authority exercised by counties in non-metropolitan areas, and districts in large towns, metropolitan areas and London boroughs.

The development of an economic focus for mainstream services has, however, been much less rapid than for specific economic development activities. The Audit Commission made stronger focusing on the mainstream a central plank of its recommended strategy in 1989. It is still a key issue in its 1999 report, where the Commission states that 'economic development services are only the tip of the regeneration iceberg. Mainstream services ...

---

13 Audit Commission, 1999, p. 84.
14 Bennett and LGA, 1998.

can play a crucial role in fostering or sustaining economic vitality for people or places. If they are badly delivered, they can deter or stifle it'.[15] It found that the 'connections are not always made as well as they could be',[16] with most mainstream service plans and economic development plans developed independently of each other. However, much of the fragmentation is stimulated by central government's narrowly focused departmental approach[17] with too much 'central policy design and implementation'. Hence, more joined-up government is a need recognised at both central and local levels.

(iii) Leadership and participation As well as using their own expenditure responsibility, local government is an important local agent in helping to gain other resources, or in providing an expertise of leadership or facilitation to other initiatives.

An important element of this role is through bidding for central government schemes and for European funds. The range of the main central government schemes, which is listed in Table 2.1, demonstrates the wide range of initiatives within which local government plays a crucial role, often in partnership with other agents. Similarly EU funds, listed in Table 2.2, have become a most important element, although their potential significance varies considerably between areas depending on the eligibility status of each area. On average, the Audit Commission found that external funds from central government and EU schemes met 14 per cent of the economic development budget.[18]

Despite its important roles as a local strategic leader, partner or bidder for funds, local government is often not as fully committed to partnership development as it should be. In a survey of local authority economic development undertaken in association with this book it is clear that whilst 94 per cent of local authorities have an economic development strategy, only 45 per cent have this developed as a coordinated statement agreed and 'signed off' with local partners. Moreover, in only 18 per cent of cases do these local partners include non-government bodies; only 16 per cent having chambers of commerce, and only 5 per cent having private companies as partners, for example.[19] Whilst many partners thus, quite properly, are other local authorities (usually at the respective county or district level), other agents are not very

---

15 See Audit Commission, 1999, p. 20.
16 Audit Commission, 1999, p. 69.
17 Cabinet Office, Performance and Innovation Unit, February 2000.
18 Audit Commission, 1999.
19 See Bennett and LGA, 1998; similar proportions are reported by the Audit Commission, 1999.

fully involved in local government strategies. Indeed in one area priding itself on a partnership approach the local chamber of commerce would 'be out of the door tomorrow if the Government wasn't insisting on partnerships'.[20] So even present partnerships are fragile. Moreover, only 56 per cent of local authority strategies envisage developments of more than 1–2 years, which is very short in economic development terms.[21]

We have therefore an awkward situation in which the key role that can be played by local government in developing its mainstream is not part of an explicit strategy in many cases. Where it is, this strategy is often very short term. And most problematic of all, the strategy is usually a 'local authority strategy' that is not a collective instrument for underpinning a broader partnership approach.

Hence, at present the local and regional economic development process is subject to developments by one of its key agents that do not follow fully the cooperative, participative process that we argue is essential to success. Whilst some of the blame for this undoubtedly rests with the fragmented structure of central government departments and funding streams, it is also clear that the separation of local authority economic development activity from other partners, and indeed from other aspects of local government mainstream services, is chiefly the result of the traditional approach of local government to its negotiations and implementation. We find this reflected to a greater or lesser extent by other agents.

2.4 Business and Economic Agents

Whilst government policy is the key focus of this book, the development of the economy is chiefly an issue of how economic agents and businesses operate, and how their behaviour is shaped by public policy. The economy is composed of individual firms, the self-employed and sole traders. It is the stimulation of their activity, startup, and growth which is a primary focus for most local and regional economic initiatives. Much can be done by central and local government, and other public agents, to influence the general climate within which business decisions are made. It is this generic influence of government on the 'rules' of the system through direct regulation, and influence on the perception of the business environment, which is a key underpinning of

---

20 Quoted in Audit Commission, 1999, p. 81.
21 Audit Commission, 1999, Exhibit 15, p. 43.

endogenous growth as conceived by Michael Porter or Rosbeth Moss Kanter which we focus on as a key element in capacity building.

From the point of view of negotiating public policy changes, however, individual businesses are rarely able to participate directly. Direct influence on government is certainly possible for large businesses that have a lot of clout and resources or may have special access routes to government departments, key politicians or senior civil servants. Indeed, there is much evidence that large companies are seeking to exert stronger direct influence on government (and the EU and other international institutions) than was the case five or 10 years ago.[22] We also find in several parts of our analysis of our case studies that individual large companies can play an important role in influencing change at both national and regional/local level. This can occur both through informal networks and through more formal processes such as membership of taskforces. Large businesses certainly need to be built into any analysis of the negotiation and power-relations structure of the policies that we examine. Nevertheless, most businesses, particularly SME and micro businesses, are too numerous and have too few resources that they have little potential to exert direct influence, and even for large businesses their opportunities for direct influence are usually quite limited. Large and small companies can also often gain greater legitimacy, appear to be developing a more generic and less self-serving argument, and can command broader access to government if they use more established channels for exerting their influence.

For these reasons business associations and a number of other intermediary bodies are often the chief medium through which the views of business influence government policy. In Britain there are several routes through which these bodies operate: nationally, sectorally, and at regional/local level. Each has to be built into our analysis of the policy negotiation process.

(i) National level At national level the premier representative business body continues to be the *Confederation of British Industry (CBI)*. This is chiefly a body representing the interests of very large firms, blue chip firms, and the leading businesses in the economy (often those with transnational operations). However, it has been concerned also to develop its role in representing SME and sector interests. To do this it has established since 1996 a SME Council and a Trade Association Council, and since 1999 it has developed SME membership of all its main policy committees. The CBI with the TUC was a key player in the 'corporatist period' of government-business relations that

---

22 See Greenwood, 1997; Greenwood et al., 1992; Grant, 1993; Bennett, 1999.

covered much of the post-war period. But under the Thatcher government after 1979 the CBI was marginalised and had to play a role more as a lobby and influence body.[23] Under Labour it has perhaps, achieved a higher status and has sometimes been able to exert influence to a greater extent. But this has been matched by a greater pressure on it to deliver business commitments to government. Some members have seen the new relationship of the CBI with Labour, therefore, as being 'a poisoned chalice'.[24] Certainly there are tensions for the CBI, as with any voluntary membership body, in seeking on the one hand to negotiate with government and on the other hand to enforce any agreement reached on its members. Since 2000 under its new Director General, Digby Jones, it has tried to develop greater distance from government recognising that it had come to be perceived as 'too cosy with government' and 'too London oriented'.[25]

As well as the CBI there are several other national bodies that represent different business interests. Chief of these, and included in our case studies, are: (i) *The Institute of Directors (IoD)*, which has 50,000 individual, not corporate membership, overlapping in part with CBI, but chiefly covering SME businesses; (ii) *The Federation of Small Businesses (FSB)*, which was established in 1974 to represent self-employed and small business people, to act as a pressure group and support its members; and (iii) *The Forum of Private Business (FPB)*, which acts chiefly as a parliamentary lobby also on behalf of self-employed and SME businesses.[26] These bodies have tended to take a stronger view about reducing government regulation, red-tape and intervention, and have lobbied against the CBI and large company interests on many issues where they see SMEs adversely affected by competition from dominant firms. Since April 2000 aspects of their role has been supported by the Small Business Service which is supposed, among other things, to represent small firm interests in the drafting and implementation stage of government initiatives and legislation.

(ii) Sector level Within individual business sectors there is a strong tradition in Britain for associations to be formed to press for specific sector concerns with government policy. The number of sector associations, and their variety, is daunting. This has led to efforts by government to stimulate mergers,

23 See Grant and Marsh, 1977; Grant, 1993.

24 Interviews with key CBI officials 1998, 1999.

25 *Financial Times*, 29 March 2000, 'A man of the business people: New CBI director-general Digby Jones aims to take the organisation much closer to its members'.

26 Interviews, and details from organization reports and website.

federations, or lead associations.[27] However, government attempts to influence the organization of the sectoral business associations have had very limited impact and the pattern remains highly fragmented and complex.

Recent surveys show there to be about 3,000 sector bodies. Of these approximately 56 per cent are trade associations and 44 per cent professional associations, but there are overlaps between the two categories. Whilst *trade associations* are predominantly corporate member bodies, *professional associations* have predominantly individual self-employed, partner or employee status business members. The membership of many associations includes all categories, and 6 per cent of sector associations self-identify themselves as both trade *and* professional bodies. Although estimation is difficult, it appears that businesses with over 200 employees on average belong to over seven associations of different types, with this number generally declining by company size so that the self-employed and sole traders generally belong to only one association or none at all.

The associations also differ greatly in size of membership and resources. Total membership of all associations is about 4.5 million which, because of duplication and the membership by employee status individuals, exceeds the estimated British business population of 3.7m businesses. The size of trade associations is generally small, 68 per cent having less than 100 members and 30 per cent have less than 30 members. But the smaller associations generally have members that are predominantly the larger companies. Trade association mean income is £1.1m, but this is highly skewed with only a tiny proportion having an income over £5m, 37 per cent have only one member of staff or less, and only 3.4 per cent have a staff of over 50. Professional associations are generally larger, only 1.4 per cent having under 100 members and 68 per cent having over 1000 members, with a greater proportion of SME members. Their mean income is £5.4m, and only 19 per cent have a staff of one or fewer, 14 per cent having over 50 staff.[28]

The result of this large and diverse pattern of sector representation is a situation that may make it difficult for individual sectors to influence government. Certainly for the development of local and regional initiatives we find them fairly peripheral in most of our studies.

(iii) Local and regional level Local and regional business bodies exist in a variety of forms. Some are specialised sector bodies represented only in certain

---

27   See e.g. Committee on Trusts, 1918; PEP, 1957; Devlin Committee, 1972; Heseltine, 1993; DTI, 1996; reviewed in Bennett, 1997.

28   All the statistics quoted here are derived from surveys in Bennett, 1997, 1998a, b, c.

locations, such as Scottish salmon farmers, English wine makers, Welsh organic cheesemakers, etc. Many sector and national bodies also have regional and local branches, e.g. CBI, IoD, FSB and many sector associations. However, the primary agent for representing interests at the sub-national level has traditionally been local chambers of commerce, and at regional level the CBI regional branches or regional groups of chambers of commerce. Because of the overlap of interests at the regional level, and Labour's greater emphasis on regions through the RDAs and devolution to Scotland and Wales, there has been some recent discussion of merger between the chambers of commerce and CBI,[29] an objective sought in the 1970s following the Devlin Report. This is unlikely to take place in the foreseeable future, and for our purposes here the primary local and regional business body is the chambers. However, we demonstrate in our case studies how the variety of perspectives of local and regional members of the business bodies influences and constrains their policy positions or salience on some key issues.

The chambers of commerce in Britain number about 50 that have reached a level of 'Approval' through an internal self-accreditation process. These are the larger chambers and the ones which offer a range of services to their members as well as representing business interests. In addition there is an unknown number, probably about 300, of 'town chambers' that are not approved. These are usually very small, most being entirely voluntary with no staff, and chiefly having only an interest in social functions and representing interests at a local level. Both approved and non-approved chambers can be important at local level in influencing economic development policy, particularly with local government. However, it is only the approved chambers that form a national lobby for local interests which we find to be of significance in the negotiation with government of the key policy developments we examine.

The Approved chambers are all accredited by, and members of, the national body of *British Chambers of Commerce* (BCC). This has been one of the key partners in the development of SBS and Business Link, and has sought a role in influencing RDAs and LLSCs. Many chambers are also providers of training and thus have become involved as contracted partners for Business Link, direct suppliers to New Deal, and contracted to LLSCs and TECs for work-based training. BCC and Approved chambers of commerce, therefore, are an important part of the negotiation process, both as business influence bodies representing varied local and regional concerns, and as local business-led

---

29 *Financial Times*, November 1998.

agents contracted to government. The Approved chambers generally have staff sizes of 20 or more and an income of £750,000 or more,[30] and are thus among the larger of business bodies.

(iv) Other economic agents As well as business associations at national, sectoral or regional/local level, there is a wide range of other economic agents that influence the negotiations in the development of government policy.

An important player in several of our case studies is *Business in the Community (BiTC)*. This is body that encourages the social responsibility activities of businesses through seeking to stimulate and to focus sponsorship of local development activities. Naturally many social responsibility activities overlap with areas of interest to government. Because almost all its members are also large companies, and are particularly strongly represented within the FT top 100 companies in Britain, BiTC can also sometimes exercise considerable 'clout'.[31] It had a particularly strong role in the field of business supports in the 1980s and 1990s through its sponsorship and championing of the enterprise agency network. This gave it an important role in the development of TECs and Business Link. However, from about 1994 it sought to distance itself from direct or major involvement with enterprise agencies and focus more attention on either sponsoring local regeneration initiatives or developing international business exchanges, and its influence on the case study areas examined in this book has perhaps tended to wane a little under Labour.

Enterprise agencies, in part supported by BiTC, were stimulated initially by the experience of the US Community Development Corporation, with the earliest examples set up and sponsored by large companies in their own localities in the mid-1970s; e.g. by Pilkington Glass in St Helens, by ICI Mond in Runcorn, by Wills Tobacco in Bristol, and by BSC in Glasgow. There were also early initiatives by local authorities to sponsor enterprise agencies, e.g. in Hackney. There was rapid growth in the number of agencies from 23 in 1981, to 245 by 1985, and 421 by 1991. This growth was stimulated by a series of government grants initiated in 1983 such that by 1988 most enterprise agencies were dependent for 45 per cent of their income from central government and 18 per cent from local government. In 1992 this funding was taken over by TECs which generally tried to consolidate the system, improve its quality, and reduce the number of separate agencies. By 1995 there had

---

30 Statistics and greater detail given in Bennett, 1996, 1997, 1998a,b.

31 Its nine founding business members were Marks and Spencer, IBM, Shell, BP, GEC, ICFC, Pilkington, Prudential and NCB.

been a reduction to about 250 agencies.[32] With the development of Business Link many enterprise agencies have been incorporated into the local partnership structures for negotiation and/or delivery of business support. In particular many enterprise agencies are responsible for key parts of the supply of business counselling and advice, particularly for startups and early stage businesses. With the withdrawal of BiTC from national championing, the enterprise agencies set up their own *National Federation of Enterprise Agencies (NFEA)* in 1994. Its representatives played a role in the negotiations in our case studies, particularly in the SBS and Business Link.

Also of relevance to Business Link and Learning and Skills Council negotiations is the *Institute of Business Advisors (IBA)*. This is an institute of individual members, many of whom, follow a path to full personal accreditation as 'fellows'. We use the IBA as a body indicative of the interests of personal business advisors.[33] They are employees of, or consultants to, government-sponsored local business support organisations. Hence, they have interests distinct from the IoD, BCC or BiTC, but have many interests in common with enterprise agencies, though with less commitment to a particular national structure.

There is also a number of other economic agents that are important in various of our case studies. The chief of these are bodies supported by government but with a business purpose or business-led board. Of relevance in our case studies, with different importance and varying policy positions in each case, are: the *National Training Organizations (NTOs)* which are sectoral lead bodies for encouraging training to meet the government standards of the National Vocational Qualifications (NVQs); they are part-financed by the industries concerned, but chiefly depend on DfEE grants;[34] the *Rural Development Commission (RDC)* responsible for the allocation of business grants and support to SMEs in rural areas; the *Commission for New Towns (CNT)* responsible for the planning and development of new town communities; *English Partnerships (EP)* which managed estates of derelict land and buildings with compulsory purchase powers and the ability to make grants and finance for the clearance and development of their sites; *Urban Development Corporations (UDCs)* with some planning powers and resources

---

32 All statistics derived from analysis in Bennett and McCoshan, 1993, Chapter 6; and Bennett, 1994, 1995.

33 Other individual member bodies that supply consultants to Business Link are the accountancy associations, particularly ACCA, and the Institute of Management Consultantcy.

34 See Bennett, 1998d, survey of NTOs.

to regenerate defined inner city areas; *Invest in Britain Bureau (IBB)* responsible with the Foreign Office for promotion of inward investment in Britain; and the *English Tourist Board (ETB)* responsible for promoting the tourist industry.

The summary here of economic agents presents a pattern of many agents, of highly varied size and resources, with many potential cleavages for division between different types of firm and different types of body. The business view is thus often divided, with competition for representation to government between large and small firms and between the national level, sector and regional/local bodies. In general, the diversity of business interests and their representative bodies is a dominant facet of their negotiations, and is strongly demonstrated in our case studies. Thus, in contrast to the position held by Marxist writers, that business interests have a privileged position because of their dominant market power and ability to coerce,[35] the more realistic position is one of fragmentation, overlap, gaps and competition between business interests that undermines their capacity to influence the public policy debate.

2.5   Social and Other Agents

A wide range of other agents also influences government in its development of policy for the local and regional economy. Much of this influence takes place outside of government departments and formal channels. Of particular importance is representation informally directly to ministers, MPs and civil servants, and via the media. The parameters which are set by government's policy objectives also stimulate the wider relevance of social and other issues. Thus Labour's attempt to shift the 'governance regime' to emphasise social inclusion and a more consultative approach has drawn a wider range of more varied agents into a position to influence economic development policy. Much of this finds chief relevance via the government's employment objectives. However, we have only found a few social and other agents to have strong direct influence on the development of local and regional economic policy. Chief among these are the TUC and voluntary bodies.

The *Trade Union Congress (TUC)* was the key partner with the CBI in the post-war corporatist period of economic policy that existed until its abolition by the Thatcher government in 1979. Like the CBI, the TUC found itself out in the cold after 1979. It also suffered from the impact of Thatcher

---

35 See e.g. Offee and Wissenthal, 1988; Offee, 1996; Grant, 1993.

reforms that reduced the importance of trade union membership in many industries, and from industrial decline in many of the main industries that had high levels of unionisation. Like the CBI and business associations, the TUC also suffers from a degree of fragmentation resulting from the very different interests of its different member unions. There can, therefore, be a danger of representing the lowest common denominator. Despite these disadvantages, the TUC has come to play an important role in a number of areas relevant to the local and regional economy and this has given it influence in the negotiations we examine. This role can often be complimentary to the employer point of view, since employees and employers have many common interests in productivity and competitiveness. However, the TUC emphasis can also conflict with employers in placing a stronger priority on social and employee benefits than most businesses would do. As well as national negotiations, trade unions also directly influence local and regional development through their membership of local bodies. There was a trade union member eventually on the Board of every TEC, despite early resistance to this. There are also trade union members on the Boards of most NTOs, on the Boards of RDAs, and LLSCs. Trade unions were also important in the advocacy, negotiation and implementation of New Deal. The TUC's more general investment of resources to develop policy papers has also been influential, often in conjunction with the CBI, particularly in the development of education and training initiatives.

The *National Council for Voluntary Organizations (NCVO)* is a representative body for the voluntary sector. Some of its interests are directly represented by the Home Office, which is the department chiefly responsible for the voluntary sector. However, the NCVO, and its member voluntary bodies, also plays an important role directly in a number of the case studies we examine. We use the catch-all terminology of the NCVO, but in practice it is often individual voluntary bodies with specific sector or other interests that are chiefly important. The development of the New Deal and the negotiations over the training elements within LLSCs and TECs are the chief areas where the voluntary sector has significance in our case studies.

2.6 The Need to Cooperate

The discussion in this chapter has introduced the main agents concerned with economic development in Britain. The scene is complex and often confused. The description of a 'patchwork quilt' used in 1989 to characterize the position has hardly changed in the following years. However, under Labour the new institutions of RDAs, SBS and the LLSCs are attempting to introduce a coordination at regional and local level to join up government programmes. They are, however, merely new coordinating bodies. Many other agents remain on the scene. Central government and local government act as two strong forces at the government level but often act independently of each other. Government also continues to act through separated departmental structures: separated between central departments, and separated between local government mainstream services and economic programmes. The businesses framework of supports is also fragmented between national, sectoral and local bodies. Hence, it is an open question how far Labour's reforms will achieve the coordination they seek. Our brief introduction to the scene here suggests that the development of local and regional economies remains a complex multi-agent activity where the need to cooperate remains very high if resources are to be marshalled effectively. 'Joining up' remains a key priority for all agents involved. Hence, exchange of information and negotiation are likely to remain key prerequisites for successful local economic development to take place.

3 Interpreting Labour's Local and Regional Economic Policy Objectives

3.1 'What Matters is What Works'

This book examines the change in approach to local and regional development evolving under Labour. Its context is a shift of governance regime: from one which emphasised a pre-eminence of market-led and business-led approaches of the 1979–97 period, to a regime in which social inclusion, cooperation and public-private partnership interrelations are emphasised as complimentary to business needs. This is both part of the 'joined-up government' idea and also part of the development of a so-called 'third way', between state of market solutions. However, these ideas are ill-defined and the role of a coherent single philosophy should not be overemphasised. The inside view of the Labour government is more one of pragmatism developing and consolidating Labour's political control by implementing an approach of 'what matters is what works',[1] which in turn has placed a considerable emphasis on consultation with the key interest groups and agents involved, including businesses. It is in this sense then, that Labour's approach can be seen more as an 'ongoing project' than as pursuing a single philosophical line.[2]

In this chapter we briefly examine the chief elements of Labour's governance regime, review academic assessments of how governance regimes can be interpreted, and demonstrate how any specific governance regime will shape different local and regional economic development scenarios.

3.2 Labour's Governance Regime

Policy negotiations depend on the power and objectives of the agents involved.

---

1 Philip Gould, 1998; Anderson and Mann, 1997.
2 Op. cit.

The outcome depends on the tradeoffs each agent is prepared to make over the period in which negotiations take place. As we shall argue, the outcome is not 'optimal' in any sense, for any one agent, for government, or for the economy as a whole. It is merely one possible outcome.

The possible outcomes that may develop are crucially dependent on the context within which agents make decisions and negotiations occur. It is this context which we refer to as *the governance regime*.[3] Regimes are the set of interconnections that relate public, private and non-profit sectors of the economy, both through formal and especially through informal relationships. An emphasis on regimes is important because it throws emphasis not just on formal government structures, but also on informal *governance* – the relations between agents and government. In a market economy, government must work with businesses and economic interests because it is they that undertake the key investment and business decisions. This is especially true for economic development policy, where government also needs the support of private sector interests to provide political and economic resources. At the same time business interests will seek to influence government to improve their profitability as well as seeking to acquire economic rents through regulatory capture.

Whilst the general form of a governance regime generally does not change radically over time, its specific emphases and the opportunities for influence it offers to different agents does change. This is clear in the focus of this book. At certain periods of time a range of practically possible options is possible; alternatively others are infeasible because of the political or economic climate of the time. Thus in the 1979–97 period many local and regional development initiatives or approaches that could have been developed were not even raised by the agents involved because they did not fit within the specific Thatcherite market-led approach of that time. The real contribution that Labour is attempting to make is to reopen some of these options by opening-up the governance regime to one in which there is a greater emphasis a social inclusion *as well as* economic needs: a so-called 'third way'. This allows a revisiting of the policy issues and hence policy initiatives outlined, as depicted in Figure 1.1. A shift in governance regime has five chief aspects.

First, there is the question of how the interests of agents involved in any set of policy negotiations is determined. The 1979–97 period excluded trade union interests in many cases, for example. The outcome of negotiations

---

3   This draws on the terminology developed by Lindberg et al., 1991, chapter 11; others refer to the concept of 'regimes of accumulation', which is somewhat more general and less clearly defined than the concepts we use here: see e.g. Elkin, 1985; Stone and Sanders, 1987; Dunford, 1990; Peck and Tickell, 1992; Kantor et. al., 1997.

between agents primarily depends on the agents included in the negotiations. Determining how the agents involved in a negotiation is to be limited is often difficult, since many potential interests may seek to influence a given negotiation. Labour's approach has sought to widen the process of consultation, particularly to social agents. In most of our discussion we analyse negotiations at a national level. However a wide variety of other dimensions may be relevant: the EU level or within a sector, region or locality, for example. The unit of analysis within which negotiations take place at a given point in time is the governance structure.[4] We focus on governance structures at the national level because this is the chief one at which the framework for local and regional economic development is set. We recognise, however, that it is at the local and regional level that exists the framework for practical implementation of most initiatives. The influence of the local variety of possible local and regional outcomes is a key aspect of our analysis since it frequently constrains or modifies how a national agent operates in a given negotiation.

Second, the shift of Labour's governance regime has sought to broaden the range of objectives of local and regional economic development, and shift the emphasis of others. It has particularly given greater emphasis to social inclusion, and also emphasised employment creation to a greater extent than wealth creation. This shift of emphasis is very clearly evident through comparison of the Audit Commission's two reports on local economic development best practice, one published in 1989 and the second in 1999. Whereas the 1989 report has a primarily economic emphasis and a secondary social one, the 1999 report gives a strong primary emphasis to the role of employment creation and alleviating long-term unemployment, with only a cursory mention of wealth creation.

Third, Labour's governance regime has placed a higher emphasis on the 'accountability' of local initiatives and central government support, particularly by stronger involvement of local government. It has shown a strong bias towards increasing local government representation on all locally based bodies, relying on a somewhat suspect credo that this develops stronger links to local democratically elected institutions which in turn should improve local involvement and citizen support. At the same time, however, Labour has not been fully content with existing local government structures and these have been reformed to place greater emphasise on corporate management and a directly elected chief executive (or mayor). Similarly, some aspects of local government roles will be increasingly affected by Labour's development of

---

4   See Lindberg et al., 1991, pp. 5–6, for example.

regional institutions: the English RDAs, the elected parliament in Scotland, and the assembly in Wales.

Fourth, Labour has tended to develop reforms which have shifted responsibility away from general purpose bodies towards more narrowly focused special purpose bodies that then have to network with each other. The key element of this has been the abolition of the TECs, which had a broad responsibility for training, small business supports and local economic development. These have been replaced by the four separate networks of LLSCs, SBS Business Link, the RDAs and an increased role for Employment Service Districts. Hence, whilst on the one hand asserting commitment to joined-up government, on the other hand, the practice has been to increase the independence of many agents and their programmes. This can be interpreted positively, as a means to focus single agents on improving specific programme delivery and achieving integration by inter-agent cooperation. It can also be interpreted negatively, as a caving in by the cabinet and prime minister to the interests of individual government departments and their Secretaries of State. Certainly the absence of transfer to RDAs of TEC training responsibilities and Business Link responsibilities, reflects victories by their respective parent departments of the DfEE and DTI against the objectives of the DETR which had tried to enlarge the responsibilities of the RDAs. Similarly, the development of the Small Business Service, the New Deal and the single gateway for welfare (ONE Service) are hybrid forms that exert the Treasury's direct influence over the DTI, DfEE and DSS, which appear to reflect a victory of Gordon Brown as Chancellor over his ministerial colleagues.[5]

Fifth, and perhaps most important, the general management context within which any government operates has shifted. This has fundamentally changed the nature of central-local relations and particularly the economic development role of government. For Labour this has led to a somewhat painful realisation that a return to simple Keynesian economic mechanisms and direct intervention in the economy will not work. The Keynesian approach that developed in the post-war period emphasised national mechanisms and fiscal policy to achieve full employment. Employment itself was conceived as a kind of 'service' that government had to provide, rather than as the outcome of particular economic or government activity. Most particularly, simple Keynesian failed because its focus on fiscal management tended to externalise decisions to the aggregate macroeconomic level very distant from the real economy. It left unanswered how government could help in specific fields to encourage endogenous growth.

---

5   A view echoed in *The Economist*, 'The Cafetière theory of government', 21 August 1999.

At a local level Keynesian approaches left little role for local government or other local agents. The key economic decisions were national ones, often developed chiefly between Government (primarily the Treasury), national industry bodies (primarily through the CBI) and the trade unions. Where there were more nuanced views, these were chiefly sectoral, e.g. via the 'mini-NEDDY' arms of the National Economic Development Council (NEDC). Indeed the chief way in which local government was conceived was as an expenditure arm of central government dominated by 'top-down' service provision and planning to provide key elements of the welfare state. This tended to underplay local economic particularities and the need to respond 'bottom-up' to individual local demands.

The recognition of a greater need to develop more responsive local and regional economic development initiatives can be seen as one of a range of responses to the need to shift away from the national, aggregate and tax-and-expenditure focus of government towards developing its contributions to the key factors underlying the economy: i.e. improving the specific components necessary for endogenous growth; encouraging the development of the competitive conditions emphasised by Michael Porter; the stimulation of local 'thinkers', 'makers' and 'traders' as argued by Rosbeth Moss Kanter; or the development of *local capacity* as argued previously by the author. Effective government has to operate through emphasis on both supply-side and demand-side aspects, and it has to be highly sensitive to local and other dimensions for meeting economic needs. This requires highly responsive and flexible forms of governance rather than top-down structures such as Keynesianism.

For businesses greater responsiveness is being achieved by placing greater emphasis on more flexible, adaptable and often smaller scale production or service units, often interlinked into complex networks of contracting and subcontracting. These networks have allowed business to respond locally, nationally and trans-nationally to changing customer choices and requirements. At the same time businesses have been able to adjust their production and delivery processes so as to be able to respond to continued and major downward pressure on unit costs. Not only is more produced than ever before, it is produced in potentially greater variety at ever lower prices.

There is some evidence that Labour is recognising the need for similar changes in government behaviour. Whilst government has been generally slower to develop flexible and more adaptable forms of governance that mirror those in the world of business, Labour's greater emphasis on local and regional agents is one way in which improved responsiveness may be achieved. But a greater role for local and regional agents is itself a considerable challenge. As a result of the greater complexity and interlinkage between economies (locally, regionally, nationally, and especially globally), local agents can no longer rely on the national government to assimilate, dampen and transmit economic signals demands to them – to 'manage' the national economy, as NEDC and Keynesian planning attempted to do. Instead, local and regional economies are directly accessed by global agents and economic trends. As a result local agents have directly to take responsibility for gathering the important economic information and signals, organising responses, and developing new delivery frameworks. This is not only a challenge for local agents. It is also a challenge for central government to 'let go' of its traditional command-and-control culture in order to permit local agents to be able to respond.

The increased emphasis on flexibility and adaptability of local and regional economies thus requires a far greater role for 'bottom up' rather than 'top down' approaches to economic development. It also requires agents to inter-relate with each other. The competitiveness, attractiveness, and effectiveness of local economies increasingly depends on how each of its economic agents contributes to local opportunities. This in turn depends on how agents interrelate with each other. This is the key aspect of local institutional capacity building that we argue underpins the necessary conditions for endogenous economic growth.

But local agents are not the sole source of local capacity. Their power and potential impact is strongly influenced by the stance that central government takes towards local bodies. This particularly influences the relative responsibilities and powers of local government, the existence and role of regional entities, and also the interface between government and economic agents through both specific supports and general regulatory regimes. Local economic capacity building thus crucially depends not only on local agents, but also on national and central government agents. The bottom-up approach is interdependent with the form of top-down initiatives and controls. It is towards assessing how far Labour's reforms tackle this important shift in up-down power relations that this book is aimed.

3.3   Interpretations of Negotiations within Governance Regimes

We will assess in later chapters how negotiations take place and how outcomes are determined between the agents involved in local and regional economic development policy. Our approach derives strongly from a strand of organizational network literature in economics, political science and to a lesser extent sociology.[6] We term our approach a *negotiations model*. Our approach is an encompassing approach that draws on various other academic concepts and ideas. We briefly summarize here the main alternative models that have been developed. There are many variants, but for simplicity of presentation we divide these models into five broad groups.[7]

Pluralism[8]

This argues that, in an open democratic system, negotiations between agents and government should allow all agents and interests to be represented. The advocacy of each interest should be able to act as a check or 'countervailing power' on other agents, and all trade-offs should be resolved as a political bargaining process. In this process agents will maximise their resources and effort given their assessment of the effectiveness they can achieve.

State-led Corporatism[9]

This is a development of pluralism that introduces government as an agent with additional power and resources. Government can intervene, it can intermediate and coerce to ensure that agents comply with agreements, and it can attempt to incorporate agents and their interests to try and ensure that they are drawn into supporting government's objectives.

The Resource-dependence Model[10]

This argues that agents operate in turbulent and uncertain situations which they attempt to control by influencing how the resources of other organizations are deployed. This can be achieved by various strategies e.g. cooption, recruitment, leverage, the granting of kudos, and offering other rewards. These strategies may be bilateral between two agents, or may be broader alliances to develop a 'community of interests' which perhaps can develop into winning

---

6   See e.g. Mokken and Stokman, 1976; Hanf and Scharpf, 1978; Stokman and van Oosten, 1994; Bueno de Mesquita, 1994; Ebers, 1997; Casson, 1997.

7   The discussion here draws on Hanf and Scharpf, 1978; Scott, 1985; Grant 1993, and Mizruchi and Galaskiewicz, 1994, to whom the reader is referred for a longer discussion.

8   Goldthorpe, 1984; Grant, 1993.

9   Schmitter and Lehmbruch, 1979; Offee, 1985, 1996; Cawson, 1985; Grant, 1993.

10 See Selznick, 1949; Zald, 1970, Pfeffer and Salancik, 1978; Cook, 1977; Benson, 1975; Burt, 1980.

coalitions. These horizontal alliances may allow an approach that is intermediate between a hierarchical 'command-and-control' system and a dispersed market solution.[11] However, strategies of influence also lead to reciprocal constraints that mean that the agents involved with each other may not be able as freely to pursue their own strategies.

The Social Class Model[12]

This suggests that as well as objective or economic reasons for inter-agent cooperation, there are also influences of social cohesion and control. A number of empirical analyses have pointed to the close similarity of social background, educational background in schools and universities, club membership and other interlocks between senior business managers, civil servants, government ministers and other key agent personnel. The combination of many personal interlocks between the individuals who are the leaders or key personnel of the main agents leads to a similarity of outlook and strengthens a 'class' view of how outcomes should develop. Taken to its extreme these interlocks may develop more into ensuring the continued dominance of their own class and social interests, or seeking personal kudos, rather than pursing the needs of the agent they manage. Developments of this model focus on the role of power-elites, dominant families and managerial control. These approaches emphasise the role of individuals who have gained almost total autonomy from the control of the interests of their agents: e.g. autonomy from shareholders in the case of large businesses, autonomy from their members for associations, or autonomy from the electorate in the case of government departments and ministers.

The Institutional Model[13]

This emphasises the laws and traditions within which agents must operate. As an agent becomes more enmeshed in negotiations with other agents in order to pursue its interests, it has to adapt its approach and views, even if this runs against the interests of its members or senior management. These mechanisms of adjustment can be formal or informal. A particular recent emphasis has been on the extent to which institutions may 'embed' the views

---

11 Williamson, 1985; Aldrich, 1976; Lindberg et al., 1991.
12 Mills, 1956; Hilferding, 1910; Sweezy, 1939; Zeitlin, 1974; Useem 1984; Mintz and Schwartz, 1985; Scott, 1979, 1987.
13 Di Maggio and Powell, 1990; Best, 1990; Granovetter, 1985; Heinelt and Smith, 1996; Goodin, 1996; Hollingsworth and Boyer, 1997.

and approaches of different agents so that they come to reflect similar outlooks even if they have developed these from entirely different starting points.

These five broad groups of academic approaches have each given rise to problems of application. Most importantly they have tended to be advocated in isolation of each other, and from other interpretations as the only possible form of explanation. A primary problem is that empirical evidence is often consistent with either one, or a number of the approaches simultaneously. This has caused a number of commentators to criticize much academic research on agent networks as 'over-theorized'. Grote,[14] for example, refers to much of the academic work as having an 'over-socialized bias'. The observation of Atkinson and Coleman[15] is particularly relevant to our case studies: that much academic literature on policy networks has discounted the ability of government and public administration to act autonomously to coerce or police networks, instead focusing exclusively on voluntary structures, social means of exchange, mutual trust and embeddedness. Hence, in the approach we develop here, we need a more encompassing perspective.

Certainly in our case studies, it is the government through its central departments and the central control of prime minister, cabinet and treasury, that is the prime mover and architect of the networks of negotiations we examine. This suggests that state-led corporatism as well as pluralism is at work. Despite this, we recognise that the scope for governmental leadership and coercion is fundamentally constrained by the need to rely on local and regional partners to respond and implement policy initiatives, who are themselves constrained by resources, social power and institutional position. Thus whilst government can lead, and we find this a key aspect of central-local relations in economic development, local partners must be genuinely committed. This means that negotiations are not simply ones of exerting leadership or control by a government or any other agent, but are as much about 'winning hearts and minds' and genuinely merging agent objectives to produce an agreed outcome that has a chance of being implemented.

Despite our unhappiness with the often simplistic approach of much academic literature, we nevertheless recognise that pluralist and corporatist approaches are at work, and that the influence of policy networks is not neutral. Once a negotiation takes place networks of inter-agent relationships affect the way in which agents operate and respond. However, whilst much of the

---

14 Grote, 1997.
15 Atkinson and Coleman, 1992.

academic literature has then focused on describing how policy networks operate, our purpose here is to analyse how outcomes are determined. Two key aspects are important to our interpretations.

First, networks of negotiations themselves influence the power of an agent. Generally the more central an agent within a network the greater is its power. This is not just the result of the resources deployed, but is also the result of the resources of other agents that can be mobilized through the structure of network interrelations. This certainly may depend on the number of 'ties' between agents, the importance of the agent, the personnel within each agent's organization with whom ties exist, and the ability of the agent to act as an intermediary.[16] Some authors have contrasted agents that act as 'hubs' which offer 'reflected' centrality, where an agent is tied to many agents, with those that act as 'bridges' which offer 'derived' centrality, where an agent is tied to a few crucial or central agents. We do not attempt to measure centrality, recognising that most studies that do so are fundamentally constrained by how centrality is measured. However, we do use (i) the concept of networks to interpret the pattern of utility losses or gains that agents receive from the outcomes of negotiations, and (ii) the form of the negotiation process itself, particularly whether government's lead has a chance of incorporating other agents in order to achieve implementation.

Second, an agent's performance may be influenced by the extent to which they network. As noted earlier, networks offer opportunities but also result in constraints. Hence, not only does an agent's power influence negotiations, but the act of negotiation also influences an agent's power. However, empirical assessments of the relation between the extent of networking and performance are ambiguous.[17] We focus in our analysis less on agent performance than on the influence of each agent on the outcomes of negotiations. However, it is important to bear in mind that an agent may be assessed by its constituents (shareholders, members, electors) in terms of the agent's perceived performance in the network of policy relations. Hence, it may be more important sometimes to appear to be closely linked with another agent (e.g. with government), particularly if this means that an agent will appear to be on the winning side. For other agents, however, it is more important that they stay close to their constituents and continue to advocate their preferences even if this means appearing to lose out in a negotiation. This balance of approaches is particularly difficult for business interests, particularly for business associations, with CBI,

16 See Galaskiewicz, 1979; Laumann and Pappi, 1976; Knoke, 1983; Miller, 1980; Mizruchi, 1982; Mintz and Schwartz, 1985.

17 See review in Mizruchi and Galaskiewicz, 1994.

BCC, IoD, FSB and others having to maintain a careful balance in order to avoid being seen as 'too cosy' with government from many of their member's point of view. Of course perceptions are only part of the problem, if agents are too cosy with government for the wrong reasons. This brings us to a third consideration.

Our third observation is to emphasise that usually the outcome of policy negotiation is not optimal from any one agent's point of view or for the economy as a whole. This has particular importance to the focus of the book on local and regional economic development. If the process of policy development to facilitate the economy cannot actually produce an outcome that is economically optimal, or at least an economic improvement, then why should government be trying to help economic development at all!

Because of the importance of this observation we enlarge on it below, and in chapters 9 and 10. We recognise from the outset that the lack of economic optimality leads us directly in our analysis to assessing not only the recent outcomes of particular negotiations, but also to assessing alternative scenarios more in line with economic interests.

3.4 Alternative Scenarios: 'Political' Outcomes and 'Economic' Outcomes

The outcomes of a given process of negotiation depend on the distribution of power, resources and agent objectives at any given point in time. These outcomes are unlikely to be 'optimal' in any sense, for any one agent, or for all agents as a whole. They represent only the result of the tradeoffs each agent makes over the period in which negotiations took place. For local and regional economic development this may present considerable challenges since there is no reason to assume that the outcome of negotiations to improve the economy actually achieve that purpose; it may achieve the reverse. This statement is a direct challenge to the concepts of both pluralism and state-led corporatism as means to implement economic development policy.

A number of commentators have argued, taking a pluralist perspective, that because of the accessibility of democratic government, all interests are represented in policy negotiations and each is held in check by the counterveiling power of the others, such that all trade-offs are resolved as a political bargaining process. State-led corporatist interpretations are similar. They argue that government intervention, government intermediation to ensure that interest groups comply with agreements, government incorporation to draw agents into the government's objectives, and social partnership leads to the joining of the disparate elements into a grand project.[18] These approaches were epitomised by the National Economic Development Council, set up in 1962 'to seek agreement on ways of improving economic performance, competitive power, efficiency', but in Middlemas' judgement led to 'arterio-sclerotic and defensive attitudes' by the trade unions and other interests, and became 'too close too government, too dependent on what government did or did not do, too subject to the pendulum'.[19]

Both pluralism and state-led corporatism underpin a perception that a politically efficient solution will produce an economically efficient solution. This interpretation underpins much of the political science contributions to this area,[20] as well as a number of economic arguments.[21] Gary Becker, for example, argues[22] that a

> political equilibrium (is produced that) has the property that all groups maximise their incomes by spending their optimal amount on political pressure, given the productivity of their expenditures, and the behaviour of other groups ... Policies that raise efficiency are likely to win out in the competition for influence because they produce gains rather than dead-weight costs, so that groups benefited have the intrinsic advantage compared to groups harmed.

An extension of the ideas of pluralism is concertation, which has been developed in Europe and underpins much of the way in which the European Commission operates. Building on Jean Monnet's concept of 'economie concertée', it is argued that a process of 'generalized exchange' can be encouraged through peak associations, direct representation, and other routes. Lehmbruch,[23] for example, argues that this process of concertation can replace the privileged access of one or a few groups by a plurality of antagonistic interests 'who manage their conflicts and coordinate their action with that of government in regard to the ... requirements of the national economy'. Marin[24] and others have argued that concertation allows the development of a general process of political exchange.

---

18 Schmitter and Lehmbruch, 1979; Offee, 1985; Cawson, 1985; Grant, 1993.
19 Middlemas, 1983, pp. 5 and 66, and quoting Selwyn Lloyd, p. ix.
20 Summarised by e.g. Lively, 1978; Goldthorpe, 1984; Grant, 1993, Greenwood, 1997.
21 Downs, 1957; Stigler, 1971; Posner, 1976; Pelzman, 1976.
22 Becker, 1983, p. 376, p. 396.
23 Lehmbruch, 1984, p. 61.
24 Marin, 1987; Marin and Mayntz, 1991.

Our approach rejects the idealistic views of pluralism, state-led corporatism, and concertation. We believe that there are many impediments that prevent politically efficient outcomes generating outcomes that improve the way in which the economy works. Whilst, it is certainly correct to focus on the bargaining and learning that occurs in negotiations to develop public policies, it is not inevitable that economically beneficial decisions are made. In fact the political process of negotiation is usually fatally flawed as far as economic decision making is concerned. Key flaws are:

- there is an inequality of opportunity, resources and ability open to different groups to represent their interests. This is the main political science criticism of pluralism.[25] But it is also a key economic feature underlying inequalities between different economic interests, between dominant firms and SMEs, and between economic and other interests. Unequal power removes the potential for pluralism or concertation to achieve economically (or socially) efficient outcomes;
- the outcomes of bargaining depend on the previous situation, particularly the strengths of each bargaining partner; it is *path dependent*. Hence, the most powerful groups in the political process at the outset of bargaining normally achieve the bias of decisions and regulations in their favour at the end of the bargaining process compared to less powerful groups. They form a policy community,[26] which tends to exclude other interests. Since power is rarely assigned with economic efficiency in mind at the outset, there is no reason to believe that the outcome of a 'politically-efficient' bargaining process will be 'economically efficient'. As stated by North, 'democracy is not to be equated with competitive markets'.[27]
- an economically efficient decision requires *full arbitrage*, whereby all trade-offs and outcomes are evaluated and resolved to achieve an economically-efficient outcome. This is never likely to be achieved in a political and administrative negotiation because of imperfect information, unequal power and resources, slowness of political and administration decision making compared to economic change and the influence of other political or administrative objectives.

Because of the outcomes of negotiations are not 'optimal' in the sense of inevitably improving the economic parameters they set out to improve, we

---

25 See e.g. Lively, 1978; Truman, 1951; see also Goldthorpe, 1984; Grant, 1993, 2000.
26 See Rhodes, 1986, 1992; Richardson and Jordan, 1979; Blank, 1978; Wright, 1988.
27 North, 1990, p. 57.

are led in our analysis to evaluating Labour's initiatives in two directions:

i) to assess how far Labour's initiatives do or do not improve the economy; and

ii) to assess how far outcomes would have been different if alternative scenarios had been followed in which the interests of different partners were given greater emphasis.

3.5   Conclusion

This chapter has introduced the concept of the 'governance regime' within which policy negotiations take place. We have sought to highlight the key features of the changed governance regime that Labour has sought to stimulate for the specific case of local and regional economic development. We have argued that there is no 'optimal' outcome as the result of the negotiations developed within any governance regime. Hence, the ultimate test of Labour's approach, of 'what matters is what works', is does the policy work?

We develop in this book an appraisal of policy negotiations based on an approach that allows comparison of outcomes with the objectives of the agents and an assessment of who gained and who lost in the negotiation process. Our approach also allows assessment of alternative scenarios that would have developed had Labour followed an approach giving greater emphasis to the policy objectives of any one of a number of the different agents involved.

The chapter has given a brief review of the main academic interpretations of how policy negotiations develop and how outcomes are determined. Generally we find this literature limited in its usefulness because it tends to emphasise the dominance of single explanatory factors: pluralism, corporatism, resources, class or institutions. Instead we develop in this book a more encompassing approach. We term this a *negotiation model*. It has no particular emphasis on who or how any individual agent or group of agents dominate. Rather, it starts from the premise that the outcome of any set of negotiations depends on the specifics of each agent's objectives, power and commitment to influence. Our model of the negotiation process encompasses each of the elements of pluralism, corporatism, resource-dependence, social class and institutional structures, with the emphasis shifting in each case dependant on the actual structures of the negotiations involved. We develop this model in chapter 4.

4 The Negotiation Process

4.1 Introduction

The concern of this book is with how agents develop negotiations on specific policy issues. As outlined earlier, these negotiations take place within a 'governance regime', shown in Figure 1.1, the priorities of which have changed in Britain after the election of the Labour government in 1997. Within this changed governance regime new policy initiatives have been developed by government to which each agent has had to respond. We develop in this chapter the negotiation model used in our case studies. Our approach encompasses pluralism, state-led corporatism, resource-dependence, social class and institutional models and does not presume that any one dominates.

We argue that the negotiation process is chiefly one of exchange. This involves exchange of information, but most importantly, it involves a willingness of agents to exchange their support or 'voting' positions, log-rolling between their desired objectives on different issues. This log-rolling exchange process is the key element which we seek to analyse in this book. However, the precise form of the negotiation process is not laid down, either by government, or its departments, or by the other public and private agents involved. Rather, negotiations depend on each agent's priorities, its internal form of governance, personalities and leadership. In other words, some aspects of the negotiation process are a choice made by the agents involved.

Because of these choices there is uncertainty about the form of the negotiation processes involved. Hence we do not assume that an exchange process of log-rolling occurs. Instead we test a variety of alternative interpretations of how negotiations take place and the way in which outcomes are determined. We do indeed find that an exchange process is the best interpretation of many of the negotiations we examine, but not all. In other cases agents choose not to log-roll but resort to conflict and lobbying.

In order to assess how the negotiation process operates we develop four alternative interpretations, or negotiation 'models'. Each model is assessed using analysis of the policy process based on information on each agent involved in the negotiation. The information on each agent includes an understanding of their policy position on each issue negotiated, their assessment of the importance of that issue (their salience or commitment to press for their position in negotiations), and an assessment of their power or capability to influence the outcomes. The information required for assessing the negotiations was obtained by an intensive set of structured interviews with the key individuals and agents involved. The process by which this information was acquired is discussed in the next part of this chapter. This is followed by a presentation of the alternative models which we use to assess how the process of negotiation takes place, how we evaluate these models against actual outcomes, and how we develop alternative scenarios.

4.2   Acquiring Information on Each Agent

Negotiations can only be fully understood by those who have been inside the process. But to acquire information from these 'insiders' is not straightforward since direct interviews may not yield a truly frank series of responses. However, the analysis in this book was considerably aided by building on research on the key agents undertaken in previous studies[1] which allowed many personal relationships to be used as entrées and means to gain a frank and informed 'off the record' briefing. In addition, over the life of many of the negotiations, one of the authors was advisor or consultant to a number of the agents involved and thus gained direct inside information. Furthermore, direct information was also derived from the proceedings of House of Commons Select Committees. However, the prime information used is the set of structured interviews. In all, over 60 interviews were undertaken specifically for the case studies in this book with the key individuals and organisations involved, including ministers and senior civil servants.

Using this process of gaining information each agent was subject to at least one intensive structured interview to gain information on: (i) the definition of the *policy issues* that are the most crucial aspects to each agent in the negotiations; (ii) the *position* of each agent on each of these issues; (iii) their *salience*; and (iv) their assessment of their *capability or power* to influence the outcome. This information was gathered in four sweeps of interviews:

1   *Interviews with experts and key negotiators:* these were used to define the policy issues and the range of possible positions and outcomes. The

---

1   See e.g. Bennett et al., 1993, 1994.

interview process was also supplemented by use of existing literature, parliamentary debates, and parliamentary committee proceedings, press coverage and other documentary sources.

2 *For all agents:* their policy position and salience was established from interview and their policy documents.

3 *For key agents:* their policy position and salience was established in interview: a check was also carried out on the definition of the key issues, and the relative power positions of themselves and *other* key agents. This allowed a process of triangulation of each agent's individual assessments of themselves and others.

4 *For the key negotiators:* a check was made on the relative power of all agents. The key negotiators in most cases were senior civil servants in the government department responsible for the chief financial resources under negotiation.

In order to be confident about the results of our assessments it is important that the best informed and key decision-makers were interviewed in each case. In large and complex organisations such as government departments this might involve several levels, ranging from political, to strategic, to implementation. Similarly within many of the key agents there is scope for a range of views, particularly where there are local bodies which may have to cope with different circumstances. Where possible, interviews were held at each relevant level and diversity assessed through local interviews and surveys. The broad pattern of interviews is as follows:

1 *Government:*

- Permanent Secretary, if possible;
- Senior civil servant responsible for implementation;
- Senior civil servant responsible for negotiation with partners;
- Minister, if possible;
- Parliamentary Committee Reports, Chairs of key committees, key members.

2 *Partners*

- Chief Executive, President or relevant director of national representative body;
- Survey of all, or sub-sample, or local interviews, of local bodies to determine:

    a) the range of local views that act as constraints on national representatives;
    b) the range of outcomes possible as a result of negotiations.

3 *Other agents:*

- Chief Executive, President, or relevant director, and/or key negotiator involved in process of negotiation.

Whilst it is impossible to be confident that every element of every agent's position, salience and capability has been fully covered, we believe that by this approach we have obtained a generally accurate assessment. The details of this process for each policy case study are discussed in chapters 5–8.

4.3   The Negotiation Process

We focus in this book on the dynamics of the process underlying the negotiations that lead to a final decision. We test a number of theories of negotiation, each of which has been specifically developed as a *quantitative* analysis of decision-making.[2] Each is also set within a broad framework that allows us to encompass the specific models of pluralism, state-led corporatism, resource dependence, social class or institutional determination outlined in chapter 3.

We assume that the key agents for each of the issues we examine are trying to reach their goals through a negotiation or collective decision making process. In this bargaining they act under various constraints deriving from their own organisations, and are also influenced by the environment at the

---

2   See e.g. Koenig and Pappi, 1993, Laumann and Knoke, 1987; Laumann and Pappi, 1976; Stokman and Van Oosten, 1994; Bueno De Mesquita and Stokman, 1994; Stokman and Stokman, 1995.

macro level. These constraints are economic, political, judicial, institutional and social. It is these constraints which define the governance regime we discuss in chapter 3.

Negotiations begin with a policy development process within each agent's organisation to frame its policy position. This might involve consultation with its members in the case of BCC, TEC National Council or the TUC. It will involve exchange between civil servants, ministers and consultants in the case of government departments. After this internal decision making, the negotiating parties develop their policy positions on the various issues related to the policy initiative in question. At this stage the agenda is formed and the negotiations with other agents begin i.e. negotiations begin to seek to transform individual goals into collective outcomes. This transformation consists of a process in which agents try to influence each other and the expected outcomes, aiming to reach their individually most preferred policy outcomes. According to Coleman (1990) this transformation process whereby individuals come to share goals is the core principle for any explanation of decision making. The approach we follow assesses a selection of collective decision making models of the process of transformation of individual goals to collective outcomes. These models share the similar basic assumptions and three key variables. The models differ in the way in which the negotiation process is modelled.

Each agent for whom an issue in negotiations is important has a preferred outcome. Issues are assumed to be unidimensional, meaning that the possible outcomes can be represented as points on a line, or as values on an underlying continuum.[3] This assumption is not restrictive. Indeed we find in our case studies that issues which at first sight appear multidimensional, are in fact a composite of several issues which can be separated into single unidimensional elements. The most preferred outcome of each agent on an issue is called its agent's *policy position*. The final stance of the agent on each issue is called the *voting position*. It is expected that the voting position can change due to the negotiation process. The outcomes of the collective decision making can be understood as the achievement of 'instrumental' goals[4] i.e. one outcome can produce benefits for one set of agents, whilst another outcome can be better for others. As a result, within a negotiation process, agents will attach different levels of *importance* to each issue. This will result in different and diverging stances of agents on each issue. Consequently agents can be expected to behave quite differently despite the assumption that they are all rational in

---

3   Stokman, 1995.
4   Lindenberg, 1990.

the sense that they are interested in maximising their welfare. Even agents in possession of the same information, and holding the same general goals, may nevertheless have radically different instrumental objectives.

We refer to the level of importance that an agent attaches to an issue as the level of its *salience* on that issue. This is a measure of the extent to which the issue is relevant compared to other issues the actor is concerned with. These two basic variables, the policy position and salience, when combined, express the value of each alternative outcome for each agent. This can be termed the utility function for each agent. The utility functions are assumed to be single peaked preference functions, i.e. utility gains or loss for any agent depend on the distance between the most preferred outcome and the actual outcome (or alternative outcomes), weighted by the agent's salience of the issue. Again, we find in our case studies that this is not a restrictive condition.

Agents differ not only in terms of their most preferred outcomes and salience, they also have different power or *capability* to influence the negotiation process, and thereby the collective outcome. The measurement of the capability of agents to influence policy outcomes reflects both their formal decision-making power and their informal weight. The formal power of agents derives from their legal or institutional position which may give them control over the financial resources or the choice of the specific decision rules that are used. This is, for example, crucial to a government department. Their informal weight is determined by many factors, among which will be the degree to which they have timely access to information and the resources (financial and personal) that can mobilize to gain access to resources.[5] These resources may also include the capacity to mobilize other supporting forces that can prevent certain outcomes. It may also be the case that some agents have considerable power because they are crucial to the implementation of a policy even though they have few resources. Our focus on local and regional development, for example throws up many cases where agents can prevent or diminish the effect of a policy by inaction or putting barriers in the way of development. Alternatively, at a local level, symbolic support is often required from local agents in order to achieve legitimacy or political credibility. The power of many business interests often relies heavily on this 'power of legitimation' even though few resources are available. This is particularly important to business bodies such as the CBI, BCC, FSB and FPB. It is also used by government and others through using support from key business leaders as a process of marketing on 'legitimation'. Recognising this

---

5   Mokken and Stokman, 1976.

phenomenon, we seek to ascribe capability of agents in our analysis in terms of the wider sense of their total power rather than merely their financial resources or formal power.

In our analysis, we test different models of negotiations. However, each model shares the same basic assumptions of agent behaviour and the three basic variables of: preferred policy positions, salience and capability. We assume that there is a set of agents: $i = 1, 2 \ldots n$, and a set of policy issues $j = 1, 2 \ldots, m$. The policy positions on issues j of agent i are X_{ij}. The preferred position on each issue is X^*_{ij}. We defined the positions on each issue j to be in a continuum a $0 \leq X^*_{ij} \leq 100$. The values 0 and 100 are defined as the extremes on each issue. They are the limits we consider to define the range of feasible outcomes given the information obtained in our interviews. The feasible range has to have at its limits the support of at least one agent. This constitutes the decision set over which our agents negotiate. Within this range, the positions of two agents, agent k and agent i, for example, can be compared by their distance apart, defined as : $| X_{kj} - X^*_{ij} |$. This is the difference between the desired outcome of agent k and agent i for issue j. The utility u^i of agent i for the position of X_{kj} will depend on its distance from X^*_{ij} i.e.

$$u^i X_k = f \, | \, X_{kj} - X^*_{ij} | \qquad (4.1)$$

The further the two positions are apart, the less is the utility to agent i for position of agent k.

We assume that each agent seeks to maximise their utility by negotiating in order to move the final outcome as close to their own position as possible. The agent will 'calculate' at least in an intuitive way the utility of different positions and pursue the one they believe is in their best interest (within the scope of the information available to them).

The weight of support (or votes caste in a voting context) for a given issue by an agent depends on the combination of their utility with their capability and their salience. Thus for agent i the weight (votes) for alternatives ℓ and k is:

$$V_{ij}^{k\ell} = c_i \, s_i \, (u^i X_{kj} - u^i X_{\ell j}) \qquad (4.2)$$

Thus the weight of support by a given agent depends on their utility for each position (which is a function of the distance of each position from the agent's desired position), but is weighted by the capability of the agent to influence the outcome c_i, and the commitment (salience) on that issue s_i.

This approach to defining a negotiating model takes account of the strength of competing agents, their interests, and their willingness to expend resources on influencing the outcome. The willingness to influence is the salience, which is itself the outcome of an evaluation by the agent of:

- their costs and benefits of action;
- their intensity of preference for each outcome;
- their constraints of total resources available (a budget constraint) given their other commitments.

The weight attached to a particular level of support may also be influenced by the extent to which the likely outcome is very different from the agent's desired outcome.

The salience attached to issues may also be affected by confusion and imperfection of knowledge about an agent's own position. In many situations with which we are concerned the agent may have a clear position but this cannot be pressed with as strong a commitment as might be expected because of internal divisions within the agent's organization. For example, national representative bodies have to represent a wide diversity of views among their members which leads them often to have to adopt a 'balanced' view. Sometimes their view can be in danger of becoming a 'lowest common denominator'. The policy positions and commitment in such representative bodies is itself the outcome of an internal voting and decision making structure. In our case studies this particularly affects the positions of chambers of commerce, TECs, local authorities and Business Links, for each of which representative bodies at national level are constrained by the range and diversity of the views of their local agents.

Uncertainty of commitment also affects government departments and hence reduces their salience in some of our case studies. For example, at a given point in time the political leadership of the department may not have come to a firm decision as to the preferred outcomes on all issues, or its position may change. This is a feature of some of the government departmental positions in our simulations resulting from the change in government since May 1997 and its policy positions on RDAs and the future of TECs. Low salience may also be the result of a department being accommodating to a range of local agent views, thus allowing the actual outcome to vary locally in some cases. For example, in the case of Business Link a strongly prescriptive approach by the DTI in its early phase up to May 1995 was replaced by a more flexible approach on certain issues, such as branding. The effect of this flexibility is to allow considerable local variation to reflect different agent positions, even though the DTI's policy preference has not fundamentally shifted. Similarly, low salience by a government department may result from a desire to allow different experiences to develop from which a more strongly desired preference may be brought forward at a later stage. In the case of RDAs, for example, the expressed governmental desire for their establishment to be an 'evolutionary process' which is 'flexible' to different regional circumstances[6] may well be replaced at a later stage of RDA development by a more prescriptive approach.

Saliences also reflect the evaluation by the agent of their potential to change the outcome. Every agent is strongly influenced by the external institutional structure surrounding the process of negotiations. This means that some possible outcomes that might be potentially desired are deemed at present to be so unfeasible that no agent takes up that position, even though it would be in their acknowledged best interests to do so. For example, the enhanced role of RDAs to take on major planning powers from local government, or to take a greater role in HE finance, is the only way in which the RDAs can become fully effective bodies in physical development and higher level skills development, but few agents are willing to take on this position given the judgement that it is at present politically a nonstarter. Similarly, in the case of Business Link partnership structures, a public law chamber of commerce system would be a greatly enhanced possible way for services to be delivered and financed, but the BCC has moved away from such a policy position because it judges it to be politically infeasible.

In interviews we found numerous examples of this kind where the effective range of the decision set of positions on any issue was severely narrowed. In our simulations we have adopted this narrower decision set as the (0–100) range of practically feasible positions as judged by the agents. We recognise that in future an entirely new set of political possibilities may open up which is beyond the range of the decision set modelled here. We have to interpret our models, therefore, as simulations within the governance regime and politically feasible set of options available at any point of time.

4.4   Alternative Models of the Negotiation Process

There are various methods of calculating the outcome of a given negotiating

---

6   Hedger, DfEE official, evidence in HoC, 1998a.

process. The choice of method depends upon the sort of negotiations which are being modelled and the extent of information that each agent has about the positions, salience and power of the other agents. In order to context our approach to the mainstream academic literature we list below the four chief models we use, and the key aspects of their calculation and their assumptions.

1 Base and compromise model This is the simplest model which ignores differences in utility and salience among agents, as well as any exchanges that may occur to policy position as a result of negotiations. The result is a prediction of the outcome O^B_j for issue j as the result of the combined influence of the policy position and power of the different agents I:

$$O^B_j = (\sum_i X_{ij}\, c_{ij}) / (\sum_i c_{ij}) \tag{4.3}$$

where c_{ij} is the power/capability of agent i on issue j. Note that in this calculation, as in most of the other models below, there is a dividing out of a given agent's power by the total power of all agents that are party to the decision. In some of the scenarios we modify this calculation to take account of what we term 'dominant' interests, which we define more fully later.

The base model can be amplified to include the influence of the commitment or salience s_{ij} of the different agents on each issue, but still ignoring the differences of utility between agents and of exchanges of positions during negotiations. This is a *compromise (base) model* since the outcome predicted O^c_j is still the mean of all agents' weighted positions and power, but now including their salience:

$$O^c_j = (\sum_i X_{ij}\, c_{ij}\, s_{ij}) / (\sum_i c_{ij}\, s_{ij}) \tag{4.4}$$

2 Exchange (log-rolling) model This model includes power and salience, as in the compromise model, but also adds consideration of the utility of each agent for different positions. Most crucial, however, it seeks to model the outcome of exchanges that occur in policy positions as a result of the negotiating process. The model assumes that all agents cooperate to bargain with each other, i.e. that agents will be prepared to take up new positions if another agent is prepared to do the same on that issue or another issue within the same set of negotiations (so-called log-rolling).

As a starting point the outcome function from either the base (4.3) or the compromise model (4.4) can be used. Using these functions, the exchange model calculates all two-way comparisons of agent positions on any issue and calculates the utility derived to each agent from a possible exchange on that issue. Comparing all such agent utilities, the two-way exchange with the highest expected utility is assumed to take place. The new position for the agents making their exchange will be between the two former positions. This exchange leads to *all other* potential exchanges for these two agents being deleted. The next exchange is then calculated on the same issue for the remaining agents, the highest potential exchange is identified, and so on until the new positions of all agents after exchange has been estimated. The final outcome function (4.3) or (4.4) can then be calculated from the new policy positions, but with the same capability and salience as at the start of the process.

The exchange process depends heavily on the salience components. An exchange of policy positions occurs because agent A is willing to shift their position on one issue on which it has a low salience but agent B has high salience, in exchange for a shift from agent B in their policy position on another issue where they have low salience but agent A has high salience. The exchanges proceed in a sequence which compares each potential exchange between those agents which receive the highest potential pair-wise gains. The agents with the strongest differences in salience, other things being equal, are normally those with the highest potential to make exchanges in order to achieve progress in negotiations. In our case studies this is usually an exchange between the chief government department involved (or the Treasury) and the key local agents that will implement the policy. Hence, our modelling focuses strongly on the central-local negotiation process so characteristic of local and regional economic development.

The exchanges that occur require a complex series of calculations which may have several solutions. If this is the case, in our models a comparison of all possible solutions is made and the mean and variance of different outcomes calculated, thus converting the assessment into a probabilistic estimate of the outcome. This approach, using the exchange model, is the chief approach that is adopted in our case studies. Further details of the assumptions it makes and the calculations involved are available in the established literature.[7]

3 Strategic Control Model: This model allows relaxation of the assumption of perfect information available to all agents. Although a level of common knowledge can be assumed to exist, the *control* an agent can exert and the

---

7   See Stokman and van Oosten, 1994; Stokman and Stokman, 1995.

level of their salience will differ considerably. Control is a new feature introduced to take account of the manipulation of information. Where agents with very different levels of resources (such as information, finance and personnel) are jointly involved in negotiations, a good estimate of their relative control can be difficult to make. The difficulties of assessment are even greater when an agent is very determined to mobilise resources, risking a high loss in case of failure. In these cases a high level of uncertainty is present that gives agents the opportunity for strategic manipulation. In the strategic control model the manipulation of control and salience is assessed in two steps.[8]

Step 1: an analytic solution is given for one single optimising agent. In this solution the optimising agent makes assumptions about the leverages of the other agents. The analytic solution can be decomposed into three elements: (i) the expected external leverage of the other agents on the issue; (ii) the evaluation of the distance of the expected from the preferred outcome; and (iii) restrictions on the distribution of leverage over the issues. The higher the expectation of the leverages that the other agents will deploy, the less an agent is inclined to allocate leverage to the issue. The higher the evaluation of the distance from the preferred outcome, the greater an agent is inclined to allocate leverage to the issue.

Step 2: an investigation is made of whether we can find a 'Nash equilibrium' if all agents optimise their leverage simultaneously.[9] Like the previous models, the strategic control model uses three variables, of capability, salience and policy positions, but now the policy positions are weighted according to the agent's interest in and control over an issue. This weighting is the leverage of the agent. The sum of the leverage for each issue gives the total leverage of that agent over all the issues in the decision set. The model assumes that an agent optimises strategic leverages over the issues in the decision set being negotiated. The strategic leverages affect the outcomes because they are shown to other agents. For the computation of the expected outcomes and consequently the optimisation of the strategic leverages, an agent has to make assumptions about the leverages other agents will show in the decision making. These are expected leverages. When more than one optimising agent is considered we need to examine the Nash equilibrium if all agents simultaneously optimise their strategic leverages. A Nash equilibrium is a profile of strategies such that each agent's strategy is an optimal response to the other agents' strategies. Since, as discussed earlier, we assume that

---

8   Stokman and Stokman, 1995.
9   The Nash equilibrium arise from the game-like character of attempts to exert strategic control. Nash equilibria are discussed more fully by Kreps, 1990.

there are continuous and single peaked preference functions, one or more Nash equilibria can exist. A Nash equilibrium cannot be derived analytically and must be estimated by an iterative process. The iterations are simulations of the process by which agents learn from each other during successive meetings and discussions. The final decision is made when no agent has any incentive to move strategic leverages from one decision to another. In this process different learning procedures can be assumed. The simplest is that agents take the last shown leverages of the other agents for granted and optimise their own leverage on the basis of the other leverages (this is termed the 'last solution'). An alternative is that the agents base their optimisation on the average values of each other agent over the past iterations (termed the 'mean solution'). In our development of the model we apply the mean solution.

4 Conflict (challenge) model In the conflict model, agents have to decide whether they will challenge other agents' policy or voting positions. This decision is based on an evaluation of the expected utilities of challenging or not challenging the position of an opponent. If agent i does challenge agent k, there are two possible outcomes: actor k will accept the challenge, or agent k will not accept the challenge and gives in immediately to the policy proposal of agent i. When agent k is challenged by agent i, the salience of agent k for an issue is interpreted as agent k's willingness to use its resources to try to influence the negotiation i.e. the probability of challenging or capitulating is s_{ij} and $(1 - s_{ij})$, respectively. If agent k accepts the challenge, there are again two possible outcomes: there is the chance (P^i) that agent i will win, and a chance $(1-P^i)$ that agent i will lose. The possibilities (P^i) and $(1-P^i)$ are based on the relative weights of resources (capability) of both the challenging agent i and the challenged agent k, taking into account the support they gain from third parties.[10] Where an agent does not challenge, the agent will take into account the possibility (Q^i) that the voting position of agent k on an issue will not change, and the possibility $(1-Q^i)$ that agent k's voting position will change anyway due to the influence of other agents also involved in the negotiations. In the latter case, there is the possibility (T^i) that this change in the voting position of agent k would be of benefit to agent i, or $(1-T^i)$ that it would be detrimental to agent i's interests. Therefore the choice of whether to challenge agent or not can produce total utility (benefit) to an agent that is positive, negative or neutral. The model uses estimates of the expected utility of each agent challenging each other agent. To this decision can be added a risk factor

---

10 Bueno de Mesquita, 1994.

q. Hence we can now define the utility function as, $u^iX_{ij} = s_{ia} \mid X^*_{ij} - X_{ij} \mid^q$. The exponent q takes account of risk-taking behaviour. For a risk-acceptant q = 0.5, risk neutrality has q = 1, risk avoidance has q = 2.[11]

Comparison of Models

The models we have introduced here differ in the way the transformation process takes place in order to reach an outcome. In the *conflict model*, the agents' perceptions of the chances of success or failure of challenging the policy positions of opponents are modelled.[12] Agents challenge opposing policy positions if they think this will result in utility gains for themselves. Depending on the perceptions of the opponent, the challenge results in a compromise or a capitulation of the opponent; or the status quo will prevail; or a conflict arises. After voting positions are shifted due to challenges, a new spread of voting positions, salience, capabilities and risk-taking behaviour will emerge. This forms a basis for new evaluations of strategies of challenging. This repetitive process of evaluations, challenges and shifts of voting positions stops if a state of equilibrium is reached, and a dominant outcome emerges. In the *exchange model* agents try positively to influence the expected outcomes through the exchange of voting positions with opponents, under the condition that the exchange results in equal expected utility gains for both agents. Realized exchanges between two agents on two issues at a time results in shifts of the voting positions of the agents. As a result the expected outcomes also shift, but not necessarily in the expected direction because of the multilateral nature of the negotiation process. After the exchange process, the outcome is determined as if a weighted voting procedure had taken place i.e. the outcome is an average, weighted by the policy and salience, of the voting positions. The *strategic control model* is more sophisticated, and more realistic for some situations in its underlying assumptions, than the other models. In the strategic control model, the assumption is relaxed that all the agents enjoy complete information about each other. Instead, the distribution of incomplete information across agents allows agents to behave strategically during negotiations. Unlike the exchange model, an agent is able to optimise the outcomes of decisions by manipulating the distribution of leverage (effective power) over a set of issues. We might expect that, over time, the agents involved in the policy process learn more about each other's preferences, salience and

---

11 See Bueno de Mesquita et al., 1985: p. 52-54; Bueno de Mesquita, 1994; p. 85-86.
12 Bueno de Mesquita, 1994.

capabilities. The assumption of complete information underlying the exchange model does not allow us to test for this phenomenon.

We test each of these models in our analysis and compare their results with the simplest approach, the compromise (base) model. We find in general that the exchange model performs best, and certainly performs best on average across all the issues and policy negotiations we assess. At first sight this may seem surprising given its rather rigid assumptions, particularly that all the agents have complete information about each other. However, the assumption of complete, or at least near-complete, information is not unrealistic for the situations we examine. This is so for five reasons. First, for all of the key agents in our negotiations there have been a series of continuous meetings and exchanges over many years on the issues we assess as well as a range of other issues. There have thus been many opportunities for each agent to learn about the other key agent's preferences, salience and capabilities. Second, we are dealing with a process in which all the key agents invest considerable time and resources, chiefly through specialist staff, in trying to find out government's and each other agent's positions. Third, many of the agents are not only national level negotiating bodies, but are made up as associations of many local bodies. This applies to local government, the chambers of commerce, TECs, enterprise agencies, and Business Link outlets. Others are associations of individual members, e.g. the CBI, IoD, FSB, FPB, and TUC. Each of these bodies has to communicate frequently with its own members, survey their opinion, keep them informed, and legitimize their national views through governing councils and executives. Although there may be attempts to keep the information and exchanges taking place within these bodies confidential, in practice this is very difficult. At local level, in particular, a fairly free exchange of information between partners takes place. As a result the positions and salience of most of these bodies becomes well known to other outsider agents. Fourth, many of the bodies make their case to government not only confidentially in closed meetings, but also openly in the press as part of a lobby process. Although this will always be carefully coloured and managed by the agent concerned, again wide dissemination of the views and salience of the agent becomes available.

Fifth, and perhaps of crucial importance, for government to be able to make its policies effective, it needs the active support of the key agents involved. It thus has to be relatively open in its own objectives and effective salience. Also for the support to be actually delivered by the key agents not only is active support needed in the negotiation phase, but continued support is needed for implementation. Government relies on local and regional partners and bodies for implementation in all the cases we examine. Indeed we argue that it is the multi-agent structure of local and regional economic development that leads to the need for a negotiation process to build capacity in the first place. As a result openness of information between government and partners, and between the partners themselves, is needed if real support is to be achieved. This is unlike a commercial negotiation where agents can be obliged to deliver after the conclusion of a negotiation, even if they subsequently regret the outcome. In a partnership process between central and local bodies, the agents can walk away from commitments if they realise they have been 'duped' into an agreement that they subsequently regret. In a very real sense, then, the process of negotiations we primarily examine is about winning hearts and minds that leads to commitment, for which relatively free circulation of information is essential.

The exchange model thus appears a priori to be the most appropriate for the negotiations we examine. We also demonstrate through our assessments that it is significantly better than other models in most cases.

4.5   Evaluation of Alternative Negotiating Models

The models to be developed in our case studies can be applied retrospectively to estimate how the outcomes were achieved of a negotiation process that is now complete. They can also be used prospectively to forecast the outcome of a negotiation process that is currently taking place or may take place in the future. Both approaches have methodological difficulties.

Retrospective analysis has the difficulty that interviews with key agents tend to be subject to an ex-post rationalisation of why an agent held a particular position or salience. Ex-post rationalisation is subject to agent's presenting a view that their positions were closer to the actual outcome than was really the case. This makes them look more successful.

Prospective analysis suffers from the difficulty that agents may not have yet fully formulated their views, which often tend to evolve during a negotiation process of long duration. For the case studies we analyse several years of negotiation were involved in each case. We cannot be sure at any point in time before the announcement of the outcome that we are assessing fully formed agent views.

In our case studies we include both retrospective and prospective analyses. The retrospective studies cover the establishment of TECs and Business Link in the early 1990s, and the establishment of RDAs and the New Deal for the unemployed in the 1997–98 period. The prospective studies cover the reform of TECs and Business Link to become the Local Learning and Skills Councils (LLSCs) and Small Business Service (SBS), respectively. However, whilst the interviews and analysis we undertook of the LLSCs and SBS were prospective, by the time of completion of the work we present here the outcomes were known. These were announced in July–October 1999. Hence for both the retrospective and prospective cases we have actual outcomes to compare with our simulations.

We evaluate the accuracy of our simulations using the mean square error criterion. This is a standard measure commonly used in assessing the performance of forecasts. It is defined by:

$$W = 1/N \sum_i (O_i - E_i)^2$$

where O_i is the observed outcome for issue i, E_i is the forecast or expected outcome, N is the number of issues involved in the negotiation and W is the mean square error. We also tested eight other evaluation criteria including the minimum absolute error, inequality coefficient, information accuracy and information gain.[13] The results were consistent across these criteria. Hence, in our presentation, we use only the mean square error criterion, and for presentation purposes the *prediction-realisation diagram*. The prediction-realisation diagram graphically compares the actual outcomes with those predicted by the simulation.[14] It provides a simple visual representation of the simulation which we find provides valuable insights into the policy process.

It should be noted, however, that the use of mean square criterion differs from the evaluations made in most other applications of the negotiation models we use here. For example, Stokman and Stokman measure the number of issues in which the simulations are accurate to within plus or minus 10 per cent. This is very simplistic. We believe that our use of the mean square error is preferable because it is more in line with standard forecasting evaluations and is more sensitive to all the differences between actual and estimated outcomes for each issue.

---

13 For a summary of the main forecasting criteria that can be used see Theil, 1966; Mincer; 1969; Bennett, 1979, pp. 573–5.

14 See Thiel, 1966.

4.6   Alternative Scenarios

The outcome of any negotiation process is unique to a particular point in time, representing the results of the tradeoffs each agent makes over the period that negotiations took place. It is in no sense 'optimal' for any one agent, or for all agents as a whole. Moreover, for a political and policy process it is also an outcome that can be opened up to new negotiations in the future. Indeed, in our case studies we examine two situations where the same issues are negotiated at a later time: first, for the development of LLSCs and TECs, and second, for the development of the SBS and Business Link.

New sets of negotiations may evolve very differently. In an earlier period not all possible policy positions may be represented. Also agent priorities may change. But most important, policy positions that were considered as totally politically infeasible at one point of time become feasible at a later point. Policy regimes shift. This allows agents to develop their agendas: in some cases it may allow them to come closer to realising their chief priorities; in other cases it may be more restrictive.

The chief focus of our analysis is on how local and regional economic development is promoted by various policy interventions. Hence, it is logical to focus on appraisal of alternative scenarios on how the dominance of different interests could lead to different outcomes. We develop alternative scenarios by re-weighting different agent power positions. We focus on scenarios associated with the key agents included in partnerships that are the chief means by which policies are implemented for local and regional economic development. We focus on scenarios associated with four key agents:

–   local business interests (the chambers of commerce);
–   national business interests (the CBI);
–   local public-private bodies (the TECs and LLSCs);
–   local government.

For each of these agents we develop a specific scenario which gives them a much more dominant position. We do this by increasing their power weighting significantly, and consequently reducing the power weight of all other agents. Comparing the different scenarios allows us to evaluate the consequence of following the priorities of one group of local agents to a much greater extent, whilst still having to negotiate a compromise with the objectives of the other agents. A general conclusion to come from evaluating these scenarios is that the priorities of local business interests and local public-private bodies such as TECs/LLSCs are crucial to the development of the local and regional economy. In contrast, the objectives of local government are generally inhibitive to local and regional economic development. These findings lead to some important implications for the future given, first, the shift from TECs to LLSCs and, second, the way in which the SBS is being developed in relation to local chambers of commerce. We spell out these implications in chapter 9.

4.7 Conclusion

The models of the negotiation process presented in this chapter provide the basis for our assessment of case studies that follow. We provide for each of four policy areas an analysis of agent policy positions, salience and capability. We then assess the outcome of negotiations using the five alternative models presented in this chapter. As noted above, we find the exchange model often to be the most accurate predictor of negotiated outcomes. This is in line with the expectation of a relatively open process of information availability. It is also strongly in line with the central theme of our argument, that to be successful, central government programmes have to use the support of the local and regional partners and other agents involved. A log-rolling thus has to take place whereby genuine changes in the positions of the key agents occurs in order to achieve an agreed outcome that has sufficient commitment of the key agents that it is likely to work. However, we also find conflict models to describe some of Labour's key developments, suggesting that some policies may be less successful, or that considerable modifications will be required before they can become successful.

For the purposes of economic development of localities and regions the actual policy outcomes are not necessarily 'optimal'. They merely reflect the outcomes achieved in negotiation between the agents involved at the time. Not all possible positions are represented, or fully represented, by the existing agents. Also at any point in time not all policy positions are considered sufficiently feasible. As a result key agents may not be able fully to pursue their chief agendas. To assess how far local and regional economic development might be better supported we introduce various alternative scenarios in our case studies and estimate their likely outcomes.

In the chapters 5–8 that follow we apply the models presented here to four case studies:

1 negotiations to develop Regional Development Agencies (RDAs);

2 negotiations to implement the New Deal for unemployed people;

3 negotiations to establish Local Learning and Skills Councils, and earlier negotiations to establish their predecessors the TECs;

4 negotiations to establish the Small Business Service, and earlier negotiations to establish Business Link.

For the last two of these negotiations we develop two sub-analyses: one for the early stages of evolution in the early and mid-1990s; and a second, for developments under Labour since 1997. These sub-analyses allow some direct conclusions to be drawn concerning the influence of Labour's change to the governance regime.

PART II
CASE STUDIES

5 Regional Development Agencies

5.1 Introduction

The Regional Development Agencies (RDAs) are a New Labour flagship. They are the most important aspect of Labour's changes to the institutional structures that influence local and regional economic development. Although RDAs are not in their early years as powerful as some ministers or other supporters would have wished, they nevertheless represent the major new agency on the scene. Also, with the abolition of TECs (see chapter 6), they are now the only dedicated general purpose economic development agent at sub-national level. On the one hand, RDAs are seeking to coordinate local activity in a more coherent way. On the other hand, RDAs are to act as a focus or 'glue' between the central government departments in order to underpin Labour's new model of more joined up, cooperative, and supportive Whitehall activity.

The RDAs were established as 'business-led' agencies with functions spanning from physical economic development to the creation of stronger links between small business supports, workforce skills, physical infrastructure, higher education and regional economic needs. Much of their design derives from Labour's detailed studies whilst in opposition, notably the Millan Report. However, the actual implementation did not fully follow this blueprint. Instead, the more typical process of negotiation between governmental departmental interests and other interested parties occurred so that in practice the development of the RDAs had all the typical characteristics of the sort of negotiations we seek to model. In this chapter we first introduce the detailed thinking lying behind RDAs and then describe the key issues subject to negotiations. This is followed by the implementation of our simulation methodology. This is used, first, to simulate the actual negotiation process and then, second, to assess alternative scenarios based on changing the structure of power relations.

5.2   The Development of the RDAs

The regional planning framework established by Labour in the 1960s had been abolished in the 1979–97 period. The only remaining formal regional bodies in England were the Government Offices of the Regions (GORs), established in 1994 to coordinate Whitehall activity. Hence, Labour was keen to re-establish a regional framework. However, a major change in its approach occurred with the launch in 1995 of a consultation paper, *A Choice for England* (Labour Party, 1995). At the same time there was a very specific and influential proposal developed by the North of England Assembly of Local Authorities (1995, 1996) for a regional government structure, and an influential report by Murphy and Caborn (1995). These reports formed the chief starting point for the detailed thinking behind regional changes in England which was set out by the Labour's Regional Policy Commission report of 1996.[1] This formed the background to much of the commitment to Regional Development Agencies (RDAs) and the possibility of establishment of regional elected assemblies that appeared as brief statements in Labour's manifesto.

The Regional Policy Commission believed that previous regional policy 'lacks a sense of strategic purpose, is centralised, prescriptive, piecemeal and inconsistent. It is dictated by remote Ministers, or by appointees to unaccountable quangos, and pays scant regard to the relative need of the different regions'.[2] The regional economic development need was argued to be a result of poor regional economic performance, unemployment or poverty: 'if any regions are underperforming, then the UK is not maximizing its economic potential.'[3] Perhaps the key element was the transfer of responsibility for decisions: 'Already, £11 billion per year is being spent in the regions on economic development, though little is determined by the regions themselves.'[4]

The Regional Policy Commission[5] followed Murphy and Caborn and the North of England Assembly of Local Authorities in proposing that the RDAs were to be 'responsible to regional Chambers, but operationally separate, acting as their executive arm in the area of economic development'. The boards of RDAs should be appointed by the Chambers, with scope for different levels of responsibility between regions. The RDAs should work within a plan drawn

---

1   Chaired by Bruce Millan, former European Commissioner for regions, and usually referred to as the Millan Report.
2   RPC, 1996, p.v.
3   RPC, 1996, p.v.
4   RPC, 1996, p. xv.
5   RPC, 1996, pp. vii–xv, and following chapters.

up by the Chamber, agreed with the Minister. The Chamber would be composed of indirectly elected representatives of local government until it was possible to establish directly elected regional assemblies. Power over Regional Selective Assistance (RSA) grants and inward investment through Regional Development Organisations (RDOs), both supported by the DTI as grants to businesses, should be reviewed with consideration given to delegating it to RDAs (whilst ensuring that regions did not compete with each other). The Single Regeneration Budget (SRB) from the DETR should be changed from a competitive challenge format to block grant allocated on the basis of need. The development bodies of English Partnerships (EP) and the Rural Development Commission (RDC) together with their functions, assets and funding should be transferred to RDAs. Many other elements of the Regional Policy Commission recommendations focused on strengthening the role of local government: in housing block grants, Tourist Boards, European funding (within RDA and Chamber planning), local economic development and sustainable development.

The Government Offices of the Region would be retained but have a greater input and be more responsive to regional economic strategies, coordinated by a single Minister responsible, at cabinet level, for coordinating and integrating regional issues. A key part of RDAs would be the development of Regional Skills Agencies, which might be integrated with RDAs. The FE sector, the Employment Service and TECs would work with the Skills Agencies and TECs should focus more on promoting employer-based training. The HE sector should also become involved as a partner, but its powers were left unchanged.

The Regional Policy Commission left the longer term future of TECs hanging in doubt, suggesting that they be fully reviewed, whilst any further mergers between TECs and chambers of commerce should be stopped, and where possible de-merged. Business support through DTI to Business Link should flow directly from GoRs rather than through TECs. Infrastructure and planning issues were seen as a key part of the RDA role in terms of strategy, but were left as chiefly local government activities.

The target of decentralizing £11 billion to regional responsibility involved transferring responsibility and involvement in SRB, EP, RDC, RSA, TECs, FE and BL, as well as elements of housing and other programmes. These changes involved the Department of Environment (which became the Department of Environment, Transport and the Regions – DETR) which is now the central government department for the regions with its Secretary of State, then John Prescott, the deputy prime minister, becoming the Cabinet minister responsible for regional coordination. The DETR previously had control over SRB, EP and RDC, as well as housing and most local authority matters. It was relatively easier, therefore, for regional changes to develop in these areas than in the policy areas involving DfEE (for TECs, FE and HE) or DTI (for RSA, BL and inward investment). It was also easier to develop decentralisation of central government programmes, than to create greater coordination of local elements. The lines for policy conflict and the need for exchange were, therefore, clearly developed from the outset.

The final form of the RDAs and Chambers in many ways follows the RPC recommendations. The structure was announced in a December 1997 White Paper (DETR, 1997), with 'shadow' chairs and boards of RDAs and Chambers, respectively, established in March and August 1998 with the final operational launch of the agencies in April 1999. However, the redesign of TECs and Business Link was not announced until June 1999, to be completed in April 2001. Hence, the subregional structure has taken time to emerge, and continued to be developed by DfEE and DTI independently of the RDAs. The absence of TECs and BL from the RDA role is a crucial gap and one which departs radically from the RPC recommendations.

During this extended start-up period considerable debate and tension emerged over the range of powers available to RDAs and the extent to which they would be able to integrate across the range of issues needed for an effective regional economic function. Tensions also surrounded the decision to postpone the development of any directly elected regional assemblies, except in London where the RDA, called the London Development Agency, is complemented by an elected executive mayor and a 25-member elected Greater London Authority. The tension over whether there should be elected assemblies for all regions continues but a decision has been postponed until the next parliament.

The RDAs were established following five guiding principles: integration at the regional level; decentralisation from Whitehall; stimulating regeneration chiefly via EP, RDC and SRB; developing partnership between local agents; and encouraging sustainable development (Richard Caborn, Minister for Regions, 1998).[6] In their initial phase of development from 1998/9 they received the following chief responsibilities.[7]

- Funding and administration of the former budgets of:
    - Single Regeneration Budget (SRB);
    - English Partnerships (EP), including the Commission for New Towns (CNT);

---

6 Hansard 304, No. 97, 14 January 1998, *Parliamentary Debates*, pp. 373–4.
7 DETR, 1997.

- compulsory purchase powers (in limited fields concerned with regeneration chiefly the same as those possessed by EP);
- Rural Development Commission (RDC);
- Development Fund.

- Preparation of regional strategies:
  - economic strategy and business support;
  - innovation strategy;
  - skills strategy/agendas;
  - regional planning guidance (e.g. housing, transport, infrastructure);
  - integrated transport strategies.

- 'Take the lead':
  - handling inward investment, working with RDOs.

- 'Work closely with', act as partners, or 'engage ... to ensure that provision takes full account of emerging economic trends' in the fields of:
  - FE;
  - HE;
  - TECs;
  - local authorities;
  - NTOs;
  - agents in sustainable development;
  - cultural agencies (arts, sport, heritage, tourism, film industry).

- 'Provide advice':
  - Regional Selective Assistance (RSA).

- Monitor:
  - TEC contributions to regional economic objectives.

- RDA to be represented in Committee structures elsewhere:
  - Regional Tourist Boards.

The DETR Supplementary Guidance[8] lists the chief programmes and responsibilities of RDAs. There are approximately 25 programmes under the heading of regeneration, 12 under the heading of competitiveness, three for

---

8   DETR, 1999.

skills, no specific programs for sustainable development, two for rural areas, and additional objectives for equal opportunities and involvement of the voluntary and community sector. These are all to be developed within national policy targets and objectives.

The major of these responsibilities derive from the budget of the DETR, which has prime responsibility for the regions. It clearly proved much more difficult than originally envisaged to bring together the DTI, DfEE, and other relevant budgets and responsibilities from other departments. The DTI fought particularly hard to keep control of RDOs in order to avoid competition between the RDAs, and between the RDAs and Scotland, Wales and Northern Ireland. In late 1997 the DTI was given the role of clearing 'indicative offers' that were made by the different regions and countries and would be managed by a 'concordat' which would govern the maximum levels of aid that could be offered to inward investors.[9] The concordat, which also covers Scotland and Wales, was finally confirmed in a rather weak form only in October 1999 and is policed by the Cabinet Office.

This arrangement has been deeply resented in Scotland and Wales who see the DTI role as a right of veto and a power to decide where investment should go.[10] Although the RDO budgets of £10.9m have been transferred more firmly within the RDAs, the 'concordant' is judged too weak to avoid competitive bidding, and the Cabinet will probably act chiefly to limit maximum aid levels.[11] However, even this structure is not judged to be stable, with regional officials judging the arrangement 'not worth the paper it's written on'[12] because effective controls are greatly diminished now that the Scottish Parliament and Welsh Assembly are established.

The DfEE has also resisted losing control of TEC, FE or HE budgets, but has played its hand cleverly by arguing for the need to maintain national standards whilst encouraging local and regional partnerships to bring coordination of strategies. Finally, in June 1999 it sought to pre-empt any further transfer of budgets to RDAs by setting up its own subregional bodies of LLSCs to succeed TECs (see chapter 7) and reducing its role in GORs. Nevertheless, two House of Commons Committees (HoC, 1997, 1998a) have undertaken enquiries into the relation of RDAs and TECs. Both concluded in favour of immediate transfer of powers of TEC responsibility to RDAs.

---

9 *Financial Times*, 5 November 1997, 'Blair passes plan to end regional aid row'
10 *Financial Times*, 17 November 1997, 'Climbdown on inward investment'.
11 *Financial Times*, 16 June 1998, 'Beckett defeated on deal to halt poaching of inward investment'.
12 Op. cit.

Government has resisted this, arguing that the first priority is 'developing a strategic vision for their regions and to build the necessary relationships'. In the longer term the government accepted that 'There may be scope to develop and rationalise further regional structures over time.'[13] Richard Caborn, the minister originally responsible for the regions and RDAs, stated that 'there is no reason why the role of the RDAs should not develop over time, as that of the Scottish and Welsh Development Agencies did.'[14] This position was reaffirmed by the then DfEE Minister responsible for TECs, George Mudie, as recently as late 1998 who stated his personal view that: 'as time passes and the regions grow in confidence and authority, the money will pass down ... When they have grown in authority and the partnerships have hardened ... we will sit back and be able to take a wide picture.'[15] However, the announcements of the independent development of LLSCs and the SBS by DfEE and DTI, and the withdrawal of these two departments from the GORs preempts further significant evolution. Hence, although the development of RDAs has been seen, at least potentially, as an evolutionary process this is unlikely to move very far in the foreseeable future.

As well as being limited by resistance to loss of powers between central government departments, the regional proposals have also been limited by resistance from local government to loss of their existing autonomy and pressure from local authorities for control over RDAs through the regional chambers. The Local Government Association (LGA) campaigned for the RDAs to be answerable to the Chambers, submitting its strategy for approval, with similar powers for the Chamber to those of the Secretary of State: for information, advice and assistance.[16] However the RDA Act and subsequent ministerial statements have instead assured RDAs a level of independence of the Chambers 'having regard' to their views in preparing economic strategies, and consulting them on corporate plans.

The result has been RDA Boards which are business-led, with about 12 members, all with a chair who is from business or recently from business. Only four of the board positions are appointed from the local councillors in the region, and members are paid. 'RDAs will have a large measure of autonomy, allowing many of the decisions on their operation to be left to their

---

13 HoC, 1998c, p.v., paras. 12 and 13.
14 Hansard 677, 1 April 1998, *Parliamentary Debates*, p. 1332; restated in speech to TEC National Conference 1 July 1999.
15 Evidence to House of Commons Education and Employment Committee, 10 December 1998, para. 7.
16 Local Government Association, Circular 71/98, 21 January 1998.

boards, in consultation with local partners' (DETR, 1997, p. 51). The initial chief executives, however, were all from public sector backgrounds, ranging from former civil servants, to positions in development agencies and funding councils or local government.

The Chambers are much larger bodies, ranging between 30–40 members in the Eastern Region to up to 115 members in the South West. Evolution has led to a smaller steering group emerging within these large bodies, as in the East Midlands. The local authority members within the chambers are dominant, but all other major local stakeholders are supposed to be represented, either directly or through consultation by the chamber or the RDA.[17]

5.3   Issues in the RDA Negotiations: Stakeholders' Perspectives

The analysis we develop here is concerned with the negotiations that took place up to and including the first year of operation of RDAs in 1999/2000. The key issues involved, determined in extensive interviews with participants and experts, are shown in Table 5.1. There are 18 of these. However, it was very clear in our interviews that these fall into three rather distinct groups.

Phase A covers the development of RDAs up to the time that detailed proposals were published in the White paper of November 1997 (although these issues were not formally agreed until the Act of Parliament was passed in July 1998). Phase B and C negotiations concern the ongoing exchanges up to April 1999, but in most cases are issues still unresolved. Phase B is distinguished from Phase C in the relative importance of the issues, with Phase C leaving issues that are still to be confronted in the longer term. We discuss each of the issues of the three phases of RDA negotiations identifying the agents involved, their policy preferences, and salience and power.

5.3.1 *Policy Issues and Positions of Agents: Phase A*

In the first phase of the RDA debate, we identify eight issues which were negotiated together. These issues include the responsibility for the Regional Selective Assistance (RSA); responsibility for the Single Regeneration Budget (SRB); whether the RDAs should take over the roles of various local agents such as the English Partnerships (EP), the Rural Development Commission (RDC), and the Commission for New Towns (CNT). There were also three

---

17 DETR, 1997, pp. 50–53.

Table 5.1   Issues involved in the RDA negotiations divided into three phases

Phase A:
Issue A.1   DTI versus RDA with respect to RSA
Issue A.2   DETR's responsibility and RDA with respect to SRB
Issue A.3   RDA versus English Partnerships
Issue A.4   RDA versus Rural Development Commission (RDC)
Issue A.5   RDA versus Commission for New Towns (CNT)
Issue A.6   Board composition: private led or public led?
Issue A.7   Chamber composition: private led or public led?
Issue A.8   Accountability of the Board: accountability to Regional Chamber

Phase B:
Issue B.1   TECs versus RDA with respect to training policy
Issue B.2   TECs versus RDA with respect to local economic development policy
Issue B.3   TECs versus RDA with respect to SME business support policy, including Business Links
Issue B.4   RDA versus local authorities with respect to transport policy
Issue B.5   RDA versus local authorities with respect to planning policy.

Phase C:
Issue C.1   DfEE versus RDA with respect to HE
Issue C.2   DfEE versus RDA with respect to FE
Issue C.3   DETR versus RDA with respect to Standard Spending Assessment (SSA)
Issue C.4   RDA versus local authorities with respect to use of compulsory purchase power
Issue C.5   RDA versus local authorities with respect to environment and sustainability policy

other issues which concern how the RDAs would be governed. These include the composition of the RDA Board (whether it would be private or public led); the composition of the Regional Chamber; and how far the RDA Board should be accountable to the Regional Chamber.

For each of these fields of activity there was an existing government department responsible for the programme. In general, most departments affected by changes were resistant to RDAs, supporting the status quo, and represented one extreme in the negotiations. Generally at the other extreme was either the DETR as the department responsible for bringing the RDAs to life, or the business point of view, which generally wanted to produce powerful and strongly integrated agents. Between these positions were local authorities, who generally favoured RDAs, but only if the chief powers they exercised were derived from central government and not from local government. Also with intermediate positions were those government departments that were not directly affected by the specific issue, and many of the more peripheral actors.

Responsibility for RSA This was one of the more disputed issues, only resolved in early 1999 after intense lobbying from several sides. At one extreme the DTI wanted to retain its responsibility for RSA. At the other extreme, the DETR as well as the shadow boards of the RDAs called for power to allocate RSA completely independently of the DTI. This position was also supported by the local authorities and the Regional Chambers. The CBI and the BCC took the view that the RDAs should be allowed to assess all bids and allocate RSA funds up to a maximum of £5m independently of the DTI. The BCC recognised that 'central Government should maintain some control over larger allocations of RSA, to prevent regions using these funds to out-bid each other for inward investment. In such situations, one region wins but the country as a whole is worse off'.[18] The outcome is that the RDAs assess all bids and make recommendations regarding the levels of support which are referred to a Cabinet committee for decision, removing some power from the DTI.[19]

Responsibility for SRB The DETR was responsible for the Single Regeneration Budget (SRB). With the establishment of the RDAs it sought to have the allocation responsibility for SRB transferred to them. Most other agents supported this. Only a small number of agents opposed this proposal. However there were a large number of agents who were conservative in their preference, particularly the other government departments of the DTI, DfEE, Home Office, and the GoR which wanted to continue the national bidding process with regional coordination and advice from the GOR and the RDA. The final outcome has been for bidders for SRB to have to submit proposals 'in accordance with the appropriate RDA'.[20] However, the government launched

---

18 BCC, 1997, p. 20; see also CBI, 1997a.
19 See *Financial Times*, October 1999,
20 DETR (September, 1998) *Single Regeneration Budget: Bidding Guidance: A guide for Partnerships.*

the 'New Deal for Communities' with pathfinders developing in Spring 1999, at the same time as RDAs were developing.[21] There thus remains a continuing tension between the role of the RDAs and central government initiatives in the allocation of regeneration funding even within DETR funding streams. The RDAs took over full responsibilities for SRB and EU funding decisions from January 2001.

Responsibility for EP, RDA and CNT Prior to the RDAs the national bodies of English Partnerships (EP), the Rural Development Commission (RDC) and the Commission for New Towns (CNT) operated separate agendas. The RDAs provided an opportunity to rationalise their functions and provide coordination at regional level. There was fairly widespread support for this development, but it was resisted strongly by the agents themselves, particularly the RDC. The BCC position was fairly typical:

> the creation of RDAs should in essence be deregulatory, simplifying organisations, programmes and procedures. The proposed RDAs should absorb the functions of the English Partnerships and the current Regional Development Organisations ... and the Rural Development Commission with certain safeguards.[22]

However, the actual transfer of responsibility of the former bodies to RDAs reduced freedom, with receipts from sales of regenerated land and property being collected centrally and then redistributed.

Composition of the RDA Board Positions on this issue were held strongly by business interests, and supported by ministers, to require RDAs to be business-led. The BCC held that the RDAs, 'should be run essentially as private sector organisations'.[23] Likewise the TEC National Council pointed out that 'most TECs are attracted to the concept of a small RDA Board, comprising a majority of private sector members. They believe that such a structure would provide for effective and efficient management, and a sharp focus on the key priorities and objectives'.[24] The White Paper and subsequent Act developed guidance for composition for Boards to be composed of 66 per cent private sector

---

21 DETR (September, 1998) *New Deal for Communities: Phase 1 Proposals, Guidance for Pathfinder applicants.*

22 BCC, 1997, pp. 1-2.

23 BCC, 1997, p. 20; see also CBI, 1997.

24 TEC National Council, 1997a.

employers and representatives, with four of the 12 members from local government or other interests. At the other end of the spectrum, the local authorities and many of the more peripheral agents argued for the RDA Board to be comprised of no more than 33 per cent private sector employers or business representatives.

Composition of Regional Chambers The DETR and the local authorities, as well as many peripheral agents, argued that the Regional Chambers should be composed of at least 90 per cent local authority representatives, with the rest drawn from private employers and other interests. Many other agents accepted the need for a strong local authority presence on Chambers in order to secure local accountability. However, many agents would have reduced the local authority role to be no more than 40 per cent local authority representatives so that a wider range of other community and local interests could be requested. This view was supported by the CBI, BCC, TECs, Business Link Network and the enterprise agencies. The outcome of negotiations was that the Chamber should be composed of at least 80 per cent local authority representatives.

Accountability of the Board The issue of accountability of the Board was a very controversial one which was lobbied for hard. The Regional Policy Commission had argued in 1996 for the RDA Board to be accountable to, and be appointed by, the Chamber. Central government departments, other than the DETR, tended to favour the RDA Board being largely an implementation agency working with programmes and targets set by Government departments and the GoR. A more extreme set of the views from the RDA shadow boards, CBI and the BCC is that the RDA should be an executive body accountable only to the minister(s) and parliament, consulting with the Chamber. The TEC National Council strongly suggested that

> the experience of TECs themselves leads us to recommend that the transfer of funding does not occur until there are robust and transparent mechanisms in place to ensure that the regional and local communities are able to contribute to the decision making process on the RDAs strategies and activities and the allocation of their resources within the regions.[25]

At the other extreme, accountability to the Chambers was sought by the local authorities, as well as by many of the more peripheral agents. They wished that the RDA Boards to be largely an implementation authority working within

---

25 TEC National Council, 1997a, b.

targets set by the Chamber which would ultimately be directly elected.[26] The outcome has been that the RDA is an executive body, working within the broad strategy set by the Chamber as well as the GOR and central departments, but able to make its decisions independently within its corporate plan which is agreed with ministers.

5.3.2 Policy Issues and Positions of Agents: Phase B

There are five issues in the second phase of RDA negotiations. These issues are much more controversial and cannot be put off for too long before being resolved. The first three issues in this phase are all concerned with the level of transfer of different types of policy responsibility from the TECs to the RDAs. These issues concern training policy, economic development policy and business support policy, including responsibility for Business Link. In each of these areas possible transfer of financial responsibility from TECs to RDAs was discussed, together with intermediate positions of giving RDAs greater or less ability to vire TEC budgets, or set up a separate Development Fund for the fields of training, local economic development or business support.

TEC Training responsibility The former training responsibility of the TECs has been retained in the new LLSCs. This represents a victory by DfEE against strong arguments from most other agents and two House of Commons Committee reports that recommended transfer. Although, the DfEE minister responsible for TECs acknowledged that further changes may be likely over the three or four years following the establishment of RDAs,[27] the development by the DfEE of LLSCs since July 1999 appears to pre-empt any further shift of responsibility of former TEC budgets to the RDAs.

TEC responsibility for Local Economic Development Policy Like the previous issues, TEC economic development policy concerns the possible transfer of responsibility from the DfEE to the RDAs. For the most part the positions of agents on this issue were the same as the last issue, although there were some differences chiefly relating to the possible role of local government rather than RDAs in taking on the TEC role. In practice the outcome has been for much of the TEC responsibility for local economic development to disappear altogether with the establishment of LLSCs. In effect, therefore, the role of

---

26 see e.g. Harding et al., 1999; Morgan, 1999.
27 George Mudie, DfEE minister, evidence to House of Commons Education and Employment Committee, 10 December 1998.

RDAs, as well as local government, has been enhanced, but with no additional finance or responsibility offered.

TEC responsibility for business support The level of RDA responsibility for business supports chiefly involves the finance of Business Link. The TEC National Council pointed out that 'it is vital that the links between the GORs and RDAs are strong and effective and roles, particularly in relation to TECs and Business Links but also in other areas of joint interest, are clearly defined and complementary'.[28] However, the DTI, which is the funding body for Business Link, has strongly resisted this change. The outcome has been largely the maintenance of the status quo, but with the DTI handing over contracting of BL to a the new body of the Small Business Service from April 2000 which will act independently of RDAs (see chapter 8).

The last two issues in the phase B negotiations concern the development of RDAs in policy areas which are chiefly the responsibility of the local authorities but outside the core area of economic regeneration, such as transport, land use, public health and housing. These are all relevant to economic development and need to be addressed by the regional chamber in the development of a broad regional strategy. However, no executive role for RDAs has been developed in these fields, despite recognition that: 'The RDA should be required to consult regional bodies such as the Highways and Environmental Agencies in the development of its economic strategies.'[29]

Transport policy The local authorities were generally opposed to any major change in transport policy, desiring to remain as the chief agent for policy decisions, regional issues being decided by discussion between local authorities. At the other extreme were the main private sector business interests such as the CBI and BCC, which argued that the RDA should have a level of independent power with regard to making transport policy decisions for a defined range of economic development purposes. The outcome has been that the local authorities remain as the chief agents for transport policy decisions and, while they have to take account of the RDA strategy as well as monitoring it, they only have to consult with the RDA where absolutely necessary.

Planning policy For planning policy, the debate was very similar to that of transport, with agents taking similar positions. The local authorities again

28 In HoC, 1997, pp. 148–9.
29 HoC, 1997, p. 151.

resisted any proposal which threatened their position as the chief agent responsible for physical planning decisions. They also opposed transfer of the compulsory purchase power from EP to the RDAs.[30] They were supported by many other central government department interests, which wanted to see minimal change, as well as a number of the more peripheral agents. The main business associations again called for more radical changes, whereby the RDA would be given independent planning powers for a defined range of economic development purposes. The BCC stated that 'it would clearly be unsatisfactory if the RDA was trying to deliver the objectives of the regional economic strategy on the one hand, and being prevented from doing so, say by regional planning guidance, on the other'.[31] Likewise the CBI argued that the 'RDAs should be strategic bodies. They should exercise their responsibility by (a) ensuring the delivery of economic development priorities (b) helping to shape regional transport and land use planning strategies'.[32] This was further suggested by an editorial in the *Financial Times*[33] which referred to the need to reform 'Britain's archaic and inefficient planning system' in favour of stronger support for business. This argument was rejected by Richard Caborn, the Minister for the Regions, who argued that improvements could be made, but radical change was not needed.[34] As with transport, the outcome has been close to the status quo: local authority planning decisions are to be monitored by the RDA, but the compulsory purchase powers of EP were transferred to RDAs.

5.3.3 Policy Issues and Position of Agents: Phase C

The last group of issues concerns the relation of RDAs to higher education (HE), further education (FE), and some aspects of the Standard Spending Assessment (SSA). A further two issues covered the role of RDAs compared to local authorities in the fields of compulsory purchase and environment and sustainability policy. Although these issues have a longer time frame, they are significant issues in the negotiations because they form part of the overall Government strategy for future possible roles of the RDAs.

---

30 LGA Circular 71/98, 29 January 1998; see also, Murdoch and Trewdwr-Jones, 1999; Morgan, 1999.
31 BCC, 1997, pp. 17.
32 CBI, 1997b.
33 *Financial Times*, editorial, 14 December 1998, 'Competitiveness'.
34 Richard Caborn, letter to *Financial Times*, 17 December 1998 'Regional Planning initiatives aim to modernise but leave the roots in tact'.

Higher education In general, most agents, including the universities themselves, opposed the transfer of any significant responsibility to RDAs for university funding.[35] However, others argued that the RDA should have full executive responsibility for some elements of HEFCE funding including the ability to vire between policy programmes (a power available in Scotland to its parliament, for example). 'The government wants RDAs to engage further and higher education fully in the regional agenda and improve cooperation between the sectors.'[36] This was strongly supported by the TEC National Council who suggested that:

> Further and Higher Education are areas which the TECs believe should be included in the regional framework. Although FE colleges and HE institutions are likely to continue as separate organisations, there is a strong argument for better integration of their delivery through planning and resource allocation with other partners in a manner directly related to regional competitiveness strategies.[37]

The DETR however, proposed that the DfEE should continue to allocate funding to HEFCE, which would take account of the relevant RDA strategy for the region. The outcome was largely status quo, according to which the DfEE allocates funding via HEFCE and other bodies. But an education development fund has been introduced. In addition in the December 1998 Competitiveness White Paper[38] a separate DTI funding stream for universities, with an RDA input to decisions, has been developed to stimulate partnerships between industry and universities in research and 'knowledge-based' industries. In the long term this opens up a wedge of leverage on university funding, the size of which depends on the government's commitment to increasing the role of regional and economic agendas in HE finance.

Further education For FE funding, most central departments sought to retain the existing arrangements whereby the DfEE would continue to allocate funding via the FEFC, with interdepartmental coordination by the GoR. The FEFC stated that 'it would not be appropriate for FEFC funds to be allocated by the RDAs. The FEFC was created under statute for this purpose; any proposals to transfer the FEFC's responsibilities would require wide

---

35 *Times Higher*, editorial 12 December 1997, 'Beware of bullies in regional cloaks'.
36 DETR 1997, p. 36.
37 TEC National Council, 1997a; see also Goddard and Chatterton, 1999.
38 DTI, 1998.

consultation followed by changes to primary legislation'.[39] At the other extreme, the DETR was in favour of the RDAs being given full executive responsibility for FEFC funding, including the ability to vire between policy programs. The TEC National Council also called for the RDA to have full executive responsibility for FEFC funding. The outcome at the first stage of RDA development in 1998/99 was very conservative: the DfEE would continue to allocate funding to the FEFC which would be required to take account of the RDA strategy for the region. This general position was confirmed in the July 1999 DfEE White Paper where, although TEC and FEFC funding for training are to be combined from April 2000, the RDA is still only involved in a peripheral way.[40] The DfEE structure has a National Learning and Skills Council linked to sub-regional LLSCs which bypass the RDAs. With this strategy the DfEE has won the battle for control of training funds and kept it away from the RDAs.

Standard Spending Assessment (SSA) The main block grant funding by central government of the local authorities in England is a revenue support grant allocated using a complex funding formula based on a Standard Spending Assessment (SSA). The DETR has the overall responsibility for the assessment and allocation of this distribution. The Regional Policy Commission recommended a role for RDAs in SSA budget allocation, and this would indeed be equivalent to the position in Scotland. This was generally supported by the business associations. However, at the first stage of development this change was opposed by all central departments and the Treasury, arguing that it would undermine their power to assure national standards. The outcome has been for no change in SSA procedures to take account of RDA issues, although in the longer term a review of SSA and local government finance is being undertaken in 1999/2000 which may lead to some changes. Any change in favour of RDAs is, however, expected to be modest.

Compulsory purchase power Several private sector business interests, including the CBI, and BCC, argued that the RDAs should have independent compulsory purchase powers in order to strengthen their planning powers for a defined range of economic development purposes (i.e. similar to that held by the UDCs and an extension of those powers previously available to English Partnerships). The BCC recommended that:

---

39 FEFC, 1997.
40 DfEE, 1999.

the RDAs are given the same powers as those contained in s.142 of the Local Government, Planning and Land Act, 1980, which gave the Urban Development Corporations compulsory purchase order powers, but 'only by agreement or, on being authorised to do so by the Secretary of State'.[41]

The TEC National Council and the DETR proposed that it would be appropriate if the RDA was the chief agent with respect to the use of compulsory purchase power for a relatively narrow range of economic development purposes, also taking into account the relevant local authorities' strategies and views. However, the local authorities, as well as most other agents and most central government departments supported the status quo, resisting any loss of their power. The outcome has been that the local authorities have remained the chief agent with compulsory purchase powers, but the RDAs have been able to achieve very limited powers in this respect for economic development purposes similar to those exercised by EP.

Environment and sustainability The local authorities' have been the main agents responsible for policies on the environment and developing sustainability, particularly through Local Agenda 21. However, the DETR (1997) White Paper made a strong statement in favour of RDAs playing a significant role in environmental policy. The main private business associations supported the view that the RDA should have independent environmental and sustainability powers for a defined range of economic development purposes (i.e. a development of the UDC model). This has so far been rejected by most central government interests and the local authorities. Other agents took a compromise position, that the local authorities remain the chief agent for environment and sustainability policy decisions, but they should to take account of the relevant RDA strategy for the region as well as having their environment and sustainability decisions available for monitoring by the RDA. This compromise was the final outcome at the initial stage, but it is an outcome that falls short of the DETR White Paper proposals so that a debate continues on how greater RDA powers for the environment can develop.[42]

5.4   Salience of Agents

The level of salience the agents attached to the alternative RDA issues varies

---

41   BCC, 1997, p. 17.
42   See e.g. Gibbs, 1998.

considerably. In part this reflects the fact that, for a majority of the agents, their concerns with RDAs were quite limited, usually focused on only one or two specific issues. There was only a small proportion of the agents involved who were interested in a majority of the issues negotiated. This applies to each of the three phases of RDA negotiations.

Phase A

Splitting the agents into groups, a first group is composed of the various Government Departments. The DETR attached the highest salience levels across the majority of the issues in Phase A, and the only issues which are somewhat less important to the DETR compared with other agents was the composition of the RDA Board and its accountability. A second group of agents is the local authorities and related interests. The local authorities had a strong salience on most issues, particularly on accountability and the composition of the Chamber. A third group of agents covers the various business interests. For a number of these agents, especially the CBI the BCC and TEC National Council, many of the issues in phase A were highly salient. For other agents in this group such as the Business Link network, the enterprise agencies and local partnerships, the relevance of this set of issues was much lower. A fourth group of agents is those which are various types of education providers. None of the issues debated in the first phase of the RDA negotiations were very important for these agents, reflecting the fact that the policy areas were not normally part of their policy agenda.

Phase B and C

For Phase B and C issues, there are some different patterns of salience to those in phase A. The first three issues of Phase B related to TECs are very important for the DfEE, TECs and GoR, where they generally have much higher levels of salience than for their Phase A issues. For the rest of Phase B and most Phase C issues, however, most central departments other than DETR are relatively remote and only have high salience where it affects their area; e.g. DfEE where their funding to TECs, HE or FE is affected. This reflects the fact that the issues debated in Phase B are more remote from many department's mainstream concerns but, where they are affected, the possible development of RDA power is much more controversial than in Phase A, particularly those affecting responsibilities of departments outside of DETR. However for the local authorities none of the issues in Phase B are as significant as those in Phase A.

For Phase C issues, many are of major significance for local authorities. Business concerns with Phase B and C are generally similar or less than in Phase A. For the more peripheral agents, such as universities and FE Colleges, a similar pattern emerges to that for the Phase A issues. The Phase B and C issues generally are of low importance to these agents except for the cases where they have a direct impact on their area of responsibility, e.g. for the HE or FE funding.

5.5   Capability of Agents

For the majority of agents, and with respect to nearly all of the issues and phases of RDA development, the agent's level of capability remains constant. The national level government departments are strongest at the level of the Prime Minister, who has had to adjudicate and balance between the DETR and other departmental interests. The Treasury is rated second to the Prime Minister, all of the other government departments rated next. The potential power of the GOR is very low, since they were not involved in strategic policy development, but are significant in the administrative relations of the RDAs. The local authorities and the majority of private sector business interests are rated approximately the same and at a medium power level. They are each important, and rival interests, which ministers have had to balance. The level of potential power of the emerging Regional Chambers and RDAs is relatively low, reflecting their newness, but we expect their levels of capability to increase over time. The average level of capability of most other agents is generally very low. However, in those areas of policy where they have greatest role (e.g. of universities in the HE phase C issues), their level of potential power is much greater reflecting their need to be involved in discussions as either allies, or to overcome their capacity to block or undermine change.

5.6   Simulations

The approach we develop in our case studies is to combine the information on the policy positions, salience and power of each agent to assess how negotiations to develop policy are likely to have evolved. We use the four models outline in chapter 4. A key aspect of our assessment in each case is to determine which model best characterises the negotiation process: compromise, exchange, strategic control or conflict. We find the process generally to be one of log-rolling and exchange, but with a key role played by central government acting in some crucial ways independently of the agent lobbies it receives. In the following presentation we first use our models to develop a simulation for each of the three phases of the RDA negotiations; we assess power relations of gainers and losers; we then assess progress in achieving the government's policy objectives for the regional economy and the potential role of alternative scenarios.

The overall accuracy of our four models, compared to the actual outcome is assessed using the mean square error criterion. This is shown in table 5.2. For each phase of the RDA negotiations, and for the overall outcome that had developed by the end of 1999, the exchange model performs best. Its performance is particularly better in phases A and C, suggest that the sets of issues negotiated in these phases were particularly subject to a logrolling process. For phase B issues, which focus on the relations of RDAs with TECs/LLSCs and local government representatives, the exchange model is still much better. However, the other models are also relatively good predictors for phase B. This suggests that the TEC/LLSC and local government relations with RDAs were influenced not only by exchange, but by a level of conflict and strategic control. The interdepartmental negotiations that led to the LLSCs being established indicates a clear victory of DfEE and DTI interests that were able to win over the cabinet against the DETR and RDA lobbies to transfer TEC powers to them.

Table 5.2   Comparison of predictions from different models for different phases of RDA negotiations

Model	Phase A	Phase B	Phase C	Total
Compromise (base) model	430.2	30.2	545.6	351.2
Exchange model	106.1	10.6	43.2	58.1
Strategic control model	527.7	98.2	291.2	342.4
Conflict model	417.7	213.0	211.4	303.6

Note: values are the mean square error differences between the actual outcomes and those predicted

The very accurate performance of the exchange model across all of the phases and issues is clear from Figure 5.1. This presents a prediction –

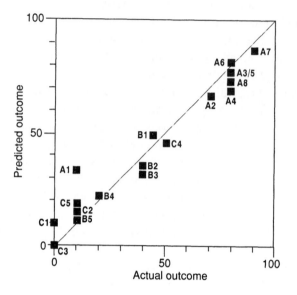

Figure 5.1   Prediction-realisation diagram for RDA negotiations (exchange model)

realisation diagram. This is a way of visually comparing the predictions of our model with the actual outcomes. The actual outcome for each policy issue is recorded along the horizontal axis; the predicted outcome on the vertical axis. Each axis is normed to run from zero to 100, with the information on outcomes given in the Appendix. There are 18 issues involved in the RDA regulations. Each has an actual outcome of the policy decisions developed (in our case up to the end of 1999). Each also has a predicted outcome. These two outcomes are plotted against each other in the diagram. The 45 degree line represents the case where all predicted outcomes are exactly the same as the actual outcomes. For the RDAs almost all of the issues do have a very close relation of predicted and actual outcomes. The least well predicted is the outcome for issues A1 and A4. These are the role of RDAs for regional selective assistance and the transfer to RDAs of responsibility for the Rural Development Commission. But even these are quite well predicted.

The high accuracy of the exchange model over all alternative interpretations suggest the importance of a logrolling process of decision making. Thus, whilst the concept of RDAs was chiefly developed by a party commission whilst Labour was in opposition, and thus was not fully negotiated, the actual implementation was based on exchanges well beyond the Labour party. The exchange process, therefore, appears to reflect Labour's consultative and consensual approach to policy development. But this has been at the expense of the rather more focused and ambitious objectives of the DETR and other advocates of more powerful RDAs. It appears that the development of consultation, exchange and logrolling has been used in part as a means by which the Prime Minister, Treasury and cabinet have been able to erode the vision of RDAs and reduce it to a more modest initiative, and perhaps a more practically achievable purpose.

5.7   Power Relations: Gainers and Losers

A key focus for our analysis is not just assessing how negotiations have evolved, but also how the power relations between agents has been influenced by Labour's policies: who is gaining and who is losing. We can evaluate this directly by using our models to estimate the utility loss or gain for each agent for each issues once the outcome is determined. The utility loss or gain of an agent is defined from our model using an amended form of equation (4.1). This is given by:

$$u^{ij} = s_{ij}(X^a_{ij} - X^*_{ij}) \tag{5.1}$$

where X^a_{ij} is the actual outcome on issue j for agent i; X^*_{ij} is the desired outcome for agent i; sij is the salience of agent i for issue j. The utility measure can be calculated for each agent and each issue, as given in equation (5.1). It can also be averaged for any agent, to give the agent's mean utility loss or gain across all issues. The average can also be calculated for any issue, to give the mean utility loss or gain for all agents for each issue. The mean over all issues and all agents gives the total utility loss or gain for the whole negotiation process: the so-called total welfare change.

Table 5.3 compares the net utility losses or gains for each agent as a mean across each issue in each phase of RDA negotiations. The most successful agents in the phase A negotiations were local government, the shadow RDAs, the GORs, CBI, BCC, DTI, DfEE and TECs, whilst the least successful agent,

Table 5.3   Net utility loss or gain for each agent across all issues for RDA negotiations (exchange model)

Agent	Phase A	Phase B	Phase C	Total (all phases)
Prime Minister	+0.010	+0.018	-0.006	+0.022
Treasury	+0.017	+0.022	+0.034	+0.073
DETR	-0.007	+0.052	+0.068	+0.113
DTI	+0.048	+0.026	+0.000	+0.074
DfEE	+0.042	-0.050	+0.012	+0.004
Home Office	+0.037	+0.102	+0.016	+0.155
GOR	+0.062	-0.038	-0.014	+0.010
Local Government	+0.121	-0.012	-0.034	+0.075
European Commission	+0.001	+0.008	+0.000	+0.009
Regional Chambers	+0.020	-0.006	+0.008	+0.022
RDAs	+0.120	+0.052	+0.124	+0.296
CBI	+0.055	+0.054	+0.030	+0.109
BCC	+0.047	+0.078	+0.028	+0.153
TECs	+0.041	-0.004	-0.006	-0.031
BLNC	+0.000	-0.038	+0.000	-0.038
LEAs	+0.002	-0.028	+0.000	-0.026
Local Partnerships	-0.013	+0.000	+0.000	-0.013
HE	+0.003	-0.002	+0.006	+0.007
HEFC	-0.002	-0.002	+0.018	+0.014
FE	-0.003	-0.002	+0.020	+0.015
FEFC	-0.004	-0.002	+0.020	+0.014
TUC	-0.019	-0.002	-0.002	-0.023
NCVO	-0.002	-0.008	-0.002	-0.012
IBB	-0.005	-0.002	+0.008	-0.001
English Tourist Board	-0.009	+0.002	-0.002	-0.009
English Partnerships	-0.020	-0.002	+0.010	-0.012
CNT	-0.010	+0.006	+0.010	+0.006
RDC	-0.001	+0.004	+0.010	+0.013
NTOs	+0.000	-0.008	+0.002	-0.006
LEAs	+0.000	-0.008	+0.000	-0.008
BiTC	+0.000	+0.008	+0.000	-0.008
Total	**+0.498**	**+0.198**	**+0.328**	**+0.997**

by far, was English Partnerships and local partners. For Phase B negotiations, the major of the more successful agents are the key private sector business interest, including the shadow RDAs, CBI, and BCC. Among the key government departments, the DETR was the most successful in the negotiations, but the most substantial losses identified are for other government departments such as the DfEE, and the GORs. For Phase C negotiations, there is a large number of minor successful agents. Most notably is the success of the agents representing the suppliers of FE and HE, as well as central departments. On the other hand, key losses identified are for the local authorities, despite the fact that the actual policy decisions reached represented very conservative changes to their status quo position. The total loss or gain over each agent and in each phase is considerable, especially for Phase A.

The average net utility losses and gains on each issue are shown in Table 5.4. The results are fairly similar for Phases A and B. In both cases there is a slight utility loss following the exchange process, but there are significant gains on individual issues for the average agent. The results for Phase C are interesting, there is an overall positive utility gain for the average agent, but overall level of losses and gains for the average agent are much lower for Phase C compared to Phases A or B. The main utility gains are derived from the increased accountability of the RDA boards, a strong decline by local government and DETR, but the protection of the status quo by FE and HE interests.

In terms of power relations our analysis confirms that central government has exercised a strong autonomy to act in establishing RDAs. But the actual outcome has reflected an exchange where many other interests have had influence. The highly conservative development of powers for the RDAs in Phase B reflects the power of strong defensive strategies played by the DfEE to protect the budget of TECs and direct it to the LLSCs, by the DTI to deflect TEC support and budgets to the Small Business Service, and the resistance by local government to erosion of its transport and planning powers. In Phase C, the strong vested interests of the FE and HE systems, again buttressed by DfEE support, has prevented major development of an RDA role in these areas. These outcomes therefore reflect a significant role for institutional and resource-dependence interpretations for how events have unfolded, but within a context of negotiated structures framed and manipulated by the state.

Table 5.4   Net utility loss for each issue for RDA negotiations (exchange model)

	Issue	Net utility loss or gain
A1	RSA	-0.020
A2	SRB	-0.001
A3	English Partnerships	+0.001
A4	RDC	+0.003
A5	CNT	+0.001
A6	Board Composition	+0.002
A7	Chamber Composition	-0.005
A8	Accountability of the board	+0.009
Phase A average		*-0.001*
B1	Training Policy	-0.002
B2	LED Policy	-0.001
B3	Enterprise policy/Business Link	+0.001
B4	Transport Policy	+0.001
B5	Planning Policy	-0.002
Phase B average		*-0.001*
C1	HE	+0.006
C2	FE	+0.008
C3	SSA	+0.002
C4	Compulsory Purchase Power	+0.002
C5	Environment/Sustainability Policy	-0.002
Phase C average		*+0.003*

5.8   Extent of Progress

The extent to which the RDA initiative has been successful in improving the economic development of the local and regional economy is too early fully to assess. The RDAs came into existence only in April 1999 and spent their first year developing their regional strategy and corporate plans. Most elements of resource allocation followed similar patterns to earlier procedures for the SRB, EP, RDC, and CNT, with many of the staff of these former bodies transferred, whilst the DTI continue to exercise the major influence over regional selective assistance, and the GOR continues to play a major role within DETR that can eclipse the RDA. The 1999/2000 year also saw the negotiations on the form of subregional areas within each region. This was strongly influenced by the DETR and government regional offices, although RDAs were given the formal role of deciding on the subregional map and arbitrating in difficult decisions.

In some regions, the GOR was crucial, in particular in the North West, and Yorkshire and Humberside, chiefly because of the inability of the RDA initially to act decisively.

Despite the early stage of development, however, a clear view is developing of RDAs from business interests. In general, this welcomes their establishment but, amongst most local agents and their national representative bodies, is critical of their limited power, their leadership, and the speed with which they have developed independence of the government regional offices and the DETR. Many aspects of regional strategies and corporate plans are seen as largely formalised or window dressing. Other aspects are criticised as merely satisfying a 'tick list' of government and departmental objectives.[43]

The criticisms have been led by the RDA Boards themselves. Lord Thomas, chair of the NW RDA, for example, has called for a review of the Treasury procedure that allocates the budget between England, Scotland and Wales (the so-called Barnett formula).[44] John Bridge, the chief executive of the Northern RDA, has called for greater flexibility of funding streams and: 'freedom to get on with the job'. 'We argued for block grants for the RDAs and that was not accepted, but it is not entirely off the agenda'. It is not a recipe for effective strategic decision-making that 'all the funds have special labels on them and you can't move money from one box to another'.[45] Bill Midgley, president of the NE Chambers of Commerce feels that the RDA is merely 'a delivery arm for Westminster and central government, not something which will fight for the region's interests and fight for a greater share of resources'.[46]

The rigidity of funding streams reflects back to departmental budgets and responsibilities and tends to undermine the scope for RDAs to be integrative. As put by *CBI News*, 'we have a situation where RDAs cover regions that are not necessarily cohesive and work with government departments that are not necessarily cooperative'.[47] John Banham, involved in the SW RDA and previously involved with the CBI and Audit Commission, is familiar with these sorts of constraints and argues that RDA 'control of strategy alone is sufficient. What really matters is control of the purse strings. Financial autonomy goes hand in hand with operational autonomy. If we chip away at

---

43 Interview comments from TECs, July 1999.
44 Quoted in *Financial Times*, 4 August 1998, 'England's regions to press for funds review'.
45 Quoted in *Financial Times*, 14 August 1998, 'Call to give regions flexibility on funds'.
46 Quoted in *The Economist*, 30 January 1999, p. 34, 'Regional Awakening'.
47 *CBI News*, December 1998, p. 32.

the former, the latter will surely weaken'.[48] Banham was also involved, through the CBI, with the set-up stages of TECs. He is aware of the analogous problems of wrestling control from central departments and the Treasury: 'If we do not get this right, the RDAs will end up like the TECs – a good idea, badly executed … smothered by bureaucracy.' If they are similar, Banham foresees that[49] 'flexibility will disappear, policy gridlock will result and good people will be deterred from getting involved. The vital regional partnership between public and private sectors will be still-born.' Similarly, the *Financial Times* editorial view[50] has been that: 'The RDAs are denied real power … they will implement their plans mainly by discussion, cajolery or bullying among a range of existing bodies … There is thus a real risk that they could become hot air factories.'

The former minister for the regions, Richard Caborn, contested this view, claiming that whereas a view can be taken 'the influence derives essentially from the control of budgets, the Government believe that the necessary influence and direction can be achieved by RDAs with the role and functions that we have given them from the outset'.[51] However, the experience of TECs is a close parallel, as is the experience of Regional Planning Boards and Councils in the 1960s and 1970s. Both TECs and the regional bodies of the 1970s were hamstrung by lack of power and financial flexibility.[52] At this stage it remains a very open question whether RDAs can deliver to their stated expectations. And doubts are continually reinforced by central departmental initiatives which are developed independently of RDAs.

Despite the difficulties the business view has been 'to make the process work'.[53] It is also clear that business has seen the RDAs as a means to strengthen its role and to make regional and local partnerships work better to achieve economic development objectives. This need is very much borne out of the evaluations of the SRB which have concluded that 'SRB partnerships could usefully review their schemes with a view to strengthening private sector representation'. Just over half of SRB schemes have been led by local authorities, only 16 per cent by TECs and a meagre 6 per cent led by either the private sector, or by the voluntary and community sector.[54] Hence, at

---

48 John Banham, Personal View, *Financial Times,* 28 November 1997, 'No easy birth for regions'.

49 Op. cit.

50 *Financial Times*, 4 December 1997, 'Talking Shops'.

51 Hansard 677, 1 April 1998, *Parliamentary Debates*, p. 1331.

52 See Bennett et al., 1994 on TECs; and Alden and Morgan, 1974 on the 1960s and 1970s regional bodies.

53 *CBI News*, December 1998, p. 32.

54 DETR, 1998, Summary, pp. 3–4, p. 8.

present there is something of a wait and see approach, with some enthusiasm to make the RDAs work as far as possible.

5.9   Alternative Scenarios

We can assess how the influence of different agents might lead to further developments by simulating alternative RDA scenarios for the future. We compare in our case studies in this and subsequent chapters four scenarios in each of which one particular agent's power is significantly increased. These scenarios offer comparisons of different business and other agent perspectives.

Scenario 1: enhancing the role of local business interests through the chambers of commerce.
Scenario 2: enhancing the role of national business interests through the CBI.
Scenario 3: enhancing the role of local public-private bodies through the TECs and LLSCs.
Scenario 4: enhancing the role of local government interests.

The way in which we implement these scenarios is uniform in this and the subsequent case study chapters 6–8. For any one scenario the power of the specified agent is increased to its absolute power resources. If its absolute power is rated at 40, for example, it is given 40 per cent of the total resources available to all other agents, with the remaining power shared among the other agents on a pro-rata basis. This gives the specified agent a dominant position, whilst still taking account of the policy positions, salience and strengths of the other agents.

Table 5.5   Comparison of alternative scenarios and actual outcomes for RDA negotiations using the mean square error criterion (exchange model)

	Phase A	Phase B	Phase C	Total
Scenario 1: Chambers of Commerce	552.1	918.2	2804.6	1279.5
Scenario 2: CBI	554.0	927.8	464.6	633.0
Scenario 3: TECs/LLSCs	1181.9	247.4	225.6	656.7
Scenario 4: Local government	1105.9	35.6	302.8	585.5
Original prediction	106.1	10.6	43.2	58.1

The four alternative scenarios are compared in Table 5.5 in terms of their accuracy. Under Scenario 1 the chambers of commerce are given a dominant position. There are major contrasts for this scenario compared with the actual outcomes, and with the local authority position of Scenario 4. The predicted outcomes would have been the most radical difference, giving RDAs much more power than the actual decisions particularly for Phase C issues, had the chamber of commerce position been given greater influence.

Under Scenario 2 the CBI is given a dominant power. Again the development of RDAs would have been more radical under this scenario but less so than the chambers of commerce. Similarly, under Scenario 3, where the TECs/LLSCs are given more power, the outcome would have been more radical, particularly under phase A, but is more conservative than the CBI and the chambers of commerce, which reflects the hybrid public-private character of TECs. However, it is clear that there is strong TEC support for a strategy for pushing ahead with a much more radical agenda, particularly for Phase C. If a greater weight is given to the chamber or TEC voice, a transfer of significant responsibility for some policy areas related to higher and further education would occur to RDAs.

Scenario 4, where the local authorities are given the power of dominant agents, is far more conservative than the other scenarios for the roles available for RDAs. Had the local authorities been more powerful, or had more account been taken of their views, the RDAs would have been even less powerful bodies than they are. Indeed, Scenario 4 is the weakest of the scenarios for all issues in the power it gives to RDAs, except for the issue of Regional Selective Assistance where, if the local authorities had had greater power, the RDAs would have been allocated full responsibility for RSA funding allocations instead of it chiefly being a central government responsibility through the DTI.

The outcomes for the different scenarios are compared in the prediction-realisation diagram shown in Figure 5.2. As can be seen by comparing this with Figure 5.1, all scenarios would have been more radical (higher up the vertical axis) on most issues, except for the local authority scenario which is almost uniformly in the lower half of the figure. As noted above, either the chambers or CBI scenarios produce the greatest deviation from the actual outcomes and shift more power to RDAs.

As in our discussion of the actual outcome, the different agent power-relations can be compared in terms of net utility gains and losses for each scenarios. The overall picture, shown in Table 5.6, suggests that for Phase A only under Scenario 4 does the average agent benefit from giving greater

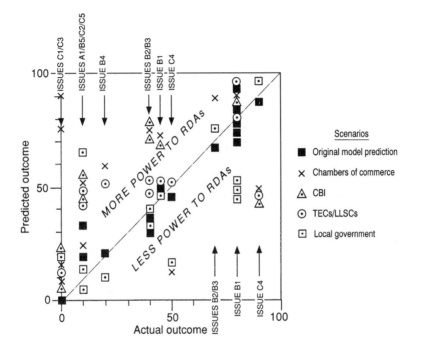

Figure 5.2 Prediction-realisation diagram comparing scenarios for RDA negotiations (exchange model)

Table 5.6 Net utility losses/gains under different scenarios for RDA negotiations (exchange model)

	Phase A	Phase B	Phase C	Total
Scenario 1: Chambers of Commerce	-0.002	-0.004	+0.001	-0.005
Scenario 2: CBI	-0.002	-0.002	+0.002	-0.002
Scenario 3: TECs/LLSCs	+0.000	+0.000	+0.001	+0.001
Scenario 4: Local government	+0.002	-0.001	+0.001	+0.002
Original prediction	0.084	0.083	0.036	

power to one of the other agents (local authorities). This accords with our earlier findings that for the regional level to develop other agents must *lose* real power, particularly local government. Development of the regional level cannot be looked at solely as decentralisation or subsidiarity from central government. Hence, any greater power to the RDAs which are business-led bodies, must lead to loss of utility to most agents since the majority are public sector governmental bodies.

For Phase B, the overall losses for the average agent are increased for each of the alternative scenarios tested compared with the actual outcomes. Indeed under Scenario 1, where the chambers of commerce have the greater power, the average agent's overall losses are considerably worsened. This again confirms that giving business a greater power radically shifts existing structures and power of the mainly government bodies involved.

In Phase C, the results are different in that, under all of the alternative scenarios tested, the average agent's net utility gain is fairly neutral, with a slight gain in each case, which suggests that more shifts may potentially occur in this area than for the issues in Phase A or B since most agents would gain. In practice, this means that the two chief losing agents (further and higher education) are likely to have their positions eroded.

5.10   Conclusion

The RDAs are in many ways a flagship for Labour's regional and local economic development policy. They have important new powers to coordinate regional and local agents across the span of economic development issues from physical infrastructure to workforce skills, SME supports and business investment. They are largely business-led and have strong support from business and most agents.

Nevertheless, they have not been given the strength of responsibility and resources the DETR, business bodies and many Labour party activities would have liked. As a result they have been criticised from the outset in lacking in flexibility, lacking authority and being more about drawing up strategy than being able to implement it. The extent to which these criticisms are true derives from the strong resistance they have received from the other central government departments affected, particularly the DfEE and DTI, and from local government that has lobbied hard to prevent loss of its own strategic economic powers. Some aspects of RDAs are coming to resemble the TECs in having ring-fenced funding regimes with insufficient powers of virement. They are also becoming similar to Labour's regional bodies of the 1960s and 1970s, that developed lots of strategies but had little or no influence on implementation. As such they may add just another agent to the scene, adding to the confusion and 'patchwork quilt' that we have identified in chapter 2.

Despite their limitations, however, RDAs are an important new development which, together with devolution in Scotland and Wales seeks to bring Britain in line with other EU countries in developing the powers of the regional level. Hence the RDAs resemble in some respects the development of regional government and/or administration that has occurred in the 1980s in France, Italy, Spain and Portugal.

The development of a new intermediate level inevitably involves tensions for the existing agents; at both central and local government levels, but also for other economic development bodies. The analysis here has demonstrated that increased central government decentralisation (subsidiarity) cannot be achieved by merely shifting central power to the regional level. Local government and a wide range of other agents is also affected.

Our simulation of alternative scenarios has demonstrated, first, that radical progress to grant RDAs more power relies on eroding the influence of both central and local government, and this is unlikely now to develop further. Second, to pursue a stronger regional *economic* agenda requires strengthening the power of business, absolutely, and relative to the power of governmental bodies. Such reforms will not increase the total welfare of all agents, because many (particularly other public sector bodies and central government departments) have to lose power.

The RDA developments so far have been achieved with modest overall increases in the utility of each agent. This demonstrates that Labour has pursued a largely consensual approach based on exchange and logrolling. This is a pattern confirmed in our models. But it also demonstrates that for RDAs to develop further will require a stronger lead by the prime minister and cabinet to erode the power of rival departments and also to reallocate some local government functions. The development of the LLSCs by the DfEE, and the development of the SBS by the Treasury and DTI, suggest that these departments and the prime minister have resolved to leave RDAs as they are and to severely limit any further developments.

However, for Phase C issues, the fact that there is a potentially high utility gain for most agents suggests that it will be this area where further development may take place. The key aspect of Phase C is the structure of further and higher education. A reorganisation of FE under the LLSCs is already occurring but this does not strongly involve RDAs. Similarly, the universities remain outside the RDA responsibility. There may be some developments of the RDA role in FE and HE, therefore. But this is likely to be some time developing. It appears more likely that most possible developments in Phase C will not be realised, and that the chief developments of Phase B have now been ruled out. Therefore, the RDAs look increasingly like a modest initiative, primarily within DETR, with some key responsibilities for Regional Selective Assistance and coordinating regeneration and EU funding, but which are unlikely to evolve further or to make major impact beyond limited areas.

6 New Deal

6.1 Introduction

The New Deal, like RDAs, is a flagship programme for Labour. It also relies on a central framework with delivery through local partnerships in Employment Service Districts. The planning for New Deal, also like RDAs, was chiefly developed whilst Labour was in opposition.[1] However, its detailed implementation involved considerable interplay of central government departmental interests, local partners and potential suppliers, and external interest groups. As a result the final outcome had many elements of a negotiated and exchange process between the main agents, although fundamental disagreements remain about process and scale of subsidy and the extent of sanctions to compel involvement by the unemployed. In this chapter we first introduce the concepts and planning developed for New Deal and then describe the issues subject to negotiations. This is followed by simulations of the negotiation process and assessment of alternative power-relations scenarios.

6.2 The New Deal

The New Deal programme is part of a more general attack by the government on the welfare-to-work transition. It involves not only specific training and job-placement programmes for the unemployed, but also reform of the welfare benefits system, the tax system, and the way in which education and training is financed, accredited and quality assured. Subsequently the New Deal 'Gateway' component has been a model also applied to welfare reform as a whole (the 'New Contract for Welfare') through the or 'ONE Service' approach.[2] The ONE Service also focuses on the role of personal advisors who act as ongoing case workers to help provide 'security for those who

---

1 See Labour Party, 1996.
2 See DSS/DfEE, 1998; HoC, 1999b; the ONE service began in pilot phase in four areas in June 1999, was extended to eight further pilots in November 1999, and is being implemented nationwide in 2000.

cannot work' and 'work for those who can'.[3] It has also seen the introduction of a sanctions regime, which has been extended to New Deal. The specific role of the New Deal is to facilitate the progress of the unemployed into work. It has been made up of two chief initiatives, a New Deal for young people aged 18–24, and New Deal for 25-plus. In addition specific elements have been developed for lone parents, people with disabilities and other special welfare groups within the unemployed.

The programme for 18–24 year olds was launched at the end of June 1997, in January 1998 it became operational in 13 'Pathfinder' areas, and covered the whole country from April 1998. The 25-plus element was begun in November 1998 in 30 pilot areas, extended to the whole country by April 1999, and extended to all over 25 unemployed from April 2000.

The overall aim of the New Deal (ND) is:

> Through work, education and training … to help young people gain the qualities and skills they need to increase their employability and to get and keep jobs … to overcome barriers to employment and build the skills needed by business. [4]

The programme has been developed in three elements, Gateway, Options and Follow-through, which together seek to achieve the final output of placing the client in work.[5]

1) The Gateway is an initial stage, lasting up to a maximum of four months, which aims to help participants either directly into work (which is the preferred outcome) or into one of the four New Deal options. The Gateway is an important addition to previous programmes for the unemployed. It is also one of the most expensive elements. It has a heavy focus on the use of personal advisors who, together with other agents, offer local counselling and support services: 'help with job search, careers advice and guidance, and preparation for and submission to a range of options'.[6] The advisor will discuss the options with the young person, find out their preferences, and agree a New Deal Action Plan which best meets their needs, which may also include a trial period to sample an option.

---

3   DSS/DfEE, 1998.
4   NDL, 1998, p. 1.
5   NDD, 1997; NDL, 1998; Donnelly et al., 1998.
6   NDD, 1997, p. 1; NDL, 1998.

2) The Options offer one of four alternatives:

- a subsidised job with an employer willing to take the participant. This is waged. The employer receives a subsidy of up to £60 per person for up to six months; in addition £750 can be made available towards the costs of providing training which can be paid to the employer, a college or another training provider;
- work on the Environment Task Force, which is waged or pays benefit plus a 'grant' of approximately £400 for up to 26 weeks;
- work with a voluntary organisation, which is waged or pays 'benefit plus' as with the environment option;
- full-time education or training up at least one day per week normally leading to an NVQ 2 and generally limited to those not already having this level of qualifications. This pays only at benefit levels plus some expenses for travel and 'exceptional expenses'.

The first three options can last for up to six months and all placements must provide, or arrange, an element of education or training of at least one day per week. The fourth option can last for up to 12 months.

3) Follow-through provides continuing support during the options 'and where appropriate, afterwards'. The level of support varies depending on individual needs and their New Deal Action Plan, with the strongest support around the final month on their options in order to agree their next steps, which can include a return to benefits before they finally secure a job. The aim has been to use the same personal advisor throughout, using the assistance of the Employment Service and other agents to find and obtain jobs.

Because the financial consequences of each option differ, and also because the political priorities among options represent a delicate balance of interests, the government has had to introduce planning assumptions for each element of the programme, although Andrew Smith, New Deal Minister,[7] has accepted that these will be adjusted to align 'the planning assumptions with the labour market realities'. These assumptions are summarized in column one of Table 6.1. As can be seen, the primary planned emphasis of the programme has been to place individuals into work, with a planning assumption that this will cover about 60 per cent of the participants, either leaving the Gateway directly

---

7   HoC, 1998, p. 58, para. 442.

or into subsidised employment. Employers had, therefore, to become a major part of the target for achievement the planning assumptions. However, the actual numbers in these options is much lower, as shown in right hand columns of Table 6.1.

Table 6.1 Cumulative outcomes and government planning assumptions for the proportion of participants in different options of the New Deal

	Planning assumptions (1998)	Planning assumptions normed to 100%	Outcomes: young people	Outcomes: 25-plus
Left Gateway directly into unsubsidised jobs	30%	30%	33.3%	16.6%
Left Gateway into benefits, other and unknown	–	–	43.4%	66.8%
Entering options, of which:	70%	70%	23.2%	16.6%
Employment (private sector)	35%	23.3%	} 5.4%	4.9%
Employment (public sector)	10%	6.7%	}	
Full-time education or training (and work-based training, for 25 plus)	25%	14.7%	10.7%	11.7%
Environment Task Force	22%	14.7%	3.7%	N/A
Voluntary Sector	13%	8.7%	3.4%	N/A

Note: the proportions in the planning assumptions in options do not sum to 100% because the assumptions are specified in the terms of 'up to' this proportion; in the second column of the table they have been normed to sum to 100%. The outcomes reported here also exclude those still in the Gateway or on Follow-through.

Source: New Deal Monitoring Statistics, DfEE December, 1999.

The delivery mechanism for New Deal is different from most previous programmes in that it involves a range of different agents, operating in different ways in different parts of the country, as New Deal Delivery Partnerships in each Employment Service District. The partners include a varying mix of:

* Employment Service;
* FE colleges;
* training organisations (public, private, voluntary);
* employers;
* TECs/LECs and LLSCs;
* Chambers of Commerce and other local business organisations;
* trade unions;
* Careers Service;
* Probation Service;
* local authorities;
* voluntary organisations.

The contracting body for these partnerships is the Employment Service (ES), which also operates the local Job Centre and allocates to each participant a personal advisor who is a member of ES staff. The ES is therefore both the manager and contractor for delivery, but it also draws on other agents chiefly for either of: (i) work placements; (ii) provision of specialist advice; and/or (iii) delivery of training. These other agents can contract directly with the ES to cover their costs of participation in New Deal, they may combine New Deal with other parts of their activities thus offering some of their own financial contributions, or may provide a voluntary input. Predominantly, however, New Deal is financed by the new money made available via the Windfall Tax. As the major addition to existing programmes, the Gateway is the main element of the greater cost of the New Deal.

A major innovation in the management of the programme is also the role of the personal advisor. This development is in line with the focal role of advisors being developed in other fields, e.g. social care, welfare benefits administration, and Business Link. The underlying concept is to develop a more client-centred service approach. Andrew Smith, the Minister initially responsible for New Deal, has said that its objective 'is essentially a client led, demand led programme and the objectives which each personal advisor is working to with each New Deal candidate is getting them into the opportunity which is right for them'.[8]

In the case of New Deal, however, client support is tempered by the important managerial role that the advisor exercises. Most important, the advisor, as an ES employee, can refer the participant for adjudication for a benefit sanction for failing to attend a part of the Gateway or options, or for

---

8 HoC, 1998b, p. 59, para. 449.

failing to apply for or take up the offer of a job. Advisors also have a range of other important powers e.g. to choose an option for the participant and compulsorily refer them to it if they have not voluntarily chosen an option by four months after their initial New Deal interview; or cuts in benefits if a participant fails to attend interviews. Advisors are therefore attempting both to offer client support and to police the system. In this dual role they differ from any other advisors the New Deal participants encounter who have no power to refer to a benefits adjudication officer.

The power of the advisor also underlines the strong integration that New Deal is seeking to achieve between the training and placements aspects of helping the unemployed and the benefits systems. This integration is an important innovation sought through New Deal.

In addition to the New Deal for young people for 18–24 year olds, the programme also includes special provision for lone parents 18–24, people with disability and 25-plus. These follow broadly similar approaches, but the level of compulsion is initially less; there are differences in the Gateway and benefit sanctions; and the system of advice and supports has additional specialist elements. For 25-plus, only the options for subsidised jobs and full-time education and training are included. Other differences for 25-plus are that the Gateway is replaced by advisory interviews, the employer subsidy is equal to £75 per week, and training is sought chiefly at NVQ3 or above.[9] Increasingly lone parent and disability aspects are being integrated into the 18–24 and 25-plus programmes but with different provisions and sanction processes.

In some areas the New Deal approach has been give the additional support in Employment Zones which cover areas of concentrated unemployment. There were originally eight of these, then extended to 20 in February 1999. Their aim is to explore new ways of giving unemployed people the opportunity to improve their employability through partnership delivery structures and greater flexibility of programmes, particularly by co-ordinating across programmes that seek to handle, on a case-load basis, individuals with major barriers to entry into the labour market.

Summing up the programme, Richard Layard, a key academic advisor to the design of the scheme before and after Labour's election to government, argues that:

> New Deal is radically different from anything tried before, first because the quality is much higher as a result of the Gateway; second, it is a universal

9   NDD2, 1998.
10 Layard, 1998.

system offering options to all clients, with continuing inactivity on benefit no longer possible; third, because of the case worker approach of the personal advisor to finding a relevant solution for each client.[10]

A key aspect that affects the negotiation is the unusual budgetary structure. This funds New Deal by a specific taxation funding stream which is managed interdepartmentally by the Treasury. This has given the Treasury even greater power in the negotiation process that it has with other government programmes. The use of windfall tax, from which New Deal funding is derived, was an election manifesto commitment. The funding levels for the New Deal element are shown in Table 6.2. The planned levels show a rise up to the 1999/2000 year, with a levelling off and decline thereafter. This projection is based on four premises by the Chancellor Gordon Brown: first, that economic growth will reduce unemployment levels in the longer term; second, that there is a cohort of unemployed young people, who have never had jobs that need to be introduced to work, who when introduced to work will not return to unemployment in significant numbers; third, that changes in the school system to improve literacy, numeracy and more general employability will significantly reduce the numbers of young people who become unemployed; and fourth, that changes in the benefit system will reduce the length of time that people are in unemployment. These planning assumptions mean that it is hoped that the specific finance needed for New Deal will be much smaller when windfall tax receipts run out and the programme becomes part of a general government expenditure. Because of lower programme volumes, windfall tax finance is now expected to last until 2002-3, crucially after the next general election. But Gordon Brown, Chancellor, has indicated continuing commitment to its support.[11]

Table 6.2   New Deal Funding derived from Windfall Tax

Financial year	1997–98	1998–99	1999–00	2000–01	2001–02
£m	172	951	1031	1021	941

Source: DfEE, 1998, Annex A; Treasury, 1998, p. 11.

A further aspect that is crucial in the negotiations has been employer involvement, since placement into jobs is the preferred outcome from the New Deal. Employers are therefore the main customers for the programme along with its unemployed participants. The theory behind the New Deal has

---

11 Speech at Labour Party Conference, 27 September 1999.

been developed in part from the Layard and Nickell argument, that what makes it difficult for the unemployed is their badging as unemployed.[12] Layard and Nickell argue that employers use unemployment as a filter in their recruitment policies. Moreover, the longer the duration of unemployment, the greater the difficulty of attaching the unemployed client to the labour market. Hence, the aspects of the New Deal which represent fundamentally new approaches are, first, to seek to attach more of the unemployed to actual jobs, rather than to training or social programmes from which the unemployed had previously often returned to the register (the 'revolving door'). Second, the New Deal has sought to build closer relations with the personnel, human resources or recruitment managers of firms, and to private sector recruitment agencies, in order to try and overcome employer resistance to recruiting the unemployed.

This approach has forced government to work with employers and private sector recruitment agencies. This gave employers a major strength in the negotiation process, particularly as a high level of political commitment and hence risk has hung on the success of the programme. This has meant that New Deal has experienced not only a greater flow of resources, but also, so far, a much higher level and more sustained commitment, at the level of the Prime Minister and Chancellor, as well as the Secretary of State of Education and Employment and senior department staff involved.

Since employers had to be heavily involved in both the delivery and some of the crucial policy design decisions in developing the programme, a mechanism had to be established to achieve this. The chief approach used has been the setting up of a Welfare to Work Task Force under the Chairmanship of Sir Peter Davis, Group Chief Executive of the Prudential. This Task Force was reconstituted as the New Deal Task Force in July 1997. It contains six business chairs or chief executives in addition to Peter Davis, two trade union general secretaries, the leader of a local authority and the senior directors/chief executive of an FE college, NACRO, Prince's Trust, Groundwork and Centrepoint. Separate Task Forces for Scotland, Wales and Northern Ireland also have chairs from company chief executives, and these are ex-officio members of the New Deal Task Force. The New Deal Task Force is complemented by a New Deal Task Force Advisory Group, of 24 people drawn from specialist agencies, lobby groups, colleges, research, the TECs, and with four business members.

The Task Force and Advisory Group make direct inputs to the policy design and act as a scrutiny body. It has been 'enormously influential' with

---

12 Layard and Nickell, 1987.

direct links to the minister on a week-by-week basis, particularly in the early days. The Task Force has been 'the key link with employers, not CBI or other bodies'.[13] More traditional lobbying and consultation on a wider scale also took place, of course, although the CBI and TUC have seen the major aspects of their concerns about policy design as chiefly met through their Task Force and Advisory Group members.[14]

In addition to inputs to design, employers had to become heavily involved as recipients of New Deal participants if the programme was to be successful. As a result the then Minister responsible for New Deal, Andrew Smith, claimed in 1998 that: 'In designing and delivering New Deal we have, at every stage, included the advice and views of business.'[15] Towards this end considerable publicity was sought through national and local advertising, the business press, at business conferences, and though business associations such as sector trade and professional associations, and through DfEE-convened national and regional conferences. Personal approaches were also made to the top 500 companies. Including SME companies as well as larger firms has been seen as a particularly difficult challenge. Special effort went into this through approaches to sector trade associations, national organisations such as IoD, FPB, FSB, and local bodies such as TECs/LECs and chambers of commerce. These bodies were seen as particularly important to disseminate awareness of New Deal, to respond to consultations and 'to add legitimacy'.[16] In local partnerships, business bodies such as TECs/LECs and chambers also play a direct role. In addition, in pathfinder areas, mechanisms for early feedback and exchange with DfEE staff, ministers and the New Deal Task Force were important. In a further 10 areas which contain a large proportion (approximately 50 per cent) of the target participants, Employer Coalitions have been set up to stimulate employer involvement and participation to 'play a vital role in engaging local employers and in advising on ways to continually improve the quality, relevance and effectiveness of New Deal'.[17] They have been seen also as 'sounding boards', 'advocates', and 'friendly critics', who are particularly 'good at understanding SMEs'.[18]

A further element of employer involvement was through Regional Assessment Panels. Formally their chief role has been to be:

---

13 DfEE interview comments.
14 CBI and TUC interview comments.
15 DfEE Press Release 257/98, 21 May 1998, p. 3.
16 DfEE interview comments
17 DfEE Press Release 257/98, 21 May 1998, p. 1.
18 DfEE interview comments.

responsible for considering the plan [from New Deal local partnerships] and making sure that all of the elements that needed to be brought together had been done ... Look at management arrangements, make sure the Gateway in particular was properly provided, that all the options were covered ... and that these were proper linkages with other regional initiatives [e.g. SRB].[19]

They were composed, like the New Deal Task Force itself, of senior business people (Chair, chief executive, director level), chaired by the ES Regional Director, and with other partner representatives.[20]

As a result of each of these mechanisms the employer power in the New Deal negotiations has been stronger than in many other programmes. It has also been drawn on at more levels, from the top political strategic level, through senior departmental programme design, to detailed implementation by taking on New Deal recruits.

6.3   Issues in the New Deal Negotiations: Stakeholder Perspectives

The New Deal is financed through a contracting process from the Employment Service (ES). The ES is an executive agency of the DfEE, but the specific new resource contributed by Government to New Deal has been met by proceeds from the Windfall Tax. This tax has been retained as an inter-departmental budget within the Treasury. In addition, the Chancellor, Gordon Brown, has retained a personal interest in the programme. This has meant that the ES, DfEE and the Treasury have emerged as the most crucial elements of the government contribution to New Deal, although operational responsibility is fielded by a DfEE junior minister. In addition, three other government departments are involved: DSS because of the strong interface developed between New Deal and the benefits system, for example through the power of ES personal advisors to sanction New Deal client benefit payments; the Home Office, because they are the government department responsible for exchanges with the voluntary sector, as well as having an interest in many New Deal clients who are ex-offenders via the probation service; and the DETR, because of the role of the environmental option and their responsibility for local government among the partner bodies. As a result considerable tensions between departments could have arisen. As recognised by DfEE 'we cannot tell other departments what to do, they are there to serve

---

19 Evidence by Mr R. Thew DfEE New Deal Project Manager, in HoC, 1998b.
20 Quoted in DfEE guidance on Regional Assessment Panel 'Champions', September 1999.

other needs'.[21] In practice, these tensions have been controlled by the dual reporting line to the Treasury and DfEE, with the Prime Minister involved directly in keeping strategic coordination on track, e.g. by writing to all cabinet colleagues in late 1998 telling them what they should do for New Deal.[22]

Operationally, New Deal is developed through local partnerships. These partnerships can be local planning and strategic bodies, and/or delivery bodies. The chief local partners include the local ES office (which is also the formal contract holder and can deliver New Deal itself), the TECs/LECs, local authorities and chambers of commerce. In addition, training providers, FE colleges, trade unions and recruitment agencies are important in varying ways within and between areas.

At a national level business leadership via the New Deal Task Force has been a crucial and powerful contribution at the strategic level of policy development, implementation of changes as a result of local experiences, and in publicity or encouragement to the business community to become involved. The Task Force, from all of our interviews, appears to have become the dominate way in which a business point of view has made itself known. Indeed, many other bodies, such as CBI, have been happy to acquiesce in this arrangement, whilst also maintaining close contact with Task Force members. Other national business bodies have been much more peripheral to the policy design of New Deal, but major efforts have been made to keep them involved with the publicity and launch of the programme.

In our power rankings, therefore, the national business bodies have low power, but business leaders (in the form of the Task Force) have a power rating equal to a government department. This recognises the extraordinarily powerful and unique position that the Task Force has been able to develop. However, the business commitment is lower than that in the government departments because New Deal is seen as 'ultimately a social programme' which business has been persuaded to support 'chiefly on the basis of the argument that it is in the national interest'.[23]

Because of the need to involve so many interests and also to develop a 'bottom up' approach to partnerships in each area, there were very widespread negotiations and a relatively open exchange process of information between agents, although the final outcomes were not without friction. These exchanges have provided a major source of evidence to this study, as well as specific interview comments, and the investigations of the House of Commons Select

21 DfEE interview comments.
22 Interview comments.
23 Interview comments from a senior business member involved in the New Deal Task Force.

Sub-Committee on Employment which has produced an important report on the role of the Employment Service and the New Deal Pathfinders.[24] For our analysis we have focused heavily on the period covered by the early experiences of the New Deal Pathfinders, and the policy developments in the early phases after its full launch from all age groups for the year 1999/2000. We have identified the chief set of policy issues, and the chief areas where ongoing debate is occurring. Our analysis identifies five main issues in which exchange between policy agents has taken place. These are listed in Table 6.3.

Table 6.3   Key issues involved in the negotiations between agents in developing New Deal

1	Length of time in the Gateway
2	Proportion of jobs subsidised and extent of public or private employer involvement
3	Size of subsidy to employer wage and training costs
4	Partnership and contracting structure
5	Flexibility of contracts

Length of Time in the Gateway

The Gateway is the four month maximum time period before a client is moved into one of the four options available. Some agents have questioned whether this is a sufficient time for some clients, particularly those of the long-term unemployed who have major literacy or numeracy problems, or have special difficulties as a result of drug abuse or being ex-offenders. This problem was a concern by agents from the voluntary and community sectors as well as employers, but has also been a concern of the local level ES staff who are personal advisors to the clients. This is an issue which became controversial following the launch of the Pathfinders and was a reflection of the practical difficulties of trying to operate the New Deal initiative when the client group was becoming more and more focused on the 'residual' element of the labour market as other parts of the target group were absorbed into work. The outcome has been to maintain the four month Gateway period with little formal distinction between client groups. However, some flexibility has been introduced for personal advisors to extend the Gateway period in special cases and to add time for some specialist training and counselling courses for particularly difficult cases. However, at the same time the sanctions regime has been strengthened so that a strong effort is being made to separate clients who evidence a genuine desire to enter employment from those who do not.

Proportion of Jobs Subsidised and Extent of Public or Private Employer Involvement

At the time of the launch of the New Deal, the planning assumption for the employment option was that there would be no more that 45 per cent of the clients in subsidised employment. This planning assumption was reaffirmed in the Government response to the Commons Education and Employment Committee Report in October 1998.[25] Exceeding this level had overall budget implications and possibly undermined the long-term sustainability of the jobs. As there appeared to be more than 45 per cent of clients entering subsidised employment in some Pathfinder areas, some ES District Managers came under scrutiny. The issue of public sector provision of places has also emerged since the number of places offered was unclear and it has been question whether the public sector could meet the targets agreed for subsidised places on offer.

Size of Subsidy to Employer Wage and Training Costs

The payment of a £60 subsidy per week to New Deal employers, and £750 towards the training costs of employers, has been criticised on the one hand as inadequate for the very difficult groups that have remained in 'New Deal'. A higher level of subsidy would have encouraged a stronger private sector involvement by firms, recruitment agencies and specialist advisers. On the other hand, a major concern raised by some partners about the impact of New Deal recognised that in Pathfinder areas New Deal could undermine existing provision in the training market. KPMG[26] recognised that if more money is seen to follow New Deal clients than work-based training for adults or other training programme participants, then providers may opt out of these programmes and into New Deal, leaving a potential lack of providers in the training market. Added to this is the concern that employers may prefer New Deal clients (who may be older and have more funding attached to them) to 16 and 17 year old Modern Apprentices, leaving the latter without training places'. In addition KPMG[27] recognised that doubt was also 'expressed about whether employers will be keen to take on non–subsidy New Deal clients, when they could wait and take clients with funding attached when they come out of the Gateway'. We have also found these tensions in local interviews.

---

24 HoC, 1998b, 1999a.
25 HoC, 1998b; HoC, 1998c, p. v–vi.
26 KPMG, 1997, p. 16.
27 KPMG, 1997, p. 16.

Some of these concerns have ebbed as the New Deal has become established, although the funding for work-based training for adults (WBTA) has continued to decline. In effect, the providers most concerned have transferred from the WBTA to the New Deal market. To this extent the DfEE approach, which has left it to local agents ('we don't have an answer'[28]), appears to some extent to have worked. However, the concern at the other extreme, of whether enough costs are available to the trainer, remains an important problem for providers of subsidised jobs and in the Gateway.

Partnership and Contracting Structure

A related issue is the sort of partnership arrangements developed at the local level. Before New Deal a range of local partners delivered unemployment counselling, pre-job advice and training, and work-readiness preparation. This included the voluntary sector, TECs, chambers of commerce, industry training bodies, private sector providers and FE colleges. The New Deal has replaced these by a strong focus on ES personal advisors, who may choose to contract the former providers, but the role of the former intermediaries or managers of the process in most areas has been replaced by the ES District manager. The ES had no previous experience of these management and advising functions, its chief role being policing and administering the job centres and the employ-ment benefits system. Concerns about this shift arose prior to the October 1997 launch of the New Deal and continues. There is also the interrelated sub-issue of who makes the decisions in terms of the local level contracts: the national level ES management, the ES District Manager, the Regional Assessment Panels, or the Task Force? The role of at least some national level decisions has had to be developed in order to be able to achieve contracts with those large employers which are located in many areas who are not prepared to undertake separate negotiations in the numerous ES Districts.

A further issue is whether ES-led partnerships should be chiefly about planning and strategy or about delivery: a distinction referred to by KPMG between strategic and delivery partnerships.[29] Also important is the size of partnerships, who are the key partners who should be involved, how the partnerships relate to the providers of New Deal, whether the ES and the partnership should be seen primarily as 'wholesale' body (managing contracts for delivery) or a 'retailer' actually providing the New Deal, and whether there should be special provision to ensure the breadth of partnerships.

28 DfEE interview comment.
29 KPMG, 1997, pp. 2–4.

Reflecting these concerns, the voluntary sector has complained that they have been excluded in some cases because they have been unable to compete with other potential partners, such as FE colleges, due to a lack of comparable 'core' resources and an absence of long-term contractual commitments to allow investment costs to be recovered.[30] Subsequent to the nationwide launch in April 1998, the voluntary sector has been granted some extra funds to overcome this problem and help them to participate. However, the partnership and contracting process remains one of the key areas of continuing concern for all former providers and connect partners.

Flexibility of Contracts

A further continuing concern, before and since the launch of the New Deal, has been the flexibility of the ES 'rule book' and contracting process. Several of the partners (e.g. TECs) wished the New Deal to take a flexible approach to the delivery of services at the local level, so that they could reflect more closely particular local needs. The discussion turned around the level of discretion of ES district managers within the central ES guidelines. In addition, many of the smaller providers, particularly in the voluntary sector, continue to complain that the procedure is too rigid. KPMG states that 'some organisations were clearly accustomed to contracting with the ES and found the process straightforward, but many of the smaller voluntary sector organisations with specialist expertise resented the diversion of their limited resources, in terms of staff and time, to filling in such forms. Some small organisations felt disadvantaged in comparison to 'regular' contractors.[31] In addition, some providers who pressed ahead with submitting bids found that the level of detail required by the application to tender was so great that they had little room to make adjustments once a contract had been awarded. One Sheffield provider refers to the contracting process as 'mind numbingly bureaucratic'.[32] The Local Government Association made the same point, adding that providers had been unable to renegotiate contract prices even when it became clear that the contract had been signed that supplementary costs (such as the requirement to offer childcare provision for New Deal participants) would be incurred.[33] The DfEE approach has been to suggest

---

30 See evidence in HoC, 1998b.
31 KPMG, 1997, p. 21.
32 Sheffield Coordinating Centre Against Employment (SCCAU) Ltd, Evidence in HoC 1998b, HC 263–III, p. 172.
33 LGA evidence, in HoC, 1998b.

that small providers who are unable to invest in the production of a bid, or set up infrastructures to provide services under contracts with no guarantee about the volumes available, are best steered towards becoming involved in consortia that include larger organisations. But this has been only a partial solution.

In addition, several providers have been unhappy about the nature of 'call-off' contracts, which expose smaller organisations to financial risk: if the number of clients is smaller than expected, then the contract may not be large enough to cover overheads. One provider argued that such contracts act as a 'disincentive to organisations who are expected to allocate premises, resources and people against uncertain through-flow of clients'.[34] Another provider pointed out that it was not feasible to set up new or innovative projects before the award of a contract, as funding could not be guaranteed, participants might not choose the option or the type of placement being offered, or they might be unable to get to the location of the project.[35] For some providers, 'New Deal provision is therefore often supported by existing infrastructure developed under other employment programmes. This reinforces the likelihood that existing providers will win New Deal contracts'.[36]

As a result concerns with flexibility to local needs continue. The Commons Education and Employment Committee has recommended that

> it will be essential, if the New Deal is to operate smoothly, for bureaucracy in the contracting process to be simplified. In particular, red tape must not be allowed to deter small voluntary and community organisations from bringing forward innovative projects tailored to local needs.[37]

The outcome by 2000 has been to maintain a standardised contracting process but with encouragement for small voluntary sector and other groups to enter consortia with larger agents through local partnerships.

6.4   Simulations

As with our other case studies, information on the policy position, salience and power of each agent is combined into four simulation models. The overall

---

34 Dudley Council for Voluntary Services in HoC, 1998b, MDP15.
35 Challenge South, Lambeth, in HoC, 1998b, NDP45; also DMD Business Services, in HoC; 1998b, p. 169.
36 HoC, 1998b,c.
37 HoC, 1998b, Recommendation 17.

accuracy of these models is shown in Table 6.4. This shows that the conflict model is the best overall predictor, considerably better than each other model, even the exchange model, with the compromise model the second best performer. This suggests that, whilst a negotiation process certainly took place, the final outcome was one primarily imposed by government; i.e. the government has acted to some extent as an autonomous agent whilst trying to involve and incorporate the key partners, particularly employers, into the policy. This would suggest a form of state-led corporatism more than any of the other academic interpretations introduced in chapter 3.

Table 6.4   Comparison of predictions for different models of New Deal negotiations using the mean square error criterion

Model	Mean square error
Compromise (base) model	674.2
Exchange model	985.2
Strategic control model	1657.4
Conflict model	500.0

The conflict model, which performs best, depends on a decision by each agent whether or not to challenge other agents. In the New Deal this has led agents to have to choose between largely accepting a template produced by Government or opting out of negotiations altogether. The fact that the compromise model also performs relatively well further supports this view. The compromise model depends on agents not exchanging positions at all but acting as voters for each option. Again, it supports the conclusion that government has chiefly imposed a template which agents have had to accept.

Figure 6.1 shows the prediction-realisation diagram for the conflict model. This can be compared with the prediction-realisation diagram for the exchange and compromise models in Figure 6.2. The conflict model is much better at predicting the outcome of issue 2, the proportion of subsidised jobs and their public or private balance, and issue 5 the flexibility of contracts. For these two issues agents effectively stood aside, or were excluded, by the template developed by Labour. The compromise, conflict and exchange models all predict well issue 3 (the scale of the subsidy), indicating that this involved a level of exchange as well as government leadership. All models perform relatively poorly for issue 4 (the partnership arrangements) although the conflict model is much the better of the three models. The exchange model is

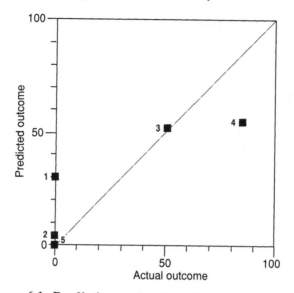

Figure 6.1   Prediction-realisation diagram for New Deal negotiations (conflict model)

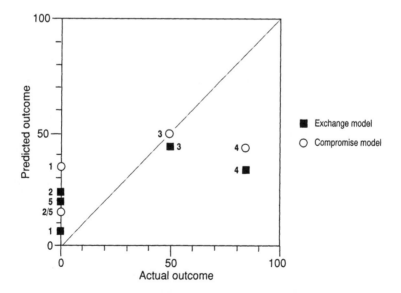

Figure 6.2   Prediction-realisation diagram for New Deal negotiation (exchange and compromise models)

by far the best on issue 1, the length of time in the Gateway, indicating that this issue was more open to negotiations. It is still a key issue with which all involved partners are having to wrestle, with the result that significant changes in the Gateway are still developing in 2000, two years after the initial operational developments.

6.5 Power Relations: Gainers and Losers

The gains and losses as a result of the negotiation process to develop New Deal can be calculated as in chapter 5, using equation (5.1). This measures the difference between the actual outcome and each agent's desired outcome weighted by their salience. The results of this calculation are shown in Table 6.5 for each agent.

Table 6.5   Net utility losses/gains for each agent across all issues in New Deal negotiations (exchange model)

Agent	Utility loss/gain
Treasury	+ 0.006
DfEE	+0.000
ES	+0.054
DSS	+0.016
Home Office	-0.012
DETR	+0.008
ES District Managers	-0.012
Local government	+0.032
TECs	-0.050
BCC	+0.022
NCVO	+0.032
Specialist counsellors	+0.078
TUC	-0.010
CBI	-0.006
IoD/FSB	-0.002
Sector associations/NTOs	+0.000
Business Leaders/NDTF	+0.082
Private recruitment agencies	-0.002
FE colleges/FEFC	-0.012
Total	**+1.120**

The most successful agents from the New Deal negotiations are specialist counsellors, the Employment Service and business leaders represented by the New Deal Task Force. Most agents gain, with the DSS, local government, BCC and NCVO also making significant gains. The main losers from the negotiations were the TECs who lost a major aspect of their responsibility for unemployment training, with small losses also for CBI, FSB and IoD who were worried about the additional burdens of a primarily social programme. Also small net losers were the ES District managers, TUC and FE Colleges who did not make the gains that they hoped for/expected. The overall net utility gain is relatively high, however, much higher than for RDA negotiations (compare Table 5.3).

The losses and gains across each issue, averaged for all agents, is shown in Table 6.6. The main gains derive from the provision of employer subsidies, the establishment of the Gateway as an improvement on previous practice, and the flexibility of contracts at the ES District level. The main losses result also from the employer subsidy, which although seen as essential to employers, were not sought strongly by most public sector agents, who form the majority of both number and power in the analysis.

Table 6.6   Net utility losses/gains for each issue across all agents in New Deal negotiations (exchange model)

Issue	Utility loss/gain
1 Length of time in the Gateway	+0.020
2 Proportion of jobs subsidised and extent of public or private involvement	+0.050
3 Size of subsidy to employer wage and training costs	-0.030
4 Partnership and contracting structure	+0.001
5 Flexibility of contracts	+0.020

In terms of power relations the analysis demonstrates central government trying to exercise a strong autonomy to shift the emphasis of the major training and contracting process for the unemployed from TECs to the Employment Service. The overall total utility gains indicate that this has been an approach from which many agents in fact gain, but their approach to negotiations is best captured by a conflict process from which some key agents withheld their challenges or were excluded. In effect this chiefly affected TECs, but other business interests in the form of the CBI, small firm bodies such as IoD and FSB, and private recruitment agencies also lost. The Chambers of

Commerce made small gains in line with their position to support New Deal in the hope of maintaining their local contracting positions for supply through local partnerships, thus de facto supporting the bypassing of the TECs.

6.6   Extent of Progress

The New Deal for young people began in Pathfinder areas in January 1998 and did not cover the whole county until April 1998, with its first outcomes following 4–12 months later. The 25-plus New Deal and other special elements began over one year later. Hence, it is still early days to evaluate New Deal. However, ongoing monitoring statistics have been made widely available by DfEE and a number of detailed evaluation studies have been undertaken which indicate the strengths and weaknesses of the initiative.

On the positive side the New Deal has become a high volume programme in a short period of time, processing over 420,000 young starts and 220,000 25-plus starts by January 2000. The outcomes, shown in the right hand column of Table 6.1 have achieved a large number of people into work, slightly in excess of planning targets for young people going straight into unsubsidised jobs. Among the options, the full time education and training option has proved most popular for both young people and 25-plus, which again reflects a positive benefit of increased personal skills and employability which further feed into jobs at a later date. In addition, the local partnership delivery process has generally worked well, although there is considerable variation between areas.[38] The programme has also been successful in stimulating a high level of involvement from employers with a relatively high level of enthusiasm and participation from SMEs.

As a mechanism for government-business collaboration the New Deal has broken some significant new ground through the special role of its Task Force. It has become 'enormously powerful', and is a very hands-on body, meeting weekly plus awaydays. It is unique in having a dual reporting line to the DfEE Secretary of State and to the Chancellor. It also has direct access from the chair to the Prime Minister. Perhaps most significant of all, the business chair Peter Davis, is a member of the relevant Cabinet committee. As such he is the only non-government member on any such committee. This particular positioning has allowed New Deal not only to satisfy the political objectives of two Government Departments, but also to bind in the Treasury's

---

38 See ES Delivery District statistics reported in HoC, 1999b, evidence.

commitments to cross-departmental spending from the windfall tax. The cabinet committee role and possibility of reference to the Prime Minister has provided both cement to interdepartmental commitment, and an ability to steer changes of both strategic and operational detail of New Deal with the highest level commitment. It has also given the Task Force a clear reporting structure and line of authority.

Because of this structure the New Deal Task Force has been able to bring a dynamic to implementation that is usually lacking in public policy programmes. Peter Davis has seen this as 'winning the battle for continuous improvement' in the programme. This is less to satisfy specific business needs (though synergies with business are certainly needed for implementation) than adoption of a management approach more akin to business. If, for example, a major company like Tesco launches a new product or service it does not stick with its initial ideas during the implementation phase, but learns from customer and manager feedback, continually reshaping product design, marketing, customer service delivery and other elements to seek out new market opportunities. Bringing a business view to New Deal has, therefore, been seen by Peter Davis as tackling some of the most crucial elements of 'government failure' noted in chapter 3.

Despite the many positive elements, there are also some important negatives. Crucial among the specific delivery aspects has been the number of participants who have left New Deal not for a job or an option, but to return to benefits. As shown in Table 6.1, return to benefits or unknown is 43 per cent of the young people and 67 per cent of the 25-plus involved in the programme, although this includes a large proportion of those with unknown destinations (62 per cent for young people and 16 per cent for 25-plus of those under this heading in Table 6.1). Among these is a very high proportion of the longest term young unemployed and 25-plus, suggesting that New Deal has done least for the most difficult participants. The New Deal has a very high proportion of cases that are difficult to 'attach' to the labour force. For example, about 30 per cent have no school or other qualifications, and a further 40 per cent are qualified only to level NVQ2.[39] Moreover, 47 per cent have been previously sentenced to a fine, prison, probation, community service, young offenders institution or have had a police warning.[40] The high level of return to benefits and unknown destinations demonstrates that integration of the benefits and New Deal employment or options approach has yet to fully

39 DfEE New Deal Monitoring Statistics, May 1999.
40 NCRS, 1999.

take place in terms of achieving outcomes into jobs.[41] Indeed the ONE Service single Gateway was not fully implemented until April 2000. The statistics demonstrate that improving this integration, and tracking those who drop out of the system altogether, remain major challenges. This is accepted by the government, Gordon Brown making the commitment to a tougher sanctions regime and a stronger emphasis on getting those on benefit into work.[42] There continues to be resistance to this tougher approach, however, from trade unions, some voluntary sector organisations and many traditional Labour supporters.[43] Indeed, it remains to be proved that the ONE Service will fully deliver the needed changes.

Interrelated with these difficulties is the high number of participants still in the Gateway (which are about one half of the cohort at any time) and the growing number on 'Follow-through' who have finished their options without a job, and who continue to need high levels of support whilst on an option. Follow through is 17 per cent of those in the New Deal for young people and 1 per cent for 25-plus[44] (these numbers are excluded from Table 6.1 which reports only outcomes). This again indicates that New Deal is only making limited impact on some of the most difficult problems among the long-term unemployed. It also confirms the difficulties of training and skill levels among personal advisors, which appear to be insufficiently robust to help participants move off the Gateway.[45]

A further tension has been the spread of outcomes from different options. Whilst the job entry rate from the subsidised employment option is good (95 per cent), it is much lower for the education and training option (55 per cent, with some outlets achieving less than 10 per cent),[46] and intermediate for the Environment Task Force (62 per cent) and voluntary sector option (67 per cent).[47] It appears that a high proportion of the relatively large numbers in the education and training option are using this as a 'resting point' before returning to benefits or having to have further follow through. Attempts to tighten up have focused on the sanctions regime, but this has not yet had time to bite on those in education and training. The 'revolving door' outcome was strongly

41 About 55 per cent of 'unknowns' in the New Deal for Young People are unemployed and a further 12 per cent are inactive: Hales and Collins, 1999.

42 Speech at Labour Party Conference, 27 September 1999.

43 See Peck, 1999.

44 DfEE monitoring statistics, January 2000.

45 See Walsh, Atkinson and Barry, 1999.

46 David Sherlock, Chief Executive Training Standards Council, reported in *Times Educational Supplement*, 31 March 2000.

47 DfEE Monitoring Statistics, May 1999.

criticized by Labour in opposition, but improvement seems to have been relatively meagre.

Other tensions relate to how business has become involved. A key element of the tensions is the gap between marketing and actuality. One issue has been launch and publicity in February 1998 far ahead of programme delivery, so that employer expectations were raised only to find that no recruits were not yet available. Driven by 'political marketing' objectives rather than economic needs this demonstrates the clear gap between government and business processes we raised in chapter 3.

A second aspect of business tension has been the gap between marketing and reality of the form of most recruits. The focus of New Deal marketing to business has been on the recruitment process: to help businesses recruit, and to reduce its cost and risk. But was this marketing ploy plausible? Most evidence suggests that businesses see New Deal as predominantly a social programme, only 3 per cent would choose to take on long-term unemployed people,[48] although many businesses have no prior preference, relying on their recruitment processes to filter the most appropriate recruit from whatever origin. However, the reality is that when recruited, employers have recognised that New Deal recruits require additional costs of internal management training, monitoring or other supports.[49] Many other employers have found the long-term unemployed to be completely unsuitable e.g. Peugeot for their high-tech production line. Peugeot found previous recruits from the long-term unemployed increased absenteeism.[50] A local employer organisation comment in a Pathfinder areas is that 'they are not going to take people on for £60, some employers say that 40–50 per cent of the unemployed don't want jobs anyway. There's also a lot of worry about "bureaucracy"'.[51] This is a view shared by many Trade Unions who feared that good quality training and apprenticeship schemes could be undermined by the job subsidy, whilst an AEEU official is quoted as feeling that 'These people will cause problems because no one likes a scrounger – a minority don't want to work at all and are quite all right on benefit and fiddle, thank you'.[52] As the numbers of the unemployed have fallen these problems have increased, so that the residual or 'hard core' of the long-term unemployed have become a more significant proportion of the group that has to be placed. The IoD found 73 per cent of employers concerned about the potential

---

48 *Enterprise Barometer*, September 1997, 3i, London.
49 E.g. in J. Sainsbury, quoted in *Working Brief*, October 1998, p. 4.
50 'Sceptics cast doubt on Welfare to Work', *Times Educational Supplement*, 15 August 1997.
51 Chief Executive of local employer body in case study area B.
52 *Times Educational Supplement*, 15 August 1997.

'unsuitable' nature of New Deal clients and were concerned about having to recruit and manage 'unwilling conscripts'.[53]

This tension is evident in the number of jobs that have lasted no more than 13 weeks. This is the period of time within which employers can most easily dismiss an unsatisfactory worker, and the period used for the definition of 'sustainable jobs'. Forty-two per cent of unsubsidised job placements and 19 per cent of subsidised job placements were terminated in under 13 weeks, 44 per cent for men, 37 per cent for women,[54] which shows that employers are often terminating New Dealers early or are unwilling to commit long-term jobs to this category of workers. A key problem, recognised by the New Deal Task Force, has been the lack of relevance of much of the full time education and training or environment and voluntary options to employer needs.[55] Although employers have been criticized for being unwilling to offer New Dealers long term jobs, it is clear that many of the participants in the programme were unsuitable for long term jobs at the time they embarked on them.

The problem of reducing the level of return to benefits, increasing the employability, reducing the take-on costs to employers, and improving the success rates into jobs for the long-term unemployed particularly among the young has thrust increasing attention on the quality of the Gateway process, the quality of the advisors, the quality of local partners, and the ability of the ES and its personnel. These are all areas needing improvement. A key business member of the New Deal Task Force feels that the main challenge is to the ES advisors, to make the advice process much more intensive:

> get away from the meeting with advisors every 2 weeks based on 'would you like to think about this', and instead institute more intense, continuous exchanges calling to a greater extent on private sector specialists and those with special skills able to help with ex-offenders, drug-takers, and basic literacy/numeracy problems.[56]

The Task Force has supported this view and in 1999 proposed transforming the Gateway into a more intensive process, with continuation of intensive advisor support for those with greatest need whilst in an option. Improving and upgrading the Gateway to make it resemble the workplace was a further

---

53 Quoted in *Financial Times*, 6 January 1998, 'Jobless Fall may Threaten Success of '"New Deal"'.
54 DfEE Monitoring Statistics, April 1999.
55 NDTF, 1999.
56 Interview comments.

recommendation of the Task Force in 1999.[57] The role of the Employment Service as local partner and contract holder has also been criticised as being too frequently perceived as policing the benefit system and lacking the specific skills required for ex-offenders and other special groups:[58] criticisms voiced by Labour itself of the previous system when in opposition.[59] The more general difficulty, recognised by the Task Force, is to equip participants whilst in the Gateway, or whilst in an option, with the necessary skills. The Task Force has recognised the need for personal advisers to be better trained, have better skills and/or attitudes, spend less time on bureaucracy, better understand employer needs, better brief the participants on what employers expect, and better understand the labour market.[60]

These tensions have also challenged the DfEE traditional approach, which has emphasised that training must involve accreditation to a qualification, which in turn has been interpreted as requiring contribution towards an NVQ. These tensions are all the greater for employers taking on employees largely for social policy reasons who are difficult to train and may lack core skills. Over 70 per cent of New Deal participants have at best NVQ2 and over 30 per cent are totally unqualified.[61] Hence, Tesco among others, has questioned whether ND training should necessarily lead towards NVQ or similar accredited qualifications.[62] Ministers have had the difficult tension to resolve of maintaining programme quality, and recognising that many company in-house training schemes do not map directly into NTO or other sectoral training structures. The DfEE have had to argue 'that employers do not have to change existing programmes, but we will send in assessors to map the training against training planned, at least 50 per cent of which must be proved to support qualifications'.[63]

6.7   Alternative Scenarios

As in chapter 5, we can assess how the influence of different agents might lead to different developments of New Deal if their views are given greater

---

57 NDTF, 1999.
58 Convery, 1997; Fletcher, 1999.
59 Labour Party, 1996.
60 NDTF, 1999.
61 DfEE, New Deal Monitoring Statistics, May 1999.
62 Quoted in *Working Brief*, April 1998, p. 2.
63 DfEE interview comments, 1 April 1998.

weight. We do this by simulating four scenarios, for increased power to chambers of commerce, the CBI, TECs/LLSCs and local government. The results are reported in Table 6.7. All scenarios produce a lower mean square error than the original exchange model, but all are higher than the conflict model. The main differences of the different agent scenarios and the actual outcomes remain the length of time in the Gateway. However, the contracting agents (issue 4) are better modelled by each of the scenarios, suggesting that it is flexibility that would be the greatest gain resulting from following any of the scenarios developed here.

Table 6.7   Comparison of alternative scenarios and actual outcomes for New Deal negotiations using the mean square error criterion (exchange model)

Scenario 1:	Chambers of Commerce	549.2
Scenario 2:	CBI	870.0
Scenario 3:	TECs/LLSCs	578.8
Scenario 4:	Local government	567.2
Original prediction:	(exchange model)	985.2
	(conflict model)	500.0

The outcomes from the different scenarios are compared in the prediction-realisation diagram in Figure 6.3. This shows the close clustering of agent views on issues 1, 2 and 5 and the considerable distance of each scenario from the actual outcome on issue 4 and issue 1.

Table 6.8   Net utility losses or gains under different scenarios for New Deal negotiations (exchange model)

Scenario 1:	Chambers of Commerce	+2.014
Scenario 2:	CBI	+3.477
Scenario 3:	TECs/LLSCs	+2.527
Scenario 4:	Local government	+2.280
Original prediction	(exchange model)	+1.120

The effect of the different scenarios on utility losses and gains is given in Table 6.8. All gains are increased compared to the original estimates of gains, with the CBI and TEC/LLSC scenarios producing the largest increases in gains overall. Despite the differences between scenarios, the main pattern is the considerable difference of all scenarios them from the original prediction.

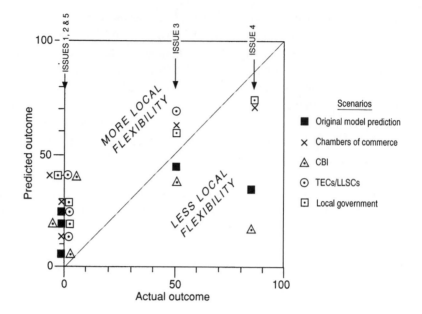

Figure 6.3   Prediction-realisation diagram comparing scenarios for New Deal negotiations (exchange model)

This demonstrates that whatever agent had been given greater power would have resulted in utility gains for the whole system, particularly for the CBI scenario which emphasises much stronger flexibility in contracting and greater incentives to employers.

6.8   Conclusion

The New Deal is a major flagship of Labour's programme of social support to the unemployed and part of a template of reform which also involves the benefits system, most directly through the ONE Service launched in 1999. New Deal has particularly high level and strong support from Gordon Brown, the Chancellor, as a central plank of his reform agenda. Its design was developed in opposition although elements had to be negotiated with the key players and partners to permit implementation.

Our analysis demonstrates that although there has been an important exchange process on some issues, the strategy and implementation of New Deal has largely followed a process of imposing a template. Thus the best model of the negotiation process is one based on assuming that a conflict approach has operated. In this approach, agents choose to participate or not by challenging or not challenging the policy options being developed. This interpretation seems to fit well the survey evidence of New Deal participation, as well as evaluations by DfEE, that a model has been imposed on partners and participants. This has worked well for the relatively work-ready. But it appears to have done relatively little for the main participant groups of the unqualified, the unwilling, or those with very low levels of qualifications or other impediments (e.g. ex-offenders). The explanation for the relatively poor record of success for these groups appears to be lack of employer involvement in local partnerships and inadequacies of the Gateway in terms of intensity, sufficient focus on job-readiness, deficiencies in capacity or skills among ES personal advisors, and the additional management, training costs or other adjustments needed by employers to cope with many New Deal participants.

The implications of a conflict model are that government has chosen to take a strong lead in which it has then had to try to involve other participants. It is a key outcome of a state-led corporatist approach. For New Deal the key involvement required is that of employers, who are essential for the achievement of the chief outcome sought, of getting participants into sustainable jobs. Our analysis demonstrates that this involvement is still very imperfect. Our analysis also suggests that major difficulties remain in the areas of the partnership arrangements, where ES leadership has replaced alternative means of job matching and advice. For this issue none of our models perform well, indicating that a particular solution has been imposed independently of expert agent inputs. The recognition by the New Deal Task Force of the need to improve the emphasis on work-readiness in the options and Gateway, and to improve personal advisor skills,[64] is a clear confirmation of the gaps in involvement with employers that our analysis demonstrates.

The assessment of scenarios supports this conclusion. Each of the scenarios assessed would produce greater gains over the whole system, with particular benefits resulting from more flexible contracting for New Deal service delivery. The overall pattern of gainers and losers from New Deal negotiations also supports the conclusion that greater employer involvement, improved ES advising skills, and greater participant work-readiness are the key problems that must be overcome. If the criterion of success of New Deal is to be the test of 'what matters is what works', there is therefore some way to go before the New Deal is really delivering on its promises.

---

64 NDTF, 1999.

7 Local Learning and Skills Councils and the TECs

7.1 Introduction

The Local Learning and Skills Councils (LLSCs) were announced in June 1999 as subregional bodies to contract for the supply of training and vocational education. They combine the resources of the former FEFC, which formerly allocated resources to the FE colleges, and the former local Training and Enterprise Councils (TECs), which allocated resources for 'work-based training'. The objective of the LLSCs is to integrate these former funding mechanisms in order to give a strong strategic structure to training, to allow a degree of rationalisation, particularly by merging colleges, and to reduce the level of power of local business leaders (that formed the majority of TEC Boards) over funds in order to make them, in the eyes of many Labour supporters, more 'accountable'.

The establishment of LLSCs is therefore a core part of the Labour government's agenda for change. However, it is part of the agenda that fell into place relatively late. In opposition and in the early years of the government there was considerably uncertainty as to whether TECs would be abolished or not.

This diffidence was borne from recognition that the TECs were a crucial part of the contracting process for training so that abolition could not be considered until an alternative institutional structure was in place. This difficulty is also reflected in the extended transition period before LLSCs finally took over fully from TECs, which covers the period July 1999–April 2001. This has caste some doubt about how training programmes would continue with what were essentially 'collapsing' organisations.[1]

The extended period of consideration of the successor to TECs, which included two major reviews over 1997–99, resulted in an extensive negotiation and exchange process between agents which can be modelled by our methodology. However, because of the long term and endemic problems of

---

1   *Working Brief*, July 1999, p. 2.

trying to find a satisfactory framework for training in Britain, which date back at least to the 1870s, we not only analyse the discussions leading up to the establishment of the LLSCs, but also analyse the negotiations that led to the setting up of the TECs. To emphasise the continuity of issues and tensions between agent views and power relations involved, we divide our presentation and simulations into two subsections in this chapter: one for the establishment of the LLSCs, and a second for the earlier negotiations that led to the establishment of TECs.

7.2   The LLSCs and TECs

The Local Learning and Skills Councils are the subregional arms of the national Learning and Skills Council. The staff at both levels are crown servants and the structure is one of a Non-Departmental Public Body (NDPB). The functions of the LLSCs are:[2]

- ensuring that high quality post-16 provision is available to meet the needs of employers, individuals and communities;
- planning the coherent provision and funding of institutions, private and voluntary sector providers, and planning for mergers where appropriate;
- developing national funding tariffs and systems for the great majority of its expenditure;
- direct responsibility for the achievement of targets for: young people; for adults (excluding level 4 for which prime responsibility will continue to rest with the HE sector); and for Investors in People;
- promoting and supporting social partnership strategies, working with others to raise the aspirations and achievements of young people and adults for learning;
- promoting equality of opportunity in the labour market;
- promoting programmes and policies such as Modern Apprenticeships, National Traineeships and Investors in People;
- ensuring an effective Education Business Partnership network exists to support the delivery of (including providing work experience);
- funding information, advice and guidance for adults;
- establishing systems for the collection and dissemination of information on labour market and skill trends; and

---

2   DfEE, 1999a, pp. 22–4.

- ensuring value for money and financial propriety, regularity and control, intervening early and effectively where necessary and ensuring that there are sound arrangements for governance, financial management and audit throughout the post-16 sector.

The membership of the national council is drawn chiefly from the consumers of education and skills, of which the largest single group is employers who will constitute 40 per cent of the total. The government has been keen to maintain a continuity from the former TECs where the majority of the Board was private sector employees. However, achieving 40 per cent employer representation on the new council was difficult and subject to considerable lobbying.[3] For both national and local LSCs the private sector is no longer a majority, even if it is the single largest group. The overall structure of the local and national bodies is shown in Figure 7.1.

The membership of the LLSCs is broadly along the same lines as the national council, but with greater variety to reflect differences in local characteristics. The LLSCs have the same general roles as the national council, but have the specific responsibilities of: [4]

- assembling comprehensive data on local client groups and participation rates in training;
- assembling data on performance of training providers;
- drawing up an ongoing assessment of local skill needs for their area, in consultation with RDAs;
- publishing an 'annual statement of priorities' for their area with a targeted action plan, which has to be 'approved by the national council, having consulted the relevant RDA';
- managing a discretionary budget to supplement the national tariffs to promote specific local approaches and improvements;
- expanding the take-up of Modern Apprenticeships, National Traineeships and other government-supported training, and promoting Investors in People (IiP) and employer workforce development.

In addition the LLSCs are responsible for:[5]

---

3   See e.g. *Financial Times*, 29 October 1999, 'Concession on training network'.
4   DfEE, 1999a, pp. 27–8.
5   DfEE, 1999a, pp. 28–9.

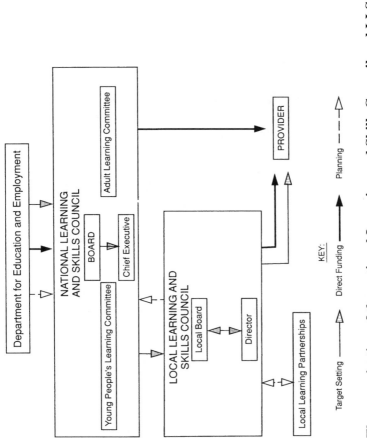

Figure 7.1   The organisation of the national Learning and Skills Council and LLSCs

Source: after DfEE, 1999, p. 30

- encouraging new training providers to enter the market subject to quality standards;
- developing local delivery plans together with Local Learning Partnerships, which have core members of FE colleges, local authorities and schools, the Careers Service, and TECs;
- developing an overall quality improvement strategy to assure quality and standards of training, probity of funding and proper complaints handling. This is undertaken in conjunction with OFSTED for 16–19 provision, and by a new inspectorate for post-19 provision;[6]
- proposing and brokering college and other provider mergers;
- improving flexibility of provision e.g. by opening up colleges in the evenings;
- providing an annual prospectus of post-16 training opportunities together with quality assessments.

This approach develops the funding regime of the former FEFC, which had progressively moved colleges towards a single tariff system with an average unit of funding, by including within it a wider range of work-based training options chiefly financed by the former TECs. This has involved both widening and adapting the FEFC approach. This has created tensions for both FE colleges and work-based training providers. In effect the decision to amalgamate government training funding into a single stream within LLSCs has put on hold, for the moment, the long-running debates on the scale of government funding for provision, the extent of local and provider flexibility within contracts, and the targets for programmes.

The reforms have also focused the training system on the single target of training. No longer is training combined with business support policy and local economic development as was sought in the former TECs. Coordination with business support is now sought by developing coterminous boundaries with the SBS and Business Link structure, and where possible through co-location of the two systems (see chapter 8). The two issues of training and business support are no longer brought together within the purview of a single management board as was the case in TECs. Moreover, the relationship between the two is likely to be largely perfunctory, with virtually no mention of the SBS developments in the DfEE White Paper 1999. It is clear that the DfEE has drawn the agenda for reform, with the DTI having to adapt to the new environment in which there are no TECs.

---

6   DfEE, 1999a, pp. 44–7.

Similarly, local economic development interests are separated from training, with the responsibility divided between local authorities and the RDAs. Again, however, the relation of training decisions to other bodies is fairly remote and, although it is too early to make a definitive judgement, it is fairly clear that the consultation process with RDAs on training provision is chiefly only at the most general level.

There has also been change in the geographical coverage by LLSCs. The former TECs numbered 75 in England at their inception in 1990/1, which was reduced to 72 by 1999 after mergers. Their average size of resident population was about 650,000 and they were mostly coincident with local authority boundaries at the country or metropolitan district level. Indeed, there was an average of 1.4 districts per TEC in metropolitan areas and 1.1 counties per TEC in the non-metropolitan areas, although in London there were 3.7 boroughs per TEC at the outset.[7]

The LLSCs are generally considerably larger and they number only 47 compared with the 75 original TECs. The target was for a minimum resident population of 500,000, with the expectation of this being larger in the conurbations. The objective was to have 'no more than' 50 LLSCs.[8] For the establishment of the TECs the objective had been a minimum population size of 200,000 and only two did not meet that criterion (St Helens and Isle of Wight). However, nearly 30 TECs did not meet the 500,000 population threshold for LLSCs so that a considerable amalgamation and change process was required to move from TECs to LLSCs.

The LLSCs were defined by the DfEE in consultation with RDAs over the summer of 1999. Although a consultation process was involved, it is clear that 'the DfEE and Government Regional Offices had their own agenda and there were not many alternative options available'.[9] The final map of LLSCs was announced in October 1999. This then guided the way in which local partners had to negotiate, and it pre-defined the local partners that had to work together in SBS Business Link areas (see chapter 8). The principles that underpinned the decision about local boundaries were that:[10] (i) they should be consistent with those of other key organisations; in practice this meant chiefly local government, but also largely worked through amalgamations rather than division of former TEC areas; (ii) should fit with local travel to work areas (TTWAs), travel to study areas and the pattern of business and

---

7 See Bennett et al., 1994, Table 5.1.

8 DfEE, 1999a, p. 29.

9 TEC Chief Executive, NW Region.

10 DfEE, 1999a, p. 29.

commercial activities; but in practice these were of only minor influence since TTWAs and study areas are much smaller than the desired LLSC boundaries (there are over 200 TTWAs in England in the 1998 definition[11]); (iii) should fit within RDA GOR boundaries; and (iv) should be at least 500,000 population and generally larger in conurbations.

In addition the LLSCs are expected to work closely with Local Learning Partnerships (also termed Lifelong Learning Partnerships, LLPs). These were set up following a TEC National Council, FEFC, and Local Government Association joint initiative which resulted in a protocol for cooperation defined at the end of 1998. This consisted of TECs, local authorities, careers service, and FE colleges at the local level, with TEC National Council, FEFC, and LGA facilitating the process at national level. The protocol led to the announcement of LLPs by David Blunkett, the Secretary of State for Education and Employment, in November 1998. They originally focused primarily on issues of school transport and national learning targets but were seized on by the government in 1999 as a means to bind in local partners whilst LLSCs were being established.[12] The outcome by mid-1999 had been over 100 LLPs with DfEE plans that these would increase to equal the number of local education authorities (LEAs) by the end of 1999. However, the DfEE 1999 White Paper attempted to put the LLPs in a more crucial position to help develop the quality of provision and increase local coherence of provision:

> It will be essential that LLPs are placed at the heart of the new arrangements ... The whole system must be driven from the bottom up ... It will be critical that the LLSCs work with the LLPs. We envisage a strong and important role for LLPs within a 'family' of organisations – not a 'hierarchy' – working together ... (with) the LLPs acting as a catalyst for collaborative action at the local level.[13]

The LLPs are thus envisaged to develop local learning targets and developing a local learning plan.[14]

The emphasis on the involvement of the FE sector and local authorities at both local and national level, with the TECs removed, has left the public sector in prime control of the provision of funding for post-16 training. The extent of employer involvement and influence has been formally reduced.

---

11 See *Labour Market Trends*, May 1998, pp. 233–6.
12 Interview comments from the TEC National Council and DfEE officials.
13 DfEE, 1999a, p. 30.
14 See *Insight*, 45, Summer 1999, p. 30; DfEE, London.

The important role played by employer-dominated TEC Boards, who controlled a specific work-based funding stream, has disappeared. The danger in this is 'there is a real risk that reintroduction of a national top-down system, with little more than a watch-dog role for employers, will reverse the growth in employer-based training'.[15] The shift from TECs to LLSCs has therefore seen a major shift in power and influence between the agents involved in training provision and strategy. We assess this pattern of change below.

7.3   Issues in the Negotiations to Establish LLSCs and TECs: Stakeholder Perspectives

The key agents involved in LLSC and TEC developments cover many central government departments and all the local agents that are concerned with training and the local economy. A first group of agents includes the main sponsoring department of the initiatives: in 1988–95 the Department of Employment (and its agency the Training Agency), and after its merger with the Department of Education in 1995 this becomes the Department for Education and Employment (DfEE). Also included are the other central government departments: the Department of Trade and Industry (DTI), the Treasury, the Department of the Environment (DoE) which was merged into the Department of Environment Transport and the Region (DETR) after 1997, and up to 1995 the Department of Employment's regional and area offices.

A second group of agents contains the main partners involved; the local authorities, the chambers of commerce and the enterprise agencies. We have also included the TEC Boards, although they were only just being established in the early stages of the establishment of TECs. They were, however, influential even in the early stages because a considerable time elapsed between the formal launch of TECs in 1988, their informal beginnings among local business leaders as early as 1987, the initiation of the process through the first TECs established in early 1990, and the completion of the established phase in late 1991. During this time TEC Boards, putative TEC Boards, as well as national business leaders, were able to exert considerable influence on negotiations.

A third group of agents is the other main private sector business interests. This group includes the Confederation of Business Industry (CBI), the British Chambers of Commerce (BCC), Business in the Community (BiTC), and a number of key individual business leaders. A fourth group of agents are those

---

15 Alan Moody, Chief Executive of CEWTEC, quoted in *Agenda*, August 1999, p. 15.

who are more peripheral to the TEC policy process. In this group we include the Industrial Training Organisations (ITOs), the Trade Unions Congress (TUC), the National Council for Voluntary Organisations (NCVO), the Further Education Colleges, the Local education Authorities (LEAs), Local Employer Networks (LENs), and local development agencies such as the Urban Development Corporations (UDCs) in existence in the 1980s and early 1990s, and the RDAs more recently.

Between these agents in the key negotiations there were many issues of broad as well as detailed negotiation. We focus here on five key issues in the negotiations over TECs, and eight issues in the negotiations over LLSCs. To some extent the greater number of issues affecting LLSCs reflects a finer level of detailed concern. Hence in Table 7.1, which summarises the key issues, the first three issues affecting LLSCs are the same as those identified as the first issue affecting TECs.

Table 7.1   Key policy issues in the negotiations concerning LLSCs and TECs

Issues concerning TECs	Issues concerning LLSCs
1 Breadth of TEC responsibility for training, enterprise and LED policy	1 Responsibility of TECs/LLSCs compared to RDAs for training policy
	2 Responsibility of TECs/LLSCs compared to RDAs for business support policy
	3 Responsibility of TECs/LLSCs compared to RDAs for LED policy
2 Size of TEC budget for training and vocational education	4 Scale of LLSC budget for training and vocational education
3 Targets for training programmes	5 Targets for training programmes
4 Number of TEC areas	6 Number of LLSC areas
5 Flexibility of use of funds	7 Flexibility of use of funds
	8 Relation of TECs and Chambers of Commerce

We discuss each of these issues below, comparing TEC and LLSC points of view. We then discuss how the salience and capability of each agent varied in the two negotiation processes: one for TECs, the other for LLSCs.

7.3.1 Breadth of Responsibility for TEC/LLSC Training, Business Support and Economic Development

The LLSCs are now focused essentially on training provision, but with coterminous areas with the SBS Business Links and a requirement to consult with, and be guided by, the RDAs in local economic development policy. The former TECs, however, had a wider range of objectives including not only training, but also business support and local economic development. There has thus been a shift from a 'broad view' to a 'narrow view' of the role of the body best able to develop training provision in the local economy.

(i) TECs The responsibility of TECs for training, business support and economic development policy was confused from the outset. The 1988 White Paper gave only short mention of business support, and this in an ambiguous form under the heading 'Training Through Life'.[16] Its main focus was on pre-existing programs such as small firm training and counselling, the Enterprise Allowance Scheme and Business Growth Training. The key plank of subsequent development proved to be the statement that TECs, would 'oversee the provision of the Employment Department's counselling and training of small firms ... they will also be the Government's link with local enterprise agencies (and seek) to ensure that provision is coordinated to maximize its effectiveness and make access as easy as possible'.[17] By the time of issue of the TEC Operating Manual,[18] business support had become the second main objective of TECs: to 'expand opportunities for local people to start their own business and to progress through training to new careers and greater prosperity'. This involved the consolidation of the DE pre-existing programs listed of Business Growth Training (BGT), the Small Firms Service (SFS), and the Enterprise Allowance Scheme (EAS). But a line of ambiguity was already evident since there was an expectation that

> in addition to its programme delivery responsibilities, a TEC will play an important role in developing information and advisory services ... new and expanding firms need information on the full array of business services available at each point in their growth cycle.[19]

---

16 DE, 1988, paras 6.17–6.23.
17 DE 1988, para. 6.22.
18 TEC Operating Manual, 1989, para. 1.2.
19 TEC Operating Manual, paras 1.10–1.11.

In addition, the potential for business support services to provide income was recognised. Hence, whilst the broad TEC mission was constrained by a funding reality that the 'Training Agency will provide core funding for information services which are the TECs responsibility (TAPs, BGT, SFS, EAS, ET)', it was also stated that 'a TEC will be encouraged to develop plans to attract extra resources to contribute towards the costs of providing more comprehensive services for local needs ... including the possibility of charging for services'.[20] Later in the Operating Manual each TEC is invited to 'establish a membership, ... may raise subscriptions, ... will be able to finance its marketing activities form the Local Initiative Fund and from program expenditure'.[21] However, by the time of the 1992 Employment White Paper[22] the TEC focus had become much more formally constrained to: (i) encouraging enterprise among young people; (ii) encouraging self-employment; (iii) maintaining a favourable business environment; (iv) offering coherent support to small firms; and (v) helping develop a wider range of sources of finance for small businesses.

The vision of TECs for local economic development was even more confused. They were given a vision to serve as a 'forum for local leaders ... to contribute to the regeneration of the communities they serve'.[23] However, this was already a crowded field with many competing agents, notably local authorities, who also considered local economic development to be their responsibility and were naturally resistant to the launch of a new body such as TECs. However, the then government saw economic development was seen as one of the key elements 'to attract and excite the right people to come on Board'.[24] Like business support responsibility, local economic development was seen as necessary for TECs to attract private sector employers to become involved.

The resistance of other agents to the development of TECs and the relative lack of their formal powers and resources, however, meant that TECs could only make relatively modest impact on local economic development. In their early stages they tended to flounder, with thinly developed staff skills and a lack of strong focus. Even by 1998 their specific economic development staff numbered only 6.7. However, by 1998 they had developed strong partnering support, and catalyst skills that had made them an important part of the economic development scene. For example, 44 per cent of TECs were involved as partners or supports to economic development projects in their areas, 34

---

20 Op. cit., para 1.14.
21 Op. cit., paras 5.3 and 5.4.
22 DE, 1992, pp. 49–51.
23 DE, 1988, p. 1.
24 Brian Wolfson, speech at London and South East Region TECs Seminar, 21 April 1993.

per cent were catalysts, whereas only 32 per cent claimed to lead these initiatives.[25] Since 1999 the economic development role has shifted to the RDAs and to local government. For the LLSCs there is a much clearer focus on training with much less confusion about seeking to integrate, within a single entity, policy on business support and economic development with training.

The tension between the broad and narrow views of the role of TECs was evident from their outset. Agents that preferred to see the TECs being allocated a minimalist role in most areas of policy at the outset sought to have TECs responsible only for unemployment training plus some role in the area of vocational education, delivered by FE colleges. Agents such as the local authorities particularly took this view. At the other extreme, the Training Agency sought that the TECs should be given a much wider breadth of policy responsibility, which included policy areas of not only unemployment training, but also vocational education, a leverage over training of people in employment (a forerunner to the current IiP policy initiative), an active role in the provision of business advice and enterprise creation, plus a special budget for LED projects which could be funded through the transfer of funds from other government departments. Other positions in between these extremes were held by the other agents. For example, the Treasury, the then Department of Education, the DoE and the chambers of commerce argued for the TECs to have responsibility for unemployment training, some role in vocational education, but also responsibility for a leverage for the training in people in employment, but little or no role for enterprise and economic development. In our expert interviews the British Chambers of Commerce pointed out that their view the TECs would have been best focused on the organisation of training for the unemployed and the further skilling of the workforce.

Agents closer to the other extreme included the TEC Boards, the CBI and Business in the Community. These agents accepted the policy objectives of the Training Agency, but argued that budget for local economic development should come from the DE and not from other government departments. The outcome of the negotiations was at the midway point between the extreme positions. The TECs were given responsibility for unemployment training, a role in vocational training as well as leverage for the training of people in employment. They were also to have some responsibility for business support as well as a catalyst role in local economic development, but received little resources for these roles.

---

25 Survey of TEC LED policy, Bennett and TNC, 1998.

(ii) LLSCs In the negotiations leading up to the establishment of the LLSCs the debate shifted. Once again a key government focus was on integrating training for the unemployed, largely focused on the work-based route and financed by the TECs, with vocational education financed through FE Colleges and funded via FEFC. But now support for integrating the business support and economic development roles had weakened. The Labour government saw these role as part of different agendas. They also wanted to reduce the power of the relatively autonomous business-led boards of TECs to make the whole system more 'accountable'. The whole debate was also wrapped up in the development of RDAs, which we have discussed in Chapter 5. Because of the additional complexity of the negotiations on the role of LLSCs, we divide the issue of the integration of work-based training and FE, from the issues of their role in enterprise and economic development policy.

Concerning *training policy* the views of agents now ranged, at one extreme, from a position that the RDAs should take over the main funding and policy role for all the objectives of training, business support and economic development. At the other extreme the DfEE wanted to maintain its control of training and education funding and was prepared to sacrifice the TEC role in business support and economic development in order to maintain its control. This was the ultimate winning position that led to the outcome of LLSCs being the new agents responsible for integrating work-based training and FE provision, but allowing economic development to pass to the RDAs and local government, with Business Link and business support passing back to the DTI. This position won against transferring all TEC responsibilities to the RDAs. The Regional Chambers, the TEC National Council, the TUC and the agents representing the FE and HE education interests all sought that the RDAs should have full executive responsibility for funding allocations to TECs with ability to vire within TEC budgets. Other agents favouring this position included the DETR, the emergent RDAs themselves, and the main business interests of the CBI and BCC. Other agents were intermediate and took the view that the RDA should have full executive responsibility for funding allocations (e.g. allocation to TECs in the region) with the ability to vire with other funds or the RDA budget. Agents with this policy position included the English Tourist Board, English Partnerships, the Commission for New Towns and the Rural Development Commission as well as the BiTC. Agents closer to the position of the DfEE included the Prime Minister, the local authorities, the enterprise agencies, the Business Link managers, local partnerships and the NCVO. All these agents supported the view that the DfEE should allocate the funding via the GoR to the TEC, but that TECs should be mandated to take account of the relevant RDA strategy for that region. The final outcome reflects a strong victory for the DfEE, supported by the Prime Minister and Treasury, in keeping control of the training budget and developing a subregional system largely independent of RDAs.

For *business support policy* the issues concerned chiefly the responsibility for Business Link and associated SME supports. The chief possibilities under discussion were transfer to the RDAs or separate control by the DTI. The eventual outcome has been DTI control within the SBS (see Chapter 8). The DfEE position supported the status quo which was for the DTI and DfEE to continue to allocate funding separately to the LLSCs. The DTI naturally wished to regain control of their funding stream independently of TECs, but this was a small funding issue for them and so they were also close to the status quo. At the other extreme was the view that the RDAs should have full executive responsibility for funding allocations for Business Link, with the ability to vire within business support policy, and an ability to vire across other policy programs. Agents with this policy preference included in the Regional Chambers, and the TEC National Council, and the more peripheral agents such as the HEFC, the FE Colleges, the FEFC and the TUC. The other extreme position was that the RDA should have full responsibility for business support policy within its own structure. Agents taking this position include the DETR, the emergent RDAs and the main private business interests such as the CBI and the BCC. Agents also close to this position include the ETB, EP, CNT, the RDC and BiTC, who argued that the RDA should have full executive responsibility for funding allocations for Business Links include the ability to vire between policy programs. The final outcome reflects a victory for the DTI, but most important, it also reflects the concern of the Treasury and Prime Minister not to support the further development of RDAs at this stage. It was also strongly influenced by the strong victory of the DfEE in keeping the LLSC budget away from RDAs.

For *local economic development policy* the positions of the various agents was similar to that for business support and training policy. Agents such as the DTI, the DfEE, the Home Office and the GORs took, at strongest, the status quo position and opposed any transfer of policy responsibility for economic development from the TECs to the RDAs. At the other extreme, the emergent RDAs, the CBI and the BCC argued for the transfer of full responsibility for economic development policy to the RDAs and for the TECs responsibility for economic development policy to be abolished. In between these extreme positions there lies a range of more moderate positions similar to those for training and enterprise policy. The outcome has been for the major lead on local economic development policy to shift to RDAs and local government, with something of a vacuum at subregional level, and a considerable gap compared to TECs in any form of formal business role at the subregional level.

7.3.2 Size of LLSC/TEC Budget for Training and Vocational Education

The second and closely related issue in the LLSC and TEC negotiations concerns the range of budget and responsibility for work-based training, FE and careers service advice. The key development of LLSCs has combined FE and work-based routes. However, for TECs far less control over FE finance was exercised.

(i) TECs In the TEC period of development, at one extreme, some agents resisted the allocation of any funding to the TECs and in effect rejected the establishment of the TEC system altogether. This position was held by the local authorities, the TUC, the FE colleges and the local education authorities. The establishment of the TECs threatened the interests of these agents with a further loss of control over their own budgets. At the other extreme, the Training Agency and business leaders sought that the TECs should be given as much budgetary control over vocational education as possible. One senior Training Agency official pointed out that at the time of the negotiations the public mood was behind this kind of initiative.[26] However, at the same time the Training Agency realised that the Treasury was unlikely to support the proposal, taking the view that employers should pay for the training they needed themselves. The Training Agency sought that the TECs should have responsibility for the budget for the careers service, and that budgetary control of 25 per cent of the FE college budget should be held back and controlled by TECs for which they could make independent policy decisions.

There was a range of policy positions between these two extremes. Agents close to the first extreme included the DTI and the DoE, who supported the establishment of the TECs, but argued that their budgetary responsibility should be minimal and limited to the DE unemployment training budget. However, a number of agents were prepared to support a more flexible approach to the funding of the TECs. The chambers of commerce, enterprise agencies, and development bodies such as the UDCs suggested that the TECs could have responsibility for the DE unemployment training budget, the careers service budget, as well as joint planning of budgetary expenditure with the FE colleges.

---

26 Interview comments.

In interviews with the BCC, it was pointed out that although BCC was highly suspicious of any move to allow the TECs a role in enterprise creation and support policy, it wanted the TEC budget to be pro-actively targeted at employers so as to encourage them to get involved in skilling their workforce. Agents close to the BCC position, but who were more flexible in their approach, included regional and area officers of the DE, Business in the Community and the NCVO. These agents supported the position that the TECs should enjoy a hold-back of 25 per cent of the FE Colleges budget which could be allocated by the TECs in collaboration with the LEAs.

The outcome of negotiations favoured this last position. However, it was a far-cry from the radical proposals initially put forward by the Training Agency. The actual development of TEC responsibility for finance of FE was particularly limited and the degree of TEC flexibility even more so. As time progressed the level of control of FE funding was actually reduced. The position was well summed up by one training provider:[27]

> the TEC budget is structured very rigidly with quite precise objectives defined for each budget heading. There is limited scope for the TECs to support or respond to training and development needs not previously acknowledged in its Business Plan. The vast majority of the TEC's budget is allocated for specific purposes before the beginning of the financial year.

(ii) LLSCs The development of LLSCs has fully achieved one of the original aims of TECs: to combine the FE and work-based funding streams. But this has been at the expense of control by employer-led boards, and the loss of business support and economic development responsibility. In the development of the review of TECs leading up to the announcement of LLSCs there was, at one extreme, the CBI, BCC, the DETR and the emergent RDAs who wanted the TECs to have an enlarged budget responsibility for work-based training, including at least some of the FE and ES budgets, but within RDA strategic control. Agents opposed to this view wanted the TECs to lose all elements of work-based training with their budget transferred to the FE colleges and the Employment Service. These agents included the Employment Service itself, FE colleges, the FEFC and the local education authorities. Other agents supported the status quo: for example the DTI, the Home Office and several of the more peripheral agents.

The final outcome leaves an ambiguous position. Whilst the ambition of combining work-based and FE funding has been achieved, the erosion of

---

27 Scope Training, memorandum of evidence, in HoC, 1998a.

control by employer interests suggests more of a victory for educational interests than for those supporting a work-based route. How effective the training developed will be can only be assessed when the LLSCs are fully operational after April 2001. Our assessment here is based on the interim evaluation possible in late 1999/early 2000.

7.3.3 Targets of Training Programmes

This issue concerns the appropriate target for the unemployment training programmes over which LLSCs and TECs have responsibility.

(i) TECs The DTI, the Treasury and the DoE sought that the TECs should be completely focused on the unemployed as the target group and that the training programmes could not be accessible people already in employment. They also sought that the unemployed applicant would be guaranteed a position on a suitable training programme. A less extreme position was held by the DE and subsequently the DfEE, who sought to have the majority of TEC funding targeted towards the unemployed, but between 5 per cent and 10 per cent of the budget made available for training of employed persons. An even more flexible view was that the main emphasis of the TEC training programmes should be placed on the training of the unemployed but with some TEC funding targeted towards those in employment through modern apprenticeships and IiP. The agents supporting this position included Training Agency area and regional area officers, the enterprise agencies and the Business in the Community. At the other extreme, agents such as the TEC Boards, the chambers of commerce and the CBI sought that the TECs should contract a broad range of training programmes which the unemployed could participate in, but that the unemployed would enjoy no special status or guarantee of entitlement to training places. The outcome of the negotiations was that the majority of the TEC budget was to be allocated to the training of the unemployed, with a small percentage of the finance (not specified, but equal to about 10–15 per cent) allocated to training programmes for those already in employment.

In effect, these national negotiations only partially succeeded in putting in place the original concept for the TECs. Moreover, as time progressed and the British economy went into recession in 1990–92, the commitment to a wider TEC responsibility for training for the employed, already on a weak footing, was further eroded. The *Financial Times*[28] headlined the change of

---

28 *Financial Times*, 2 April 1991.

TEC focus as 'Conceived in good times, born in bad'. In the launch phase of TECs in 1988 the talk was all of a demographic downturn and skill shortages. However, by 1990/1 there was a deep recession with no problem of skill shortages. Instead TECs were thrust back to the old MSC staple of training the unemployed which, although an important issue, undermined the commitments which Boards signed up for.'[29]

(ii) LLSCs The situation changed significantly under the Labour government. The unemployment programmes have become progressively taken into the New Deal, with the former work-based Learning for Adults and Youth Training almost entirely absorbed into New Deal by early 2000. This removed the more general training budget available for TECs, except in the work-based areas of Modern Apprenticeships. The development LLSCs, therefore, represents an important shift, not just in the responsibility for unemployment programmes, but also in the way in which local input occurs to vocational training and FE provision.

In the negotiations leading up to the announcement of LLSCs, the Treasury, the DETR, the DTI, the Home Office and the TUC held the position that the TEC and former TEC programmes should be completely focused on the unemployed, who would be considered a guarantee group. At the other extreme, the main private business interests such as the CBI, BCC and the TEC National Council still hoped that the LLSCs would be able to contract a broad range of training programmes for the employed in which the unemployed would also be free to participate, but with no special status or guarantee of entitlement. The DfEE, the FE colleges, the FEFC and others had supported a position in which the TEC funds should be targeted on the unemployed, but accepted that between 5–15 per cent of the budget could be used for (re)training of those already in employment.

However, late in the process of discussions, in early 1999, the DfEE, but with support from FEFC, radically changed its position. Since the unemployed had become chiefly supported financially by New Deal, the DfEE took the opportunity of combining the rump of the remaining TEC work-based training programmes with FE funding. This has meant that LLSCs have no specific remit or target for the unemployed, although much of the provision is available to both employed and unemployed. We simulate here the DfEE and FEFC position in early 1999, prior to their crucial change in position.

---

29 Bennett et al., 1994.

7.3.4 *Number of LLSC/TEC Areas*

The LLSCs areas were defined by the DfEE and RDAs with some consultation with local partners. The final group of areas to emerge was 47, which was close to the DfEE expectation of 'no more than 50'.[30] The areas covered by TECs, however, emerged from a more bottom-up process of negotiations between the various local agents.

(i) TECs The TEC boundaries were supposed to develop from a well-reasoned TEC bid which reflected the business needs at the local level. However in practice a series of other institutional constraints on the boundaries fundamentally undermined the business-led bottom-up process. For a start, the Government sent out conflicting messages regarding the boundaries for TEC areas. The White Paper stated that 'the government did not intend to prescribe boundaries … but in general they are likely to be based on subdivisions or, in certain circumstances, aggregations of the existing 57 Training Agency areas (in England and Wales)'.[31] This was in direct conflict with the TEC Prospectus,[32] that 'there are no predetermined geographical boundaries … the prospective TEC should consider what boundaries best reflect the economic, geographical and travel-to-work patterns'. This conflict in messages reflects a shift by the DE and government in the set-up phase of TECs to recognise the importance of local government boundaries, and the pressure from local authority and LEA agents who resisted attempts to undermine their boundaries. There was also considerable resistance from the DE and its regional and area offices to any adjustment of their boundaries.

These positions are clearly reflected in our interviews. At one extreme, agents such as the DTI, the Treasury and business leaders wanted the number of TEC areas to be limited to about fifty. Other agents sought a slightly higher number of TEC areas, e.g. the Training Agency and the area and regional offices of the DE. At the other end of the policy spectrum agents such as the enterprise agencies, the local authorities, the NCVO, the FE colleges and the LEAs all advocated that there should be more than a hundred TEC areas, which would imply that there would be a TEC in every local authority area that had educational responsibility. A less extreme position than this, by the CBI, the BCC, LENs and the TEC Boards themselves, recognised that it was necessary to reflect the views of local business partners, who often related to

---

30 DfEE, 1999a, p. 29.
31 DE, 1988, p. 43.
32 DE, 1989, p. 6.

specific local education authority areas (as in the case of LENs) or other smaller structures of chambers of commerce. The LENs were Local Employers Networks, established in 1987 as a preceding initiative between BCC, CBI and the DE to bring together employer demand and FE college supply of training in each of 132 areas in England. The LENs experience fed directly into the establishment of TECs with many LEN board members and LEN areas carrying-over into TECs, particularly in metropolitan areas.[33] In the end 82 TEC areas were established, 75 in England, seven in Wales. Of these three in England and one in Wales had disappeared through merger by mid-1998.

The small size of the many TEC areas produced continued pressure for reform. A DfEE Efficiency Scrutiny in 1994[34] took up the proposal of Bennett et al. (1994) that about 50 areas would achieve a more effective and efficient system. This was echoed by the HoC Employment Committee,[35] which recommended:

> that the Department of Education and Employment, in consultation with other bodies, review the boundaries of the TEC areas to consider whether they constrict the ability of TECs to engage with the local labour market; and whether they allow TECs to collaborate as effectively as they might do with other agencies.

The government's response in 1996 was to reject this proposal, arguing that:

> The existing network of TECs reflects the views of local partners, particularly the private sector, on the most sensible boundaries in the context of local labour markets. We have no evidence to suggest that either the size of TECs or their current boundaries are a constraint on effective performance. If local partners believe that changes in boundaries are necessary, in the light of developing labour markets, then we would look at individual cases on their merits.[36]

Moreover, Sir Michael Bett, Chair of the TEC National Council, denied that there were too many TECs. Some of the small TECs, he pointed out, produced some of the highest performance. Sir Michael stressed that the TEC structure had evolved naturally, through the TEC bids: 'they did not grow up because they were in accordance with some planned arrangement across the country. If there are too many TECs it is because too many communities want a TEC'.[37]

---

33 See Bennett et al., 1990; Bennett and McCoshan, 1993, pp. 180–85.
34 DfEE, 1995.
35 HoC, 1996c, p. xxxiii.
36 HoC, 1996b, p. ix.
37 HoC, 1996, p. 69.

(ii) LLSCs The position for LLSCs reflects the alternative approach of pre-defining boundaries which local partners then bid or organised to cover. The RDAs nominally took the lead in drawing up LLSC areas, although the main secretariate leadership came from the GORs. In practice it was difficult to resolve differences emerging from using the different criteria of consistency with former TEC areas, fit to TTWAs, the pattern of business activities, and the requirement to have a population of over 500,000. Even after the first announcement of the LLSC areas in late October 1999, two former TEC areas (Oldham and Rochdale) were still not assigned to a new LLSC area.

The process was very much imposed from above. The Secretary of State at the DfEE decreed the target of 'no more than 50' and this was passed down the line to RDAs. One RDA, in the North West, tried with local partner support to deviate from this norm. It proposed 12 or 13 areas compared to the six or eight it was deemed to merit. It was quickly told to think again: 'they misunderstood the task they were to undertake'.[38] Partner concerns were, therefore, largely ignored unless they fell in line with the search for larger geographical areas.

The outcome[39] has been a pattern in which the LLSCs almost all fit to local authority boundaries at the non-metropolitan county level on to groups of metropolitan districts largely fitted to the former metropolitan county areas. The unitary districts of local government are in all cases grouped into their respective non-metropolitan county areas. Only six non-metropolitan counties are grouped (Devon with Cornwall; Oxford with Buckinghamshire; East and West Sussex); only one former metropolitan county is divided – the West Midlands where the Black County, Birmingham/Solihull and Coventry/Warwickshire have three separate LLScs. London is divided into 5 LLSCs involving the most complex subdivision of the former seven TEC areas.

The coterminosity with SBS business support areas is close except for one additional SBS area each in Lancashire and Manchester, and the servicing of London by one SBS with five local delivery operations. This led to 45 SBS areas compared to 47 LLSCs (see chapter 8).

7.3.5 Flexibility of Use of Funds

This issue concerns the degree of autonomy of TEC or LLSC finance from detailed DfEE specification, particularly the extent of local power to move funding allocations from one programme area to another (virement).

---

38 NW GOR interview comment, October, 1999.
39 DfEE, 1999a, Press Release 473/99, 28 October.

(i) TECs The 1988 White Paper argued that only employers could:

> link training plans with business plans ... Employers themselves must assume active leadership in preparing and maintaining a skilled workforce and in creating a climate conducive to business development, self-employment and job creation.[40]

> Planning and management of enterprise and training need to shift from the public to the private sector. Employers are best placed to identify key skill needs and to ensure that the level and quality of training and business service meets these needs.[41]

The Training Agency recognised that an important element for the success of the TEC initiative was the need for senior business executives to become involved in the operation of the initiative. However, in order to draw these business interests into the operation, it was recognised that a devolution of funding control to the TEC level was required. This raised the related thorny question of how to ensure adequate accountability for the expenditure of public money; a cultural shift in accountability was required as far as the DE was concerned. 'The lack of trust implicit in the system of accountability of TECs is therefore a crucial constraint on development'.[42] Cay Stratton, the chief adviser to the government in the TEC development phase, saw this balance resolved through performance standards. She argued that TECs would not be 'converting public funds into unrestricted grants. Government can, and should, set clear program objectives and rigorous performance standards. But accountability should be measured against outcomes, not inputs and process'.[43] This balance of flexibility and accountability was however, never satisfactorily resolved with the result that business leaders continued to be frustrated by the lack of flexibility of TEC finance, whilst government and civil servants, parliament and the NAO were continually frustrated by the lack of their control.

In our analysis we found a considerable range of views. Agents such as the Department for Education, the Treasury, the DoE, the TUC and the LEAs objected to the TECs having any capacity freely to move funds from one policy programme to another, or even within programmes. These agents supported the position that the TEC funding blocks should reflect Treasury and Parliamentary budgetary lines. There should be no virement. Audits should

---

40 DE, 1988, pp. 30, 39.
41 *TEC Prospectus*, DE, 1989. p. 4.
42 Company interviewee, 1994; see also Bennett et al., 1994.
43 Stratton, 1989, pp. 72–3.

follow all programmes to the final recipient, through the TEC. The negative reaction to flexibility by departments other than the DE reflected the fact that they felt that their own control of funding could be threatened. The Treasury was also opposed to the concept of devolved funding, over which private business interests would have influence, on the basis that it would be difficult to ensure public accountability and their view that businesses should pay for their own training. The local authorities had a slightly less extreme position and sought that the TECs should be able to allocate any surpluses flexibly, though they were unhappy that surpluses became high.

At the other extreme, agents such as the Prime Minister, the Training Agency, the area and regional offices of the DE, the TEC Boards, the chambers of commerce, the enterprise agencies, the business leaders, BCC and the CBI all supported the view that the TECs should be allocated a 'block grant' with general performance targets. They also wanted a single audit approach, stopping at the level of the TEC itself; i.e. not going through to the training provider. The TEC National Council argued that the

> weight and bureaucracy associated with many program rules is substantial, and can hamper or prevent desirable local flexibility [Moreover] Training providers complain of the excessive auditing requirements which the TECs impose on them as a result of contractual pressure from Government.[44]

John Banham, then director general of the CBI, called for an increase in the flexibility of funds so that Boards could 'decide their priorities just as they would do in their business life. This requires that TEC funds should come in the form of a single block'.[45] In the end, the policy on this issue was much closer to the position of the Treasury. The vast majority of TEC funding had to allow Treasury and parliamentary budgetary lines of accountability to be audited through to the final recipient, but there was some flexibility for an initiative fund, as well TEC autonomy with respect to use of budgetary surpluses.

(ii) LLSCs In the review period leading to the replacement of TECs by LLSCs the arguments over flexibility and accountability continued with similar positions held by most agents. The result was a stalemate between the local agent and business demand for more flexibility and the Treasury's unwillingness to give it. The unjamming of this stalemate was found by Labour in greater control via the NDPB model.

---

44 HoC, 1996c, Vol. 2, p. 70; Vol. 1, p. 44.
45 Banham, 1992, p. 8.

The LLSCs have been given a different approach from the outset. As NDPBs staffed by crown servants the flexibility issue has been resolved in favour of managerial discretion within the public sector with formal accountability governed by standard public sector auditing and parliamentary scrutiny. The formal position is that LLSCs have budgetary control for work-based training (the former TEC funding stream) and 'agree allocations' to FE colleges. They are able to vary national funding tariffs locally.[46] However, considerable uncertainty still surrounds the degree of practical flexibility, with DfEE and Treasury interests still keen to keep it restricted. It thus remains to be seen how far LLSCs will be able to exercise an effective level of flexibility within this framework.

7.3.6 TECs and Chambers of Commerce

A further issue which we analyse in the reform process to develop LLSCs, but which was not a concern in the early stages of establishing TECs', was that of merging TECs and chambers of commerce, to form Chambers of Commerce Training and Enterprise (CCTEs). By 1998, 13 CCTEs had been formed, after which a moratorium was in place until the establishment of LLSCs. One scenario for the future of TECs was for all TECs to evolve in this way to become CCTEs. This was seen as offering an advantage of accountability through a 'membership' structure, i.e. TECs would be 'owned' by business interests through their Chamber.[47] However, this approach met much resistance particularly from the government regional offices, traditional Labour supporters, some local authorities and some TECs themselves. Not all chambers were in favour either. Indeed, the concept was very divisive within both TEC National Council and the BCC. It did, however, find initial favour within DfEE, DTI and CBI.

With the division of views between different TECs and different chambers it was only possible for a cautious approach to be developed by TEC National Council and the BCC. This severely weakened their position in negotiations. It is not surprising, therefore, that in the end the establishment of LLSCs took no particular account of CCTEs. They were treated like any other TEC. For the CCTEs themselves the transition to LLSCs and SBS Business Link areas was also no easier than for other TECs. The outcome, then, was for TECs and chambers of commerce to become separate agencies with LLSCs formed from

---

46 DfEE, 1999a, Press Release 473/99, 28 October.
47 See BCC, 1998, *The Future Chamber*; Bennett et al., 1994, chapter 12.

rump elements of TECs and the chamber element of CCTEs to become chiefly involved with the franchises for SBS Business Links (see chapter 8).

7.3.7 Salience of Agents

As the sponsoring body, the Department of Employment's executive body of the Training Agency initially had the strongest salience on most issues. Their role was taken over as the main concern of the DfEE in negotiations about LLSCs. The Treasury was also extremely concerned about two of the LLSC and TEC issues: the targets of training, and the flexibility of the budget. Given the overall emphasis in these negotiations on the use and control of substantial amounts of public finance, this is not surprising. Other government agents, including the DETR/DoE and the TA regional and area officers of the DE, register lower levels of salience with the exception of one or other of the issues.

The main local partners have high salience on most issues. The only partner in this group for whom these issues were not as important was the enterprise agencies because they felt, as a supplier to the system, they would survive in some form whatever happened. The local authorities were particularly concerned about the number of areas which were to be established, the breadth of the responsibility for training, enterprise and LED, and the scale of the TEC/LLSC budget. The issue of the breadth of policy responsibility was of most importance for the chambers of commerce, followed by the appropriate target for training.

7.3.8 Capability of Agents

In the policy negotiations the level of capability varied across the agents involved and was not the same for all of the LLSC/TEC issues. However, where differences in agent capability do occur they usually refer to just one or two agents, where they have particular concern or expertise about a particular issue. For the central government departments, we have used the same approach for LLSC/TECs as for the other policies analysed in the other case study chapters: the individual government departments generally have high capability, reflecting their high levels of administrative and financial resources, strategic information and the time that the government officials have at their disposal during the negotiations relative to many of the other stakeholders involved. However, the Treasury has the highest level of capability reflecting its overall control of expenditure across the various sectoral government departments. But, where there is one particular government department which has lead responsibility for the policy area being negotiated, then this government department is also usually rated highly as it is the most highly resourced stakeholder directly involved in negotiations. If the Prime Minister (or Cabinet) is identified as being *directly* influential in the negotiations, then this is also given a high rating. With respect to the power of regional and local area officers, the most influential were the area officers and GORs. However, the GORs are seen as quite constrained, as observed by one interviewee, the DfEE took the strong view that GOR was 'there to serve ministers, rather than have its own agenda'[48] and this has led to strong central control, or a 'command and control' system,[49] even after the introduction of RDAs.

Among the other agents none of the main partners were as powerful as the government departments. The TEC Boards in fact prove to be the most highly resourced agents in this subgroup, followed by the local authorities, the BCC and the enterprise agencies. Several interviewees suggested that it was the TEC Board's Chairmen who were more influential that their Boards, but others suggested that the chief executives were the main power source in TECs. In LLSCs the Boards are even less powerful compared to the senior staff. Other business agents, the CBI, individual key business leaders, and BiTC were, on average, as powerful as the formal partners in the TEC phase of development. But this is not true in the setting up of LLSCs.

Hence, although there are many agents who may have participated in both the LLSC and TEC negotiations, only a small number of these agents were really powerfully or strongly concerned about the issues. Also only a minority of the interested agents are concerned about *all* of the LLSC/TEC issues to be negotiated; most agents are chiefly interested in just one or two issues. Power is very unequally shared, with the key sponsoring department of the DfEE (or for TECs the DE and Training Agency) have uniquely the greatest power and salience. As we shall see, this combination of salience and power makes them the dominant player in establishing both LLSCs and TECs. If the DfEE decides it wants to make a change, and it can carry the Treasury and cabinet with it, then the change will occur; the concerns of other partners and agents can be largely ignored. The LLSCs and TECs exist, therefore, because the DfEE wants them; not necessarily because they are the best way of tackling the chief issues involved for local and regional economic policy. They are an example of state-led corporatism, as outlined in chapter 3.

---

48 Interview comments from former DE regional director, 1998.
49 Interview comments from DE senior director, 1998.

7.4   Simulations

As with our other case studies we combine the information on policy positions, salience and power of agents through use of four simulation models. The overall accuracy of each model is shown in Table 7.2. The exchange model is by far the best predictor for the negotiations for the development of TECs, but is marginally worse than the compromise model for the negotiation of LLSCs. The strategic control and conflict models are by far the poorest models in both cases.

Table 7.2   Comparison of predictions for different models of the TEC and LLSC negotiations using the mean square error criterion

Model	TEC negotiations	LLSC negotiations
Compromise (base) model	111.0	1432.9
Exchange model	52.8	1517.5
Strategic control model	459.0	2594.9
Conflict model	1282.6	2050.7

The higher accuracy of the exchange model in the case of TECs confirms that a log-rolling process occurred in the set-up phase of TECs, particularly influenced by the emergent TEC Boards. Despite the fact that a number of agents were initially very resistant to the setting up of TECs (notably local government and the TUC) their salience and power was insufficient to have major influence on the outcome, but they did have some important influences on issues such as the number of TEC areas.

The poorer accuracy of the exchange model for the negotiations surrounding LLSCs reflects the situation that many aspects were announced by government without detailed prior negotiation. The previous period of two TEC reviews over 1997–99 had demonstrated to Labour that major development would not occur through consensual exchange. Most important, the cabinet had eventually decided to back the DfEE view, that LLSCs should remain directly under the DfEE rather than being transferred to the RDAs, against the recommendations of two House of Commons Select Committees[50] and the objectives of the DETR and some leading ministers. The LLSCs were, therefore, mostly the outcome of a DfEE/Cabinet/Prime Minister imposed

---

50 HoC 1997, 1998a.

solution to a difficult problem. They did not reflect a typical exchange and log-rolling process.

The contrast between the outcomes of the two sets of negotiations is evident by comparing the prediction-realisation diagrams in Figures 7.2 and 7.3. These compare the actual and predicted outcomes of negotiations based on our models. The way in which these diagrams is constructed is described in chapter 5. In the negotiations leading up to the establishment of TECs there is a close relation between predicted and actual outcomes (Figure 7.2). Only for issue 5, the flexibility of use of funds, is the exchange model a poor predictor. The Treasury resisted this flexibility despite it being favoured by all other major agents.

In the case of the LLSC negotiations, however, the relation between the exchange model predictions and actual outcomes is much poorer (Figure 7.3). Only for the issues of breadth of responsibility for LLSC training policy and the number of LLSC areas is the exchange model a relatively good predictor. It is particularly poor for prediction of the relation of TECs/LLSCs and chambers of commerce, and the targets for training, where the TEC experience was largely ignored. The exchange model predicts that most TECs/LLSCs

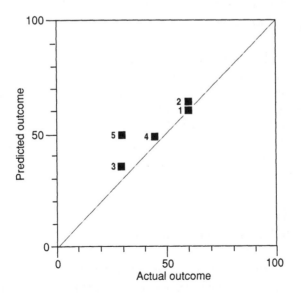

Figure 7.2 Prediction-realisation diagram for TEC negotiations (exchange model)

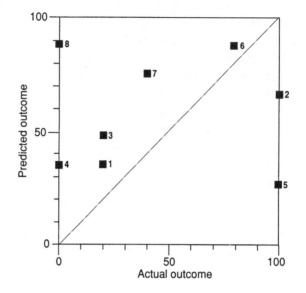

Figure 7.3 Prediction-realisation diagram for LLSC negotiations (exchange model)

would merge with chambers of commerce, but in effect the government abolished this option by making LLSCs branches of a central government body. The targets for training in the exchange model predictions reflect a strong employer work-based emphasis, but the government has decided (i) to merge work-based training with FE college funding with very uncertain outcomes for employers, and (ii) to transfer the chief responsibility for unemployment training to the Employment Service through New Deal (see chapter 5).

7.5   Power Relations: Gainers and Losers

We can assess which agents have gained and which have lost in the negotiation process by calculating their net utility loss using equation (5.1). This measures the difference between the actual outcome and each agent's desired outcome weighted by their salience.

Table 7.3 compares these net utility gains and losses for each agent as a mean across each issue. From the TEC negotiations, for those agents with high salience, the most successful agents are TA regional and area offices, CBI and BCC; the least successful agents are the local education authorities, TEC Boards and the DETR. For the LLSC negotiations there are few major gains made by any agent. The Treasury, prime minister and other government departments all make small gains, as do business groups such as BCC, CBI and BiTC. But most significant are the losses by DETR, FE colleges, LEAs and the Employment Service who all hoped to gain more directly from the demise of TECs. Interestingly the DfEE, although gaining politically out of the development of LLSCs, has neutral utility loss/gain over all issues because the development of LLSCs in fact changes virtually nothing in favour or against all the familiar issues of training targets and flexibility. All the key issues rest with implementation, not with political bargaining.

Overall the TEC negotiations give an average utility gain to most agents whilst LLSCs give an average utility loss. This is partly the result of the larger number of agents involved in LLSC negotiations via the RDA reforms for which there would have been added synergy and hence utility gains for TEC programmes if TECs had been combined to RDAs.

Comparisons of mean utility losses and gains on each issue, as a mean for all agents, are shown in Table 7.4. The main gains for TEC development where from the flexibility of funding offered (despite its limitations), breadth of training policy combined with business support and economic development, and the broadening of targets for training. For LLSCs the main gains result from improved targeting of training and business support policy. Utility losses now result from the scale of training budget (because of the challenge to the work-based approach) and from the loss of potential to develop CCTEs.

In terms of power relations our analysis confirms that central government exercised the key control over both TEC and LLSC negotiations. However, for TECs the outcome eventually reflected a log-rolling and exchange process between agents. This is the type of process modelled well by an exchange model. For LLSC negotiations, however, the exchange model is very poor. The key agents make large utility losses. The LLSCs have a strong character of being imposed on the chief agents, particularly TECs, LEAs, FE and the DETR that have the highest losses. In contrast business interests make modest gains. Overall, therefore, our analysis confirms the strong role of the central state as a coercive force, rather than a consensual facilitator of change in this case.

Table 7.3   Net utility losses for each agent across all issues in TEC and LLSC negotiations (exchange model)

Agent	TEC negotiations	LLSC negotiations
DTI	+0.004	-0.003
DfEE	-0.006	0.000
Treasury	+0.008	+0.002
DETR/DoE	-0.016	-0.022
Prime Minister	-0.004	+0.004
Other government departments	–	+0.001
TA/MSC	-0.116	–
GORs TA regional and area offices	-0.004	+0.011
Local government	+0.004	-0.010
Emergent Regional Chambers	–	-0.009
BCC	+0.180	+0.010
Enterprise agencies	-0.008	+0.003
TEC boards/TNC	-0.038	-0.006
BL NC	–	-0.003
BiTC	-0.034	+0.006
CBI	+0.036	+0.002
Business leaders/emergent RDAs	-0.010	+0.011
NTOs	-0.004	+0.001
TUC	+0.000	-0.002
NCVO	-0.006	+0.006
FE Colleges	+0.002	-0.012
FEFC	–	-0.008
LEAs	-0.122	-0.016
LENs	-0.004	–
Employment Service	–	-0.012
HE/Universities	–	-0.003
HEFC	–	-0.004
Invest in Britain Bureau	–	-0.004
English Tourist Board	–	-0.004
English Partnerships	–	-0.004
Commission for New Towns	–	-0.000
Rural Development Commission	–	±0.001
Other local development bodies/ local partnerships	-0.004	+0.012
Total	+0.700	-0.370

Note: a gap is shown in each column where the agent was not in existence or was not important in the negotiations concerned.

Table 7.4   Net utility loss/gain for each issue in TEC and LLSC negotiations (exchange model)

TECs	TEC gains/losses	LLSCs issues	LLSC gains/losses
1 Breadth of TEC responsibility	+0.021	1 LLSCs and training policy	+0.019
		2 LLSCs and business support policy	+0.021
		3 LLSCs and economic development policy	+0.009
2 TEC training budget	+0.012	4 LLSC training budget	-0.002
3 Targets for training	+0.017	5 Targets for training	+0.016
4 Number of TECs	-0.010	6 Number of LLSCs	+0.005
5 Flexibility of the funds	+0.028	7 Flexibility of use of funds	+0.012
		8 TECs and chambers	-0.001
Total	+0.700		-0.370

7.6   Extent of Progress

The TECs and their programmes have been subject to a large number of evaluation studies. However, the LLSCs are, as yet, too new for any evaluations, but there are indicators of their likely performance.

The main budget of TECs, and where their mission was clearest, was for training. This is also where their greatest achievements lie. Their flagship programme of modern apprenticeship had reached 100,000 over the four years 1995–99, and over the same period over one million people have acquired qualifications through TEC-funded programmes.[51] The unit cost of government-financed workforce training has been driven down to about 25 per cent of its 1992/3 costs by 1996/7, whilst the average NVQs or positive outcomes per learner has more than doubled over the same period.[52] Hence TECs delivered enormous efficiency gains and increases in effectiveness over their lifetime. In addition, TECs, together with other training providers, have made a significant contribution to increasing the level of employer spending on training from about £100m per year in the mid-1980s to £700m by 1997. Associated with this, over 12,000 employers were recognised as IiP by 1999.[53]

---

51 DfEE, 1999a, p. 16.
52 HoC, 1996c, Figure A, p. lv, updated with TEC annual performance tables.
53 DfEE, 1999a, p. 16.

In the fields of business support some evaluation studies indicate that those firms helped have generated an additional £33 of turnover and £3 of additional investment for every £1 spent by TECs.[54] Despite having to promote a rather independent branding as Business Link, TECs can also take considerable credit for the establishment and success of the BL system for which they were the contract holders until April 2000.

In the field of local economic development, TECs have become important partners with local government and other bodies, signing off and being key strategic partners in 37 per cent of local authority strategies, and being key facilitators of local partnerships through their own strategies in most other areas.[55] Government has found TECs a useful means to develop SRB and EU structural funding management and delivery so that they were crucial participants in most local and regional initiatives during the 1990s.

Despite these many positive contributions there had been a number of criticisms since their inception. Most important to many Labour party activists was their affront to local accountability. They gave majority control of their boards to business members which was argued to cut across the local democratic accountability to local government, FE college interests, and other lobbies. Although a code of conduct was established in 1996 for local consultation, appointment to the boards, complaints handling and similar matters, the changes achieved were not enough to satisfy ideological opponents of business leadership.[56] Similarly, the key mission of TECs to combine training with business support and local economic development, was seen as one of their chief areas of ineffectiveness. Heseltine's launch of the BL initiative was a de facto criticism of TEC performance in this area which created an uneasy rival funding structure through the DTI as well as DfEE.[57] Evaluation of TECs in the 1990–94 period found them 'floundering' in the field of economic development.[58] Although later studies find them to be more effective and more collaborative,[59] they never achieved, or were never allowed to achieve, the strong economic development focus of Scottish Enterprise north of the border.

Moreover, there were also criticisms of TEC efficiency. Whilst the unit costs of training had been driven down strongly, the main effect of this was to create surpluses that could be used for other purposes, chiefly business support and economic development. This was the desired model in the TEC launch

---

54   DTI, 1996; quoted in DfEE, 1999a.
55   Bennett and LGA, 1998; Bennett and TEC National Council 1998.
56   See Bennett et al., 1994.
57   See chapter 8.
58   Bennett et al., 1994, chapter 10.
59   Bennett and TEC National Council, 1998.

phase. But it created intense political problems since it remained uncomfortable that money assigned by parliament for training within the DfEE remit was being used for other purposes, especially since UK skill levels and large socially disadvantaged groups needing training appeared to remain as stubborn problems. Indeed the whole issue of the size of TEC surpluses, especially those unspent and used as running balances was politically very decisive.[60] Moreover, various studies demonstrated that the small size of many TECs and their excessive pay structures led to considerable management inefficiencies.[61]

The chief reasons for dissatisfaction with TECs cited by the government, however, threw the criticisms in a different direction. These focused on the fragmentation and lack of coherence, on 'a bureaucratic minefield' between TEC, FE college and sixth form school provision which resulted in 'the current system ... failing a significant section of the country, often the most vulnerable and disadvantaged'. It was also failing to overcome skill shortages, gave patchy support, advice and guidance, and there were important deficiencies in the quality and thoroughness of the training inspection regime.[62] Even the TECs flagship programme of modern apprenticeships was strongly criticised for the small number of qualifications it delivered, mainly as a result of trainees leaving prematurely to take on better paid jobs before their qualifications were fully accredited. Only about 32 per cent of leavers achieved qualifications in 1999, 'less than the much criticised 64 per cent level achieved by equivalent FE college leavers'.[63] The DfEE position drew heavily on the second report of the Skills Task Force and the first report of the Training Standards Council,[64] which both identified problems of quality, coherence, matching skill needs to provision, and defects in the careers advice system. There was also a running concern about some FE college viability, the need for inter-college mergers and school sixth form college mergers that could increase coherence of provision into integrated tertiary system. The Secretary of State for Education and Employment, David Blunkett, also had something of a template for tertiary reform in his mind, developed from his time as leader of Sheffield City Council.

The balance between TEC's considerable achievements and the long-running criticisms was finally resolved in favour of a focused approach on training, passing responsibility for economic development to RDAs and local government, and for business support to DTI. The LLSCs have therefore a

---

60 See e.g. HoC, 1996c, evidence.
61 see DfEE, 1995; Bennett et al., 1994.
62 DfEE, 1999a, pp. 16–21.
63 ONS statistics; quoted in *Times Educational Supplement*, 17 September 1999, 'Youth Scheme fails to deliver'.
64 STF, 1999; TSC, 1999.

simpler agenda which should allow more coherent support from their parent ministry the DfEE. However, there is one key concern among agents which is leading to considerable doubts about how far they can succeed. This is their perceived takeover by FE and educational interests. Business leadership of TECs, for all its faults, did assure a strong focus on work-based training and work-relevant qualifications. Merger with the much larger FE college system has thrown this into doubt with both TUC and CBI critical of LLSCs in their Annual Conferences in 1999. The move to LLSC organisation has also coincided with a shift in FE college governance to remove the majority membership of business and non-educational interests among governing boards,[65] a change which even the *Times Educational Supplement* referred to 'off message' compared to Downing Street's more pro-business approach.[66] There has also been a shift in the definition of NVQs towards greater control by educational supplier interests by merger of the specific NVQ council into the Qualifications and Curriculum Authority in 1996. At the same time the role of industry lead bodies in definition of NVQs is seen as still too dominated by DfEE interests and finance, with sector bodies such as National Training Organisations still patchy and overly dependent on DfEE rather than industry leadership.[67]

Thus, whilst LLSCs offer considerable scope for a better focus of training provision, and a greater coherence between different governmental funding streams within DfEE, there is considerable doubt about how appropriate the training provision will be. This leads to obvious concerns from business interests which can be assessed through different scenarios.

7.7   Alternative Scenarios

We compare four scenarios where one particular agent's power is increased significantly, to one half of the total power available to all agents. These scenarios are used to simulate the potential effect on outcomes of the dominance of that agent: in our four cases, the chambers of commerce, CBI, TECs/LLSCs, and local government.

The four scenarios are compared in Table 7.5. All scenarios result in lower accuracy for the simulations rather than the original model. This is because the dominant agents are each seeking a more radical solution than desired by

---

65 From 1 August 1999 business members of FE college governing boards can be no more than one third of the total; before this date they had to be at least one half of governors with limits also set on their participation for a quorum to exist.

66 *Times Educational Supplement*, 30 July 1999, 'Blunkett "off message"'.

67 Bennett, 1998d, Survey of ITOs and NTOs.

government. In these simulations the CBI is the most radical agent in the TEC negotiations. It particularly worked for greater TEC powers on issues 1,2,3,5. The chambers of commerce and TECs themselves are the next most radical, particularly on issues 4 and 5. The local authorities are least radical, except for the issue of the number of TEC areas. These positions are illustrated well in the prediction-realisation diagram Figure 7.4.

Table 7.5   Comparison of alternative scenarios and actual outcomes for TEC and LLSC negotiations using the mean square error criterion (exchange model)

	TEC negotiations	LLSC negotiations
Scenario 1: Chambers of Commerce	293.0	1545.4
Scenario 2: CBI	347.0	1597.7
Scenario 3: TECs/LLSCs	282.8	1055.1
Scenario 4: Local government	251.8	2280.4
Original prediction	52.8	1517.5

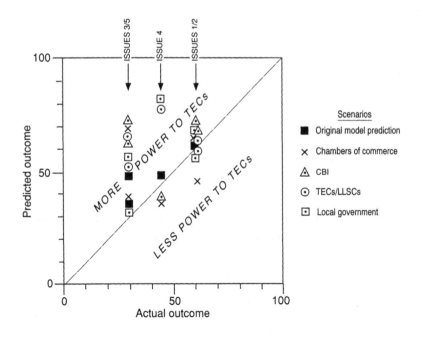

Figure 7.4   Prediction-realisation diagram comparing scenarios for TEC negotiation (exchange model)

For the scenarios with respect to LLSCs, the CBI and the chambers are the most radical in favour of more power to LLSCs, particularly on training policy, economic development policy and flexibility of use of funds. They are less radical on changes in business support policy and on shifts in targets for training programmes. Local government, in contrast, is most radical in wanting a larger budget from training, and least radical on responsibility for changes in business support policy and targets for training programmes. These contrasts are illustrated clearly in Figure 7.5.

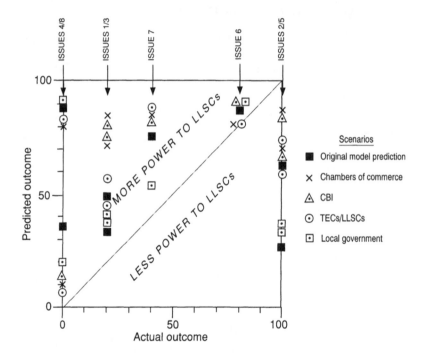

Figure 7.5 Prediction-realisation diagram comparing scenarios LLSC negotiations (exchange model)

As in the discussion of the actual outcomes, the different scenarios can also be compared in terms of how they affect net utility gains or losses. This is shown in Table 7.6. The original prediction of the outcome of the TEC negotiations gives a net utility gain. Under the chamber and CBI scenarios this becomes a loss. The TEC scenario is a welfare neutral approach among the agents, whilst the local government scenario produces a reduced utility loss. As with the simulations of RDAs, therefore, developing a more strongly

Table 7.6   Net utility losses or gains under different scenarios for TEC and LLSC negotiations (exchange model)

	TEC negotiations	LLSC negotiations
Scenario 1: Chambers of commerce	-0.005	+0.090
Scenario 2: CBI	-0.004	+0.074
Scenario 3: TECs/LLSCs	0.000	+0.064
Scenario 4: Local government	-0.001	+0.101
Original prediction	+0.700	-0.370

business-led local body leads to decreases in utility for the average agent because so many are public sector bodies or government departments that stand to lose power. To have increased TEC power further, therefore, would have required a strong cabinet commitment to reduce the influence of related government departments and other public bodies. It is not difficult to see why development of the TEC agenda as originally conceived, as a stronger business-led local body, ran into the sand.

The overall utility losses for the scenarios associated with LLSCs, shown in Table 7.6, demonstrates considerable utility gains if any of the scenarios favoured by the agents given more power in the scenarios had been followed. The local government scenario increases overall utility most, because it combines public sector and local gains. But the chamber of commerce scenario also offers considerable gains, with the CBI and TEC scenarios closely behind. Each of these scenarios involves policies favouring closer integration of training with RDA programmes. It is the potential fracture of policy resulting from keeping LLSCs and RDA distinct that leads to the average utility losses for the establishment of LLSCs. This would have been reversed if either the business or local government points of view had been more strongly followed.

7.8   Conclusion

The TECs were not a Labour initiative and were deeply resented in their early years by many Labour supporters and agents such as local government and the TUC. However, after about 1995, they began to achieve a stronger level of acceptance among most agents, with trade union members on the Boards of all TECs and a strong collaboration between local authorities and most TECs by the time of their abolition. Nevertheless they still offended Labour ideas about accountability which are unsympathetic to business-led boards for arms length bodies. Hence, their reform was inevitable.

The actual reform, to abolish the TECs and replace them with LLSCs, was however something of a surprise which was announced in June 1999 relatively late in Labour's programme, over two years after taking office. The difficulties of replacing TECs in part derived from the need to develop ideas about alternative bodies to take on the contracting role for work-based training. In part it also reflected the tensions between different central departments that were difficult to resolve. And the delay also reflected the extent of rapprochement that TECs had achieved with local and national partners. Indeed in the parliamentary debate following the announcement of their abolition it was many Labour MPs that were most critical,[68] being concerned about the consequences for their constituencies resulting from the abolition of TECs.

Also, despite their hostile birth, TECs had in their later years established a level of consensus among the main agents with which they worked, particularly business bodies. As a result their final structure, as shown in our analysis, is represented well by an exchange model that is based on close interchange of positions between agents.

The LLSCs which replaced TECs have not been developed as a consequence of intensive negotiations, they were merely announced to a shocked and surprised audience at the TEC National Conference in July 1999. Our exchange model poorly predicts their structure. It is particularly poor in predicting their level of responsibility for economic development policy, business support policy and their relation with chambers of commerce. The poor performance of the exchange model for LLSCs reflects the reality: that the form of LLSCs was decided by DfEE in isolation from the other main agents, and its best model as a conflict. Two years of intensive exchanges covering two reviews of TECs, from 1997–99, had failed to find a negotiated solution that satisfied the government's perceived needs. These two years also saw the development of the flagship initiative of the RDAs. TECs had to be adjusted. But the interdepartmental rivalry in the new government made the form of adjustment uncertain until RDAs were established and inter-ministerial fault lines were clearer. The outcome of the subregional structure of LLSCs under the DfEE separated from RDAs reflects a clear victory for the DfEE over the DETR; or a victory for David Blunkett, with support from the Chancellor and Prime Minister, over John Prescott.

The analysis we have developed demonstrates the clear role of the state as a leader of change on these initiatives and gives little support to explanations

---

68   See *Hansard*, 1 July 1999.

based on the resource-dependence, social or institutional theories outlined in chapter 3. The analysis also shows how a strong state leadership can produce outcomes out of line with the views of key agents on how policy should have developed. The form of LLSCs is far from the structure of close integration with RDAs favoured by business interests, local government and most other agents. Ironically, the fracture between LLSCs, SBS and the RDAs also appears to be in conflict with Labour's proclaimed desire to be developing 'joined-up' government. The gap of rhetoric and reality is analysed in detail in chapters 9 and 10.

The nature of the power-relations structure evidences a strong shift away from high utility gains for business interests compared to TECs, even though TECs had in no respect satisfied the desires of business, particularly for budget flexibility, or breadth of responsibility. Instead, for LLSCs, the main utility gains are for central departments, with also strong alarms about the quality of work-based training and vocational skills as a result.

This finding is somewhat at odds with our assessment of Labour's approach for RDAs. There we found that the RDA structure on the whole sought to support the business point of view, though like TECs not to the extent the CBI, BCC or other business interests desired. The contradiction between the two initiatives can be interpreted in two ways. First, that in political decisions it is rarely possible to develop a completely rational approach across all agendas even when they are clearly interlinked as LLSCs and RDAs are.[69] Alternatively, although not stated explicitly nor perhaps an explicit aim of policy, the contradiction is resolved by recognising that economic development policy has moved departmentally, from DfEE to DETR; and similarly that business support policy has moved from DfEE to DTI. This interpretation would suggest that the end of TECs also reflects the final end of the process of dismantling of the ambitious skills-led economic development agenda that had been built up by the MSC in the 1970s and 1980s. Whereas the TECs were the Conservative's answer to the MSC empire (to decentralise it), Labour has sought to establish more traditional vertical departmental lines of responsibility (in effect to break up the old MSC concept altogether). This interpretation generates some interesting insights into what joined-up government really means under Labour. It appears to rely on a joined-up approach through national interdepartmental liaison and regional bodies rather than locally. We develop this interpretation further in chapter 9.

---

69 See e.g. Grant, 1993.

8 The Small Business Service and Business Link Initiative

8.1 Introduction

The Small Business Service (SBS) and Business Link (BL) initiatives seek to offer support to SMEs through local partnerships. Launched in 1992 by the Conservative Government, Business Link had a high level of cross-party support, with both Labour and Liberal Democrats claiming to have invented the idea. In government, therefore, Labour at first did not seek to change BL radically. However, for a variety of reasons, chiefly related to the abolition of TECs (see chapter 7), BLs were restructured in the period running up to April 2001 following the development of the SBS.

The creation of a Small Business Service was announced from the Treasury by Gordon Brown in March 1999 Budget, with detailed specification subsequently developed under Stephen Byers, Secretary of State for the DTI. Detailed proposals, and a formal consultation process on the form of the SBS, were launched in June 1999 (DTI, 1999a, 2000). The SBS reconstitutes BL as a network of outlets which are contracted to the SBS since April 2000. The objectives of the SBS BL system are to provide information, advice, help with government grants, and a referral service to other public and private sector suppliers. The principles which the SBS is seeking to satisfy cover two areas: regulation, and the structure of business support, but they overlap (DTI, 1999a, pp. 18–20, 29).

1 Regulation

- The SBS should perform as a strong and independent voice to advise on the interests of small businesses to ministers.
- The SBS should work with commercial providers of advice and support, not in competition with them.
- SBS should make use of best possible electronic delivery methods, as well as offering other choices.

- SBS leaves regulators responsible for information about their regulations
- Principal approach will be to signpost to specialist sources of advice both from regulators and from commercial sectors.

2   Business Support

- Improve coherence and quality across the range of government support for small business.
- Putting the needs of small business first, before the needs of the provider.
- Capitalise on opportunities of new technology and e-commerce, particularly for businesses in remote rural areas.
- Contribute to government's wider economic and social objectives
- Take account of support available elsewhere.
- Provide a single gateway for all government services directed primarily or mainly to small businesses.

We chiefly focus on the business support function of the SBS which is referred to as SBS BL. We analyse how the negotiations evolved in the development of BL from 1992 until its main establishment in 1995. We then assess how the negotiations continued to evolve between 1995 and 1999 until the establishment of the SBS BL system. We compare predictions of the form of evolution of BL with its actual development, and we also compare the SBS BL with alternative scenarios.

8.2   The Business Link Initiative

The Business Link (BL) initiative was originally announced by Michael Heseltine, then President of the Board of Trade, in July 1992. The aim was to establish local partnership bodies in England, funded by DTI, to provide a range of support services to small and medium sized enterprises (SMEs). A prospectus was published in December 1992 opening a bidding process for the first what was originally termed 'One Stop Shops'. The term Business Links was coined as a marketing brand in England from mid-1993. After early 1994 bidding in England was replaced by a national assessment process whereby all areas were expected to develop BLs subject to a set of criteria judged by an Assessment Panel. In Scotland Business Shops, and in Wales Business Connect, followed a different approach which is not included here. A summary of the history of Business Link in England from its inception

Table 8.1   Business Links Timetable of Development 1992–95

July 1992	First announcement of 'One Stop Shops' by Mr Heseltine.
November 1992	Announcement by Mr Heseltine inviting bids.
December 1992	Prospectus published on how to make bids.
29 January 1993	Closing date for bids.
early March 1993	Presentation of proposals to DTI by bidders.
1 April 1993	Start-up phase to begin pilots. Of 58 bids, 20 were shortlisted, and 15 were accepted, plus a special London 'Development Bid'.
May 1993	Implementation Strategy Group (ISG) set up. Various subgroups also established to advice on IT, branding, finance etc.
July 1993	BL brand selected.
February 1994	National launch planned for February is postponed and to be replaced by a 'low key' approach.
end of April 1994	26 local BLs established.
June 1994	Announcement that 'from April 1996 all DTI funded business support services for SMEs would normally be delivered through BLs'.
September 1994	The predecessor DTI programme of the Enterprise Initiative is finally closed.
March 1995	DTI internal audit warns that BLs are financially 'at risk'.
April 1995	First draft of *Operational Manual* of BLs printed.
4 May 1995	100 BLs now open (in pilot stage at least).
*24 May 1995	Meeting of partners with Heseltine on 'prescription'.
28 May 1995	Announcement that Commons Trade and Industry Committees is to start enquiry into BLs.
May–June 1995	Baseline study of awareness of support network undertaken (MORI).
June 1995	Restructuring of Manchester BL to save money and develop joint branding .
July 1995	Change of Small Firms Minister from Baroness Denton to Richard Page. Publications of BCC Report *Engaging the Business Community.*
August 1995	Business Link Network Company (BLNC) goes operational.
October 1995	Final draft *Operational Manual* agreed (with reduced level of prescription).
31 October 1995	Launch of network and final *Service Guide* launched.
November 1995	and following: Review of branding continues, with flexibility introduced via 'Dual' and 'Corporate' branding.

until the end of 1995 is given in Table 8.1. The continued evolution is summarized later in this chapter in Table 8.4

It is important to understand that a process of development occurred over a significant period, from announcement until the establishment of the first local BLs. In the early phase the initiative was limited in finance from existing DTI budgets and was dependent on competitive bids. After 1994 the initiative was explicitly national (to the *whole* of England). Moreover during this period a process of continuing debate and elaboration occurred that involved negotiation between the main partners and the funding Department, the DTI. The development of BLs thus has attributes of a negotiated policy process, led by government, which can be simulated by the decision making models we use below. However, an important change in policy development occurred in May 1995 when a meeting of the main partners took place with Mr Heseltine. This led to a significant reduction in the level of 'prescription' by the DTI. We discuss and model the process of BL development up to May 1995 in the first empirical section of this chapter. Then, in later sections we extend the discussion and modelling from the period since May 1995.

The chief objectives sought for BL as specified in the DTI (1992) *Prospectus* were:

- to bring integration and *coherence* between the main suppliers of enterprise services, particularly TECs, Chambers of Commerce and enterprise agencies, as well as local government;
- to achieve this by *partnerships* with these agents;
- to improve the overall *professionalism* and *quality* standards to the best in Europe;
- to have a *physical presence* – an office/shop with maximum co-location of partners;
- to develop a network to cover whole country;
- to combine DTI resources with local inputs from partners;
- but to move to 'self-sufficiency' as rapidly as possible; in part based on charging fees for services;
- to be bound by a contract to government through TECs, in partnership with other agents, thus aligning partners and TECs within a single framework set by DTI.

This approach required, therefore, not only government-funded bodies such as TECs, but also independent entities such as Chambers of Commerce, enterprise agencies and local government to collaborate with each other. A key agenda, which was only partly hidden in Heseltine's approach, was to develop closer working relations between Chambers and TECs, probably in part to fulfil a concept he had developed whilst 'in the wilderness' after he resigned from Mrs Thatcher's government in 1986. This concept sought to introduce to Britain a chamber system of equivalent quality to that in Europe, although with a different financial background (Heseltine, 1989).

Also important in influencing the DTI position was a review set up by Heseltine on his return to the DTI in early 1992. This sought to reassess the whole range of DTI supports to business. The steering group for this review included Heseltine, the Small Firms Minister, the Chambers, TECs, CBI, local authorities, National Training Task Force, and Business in the Community. This Review criticised confusion between providers, lack of strong involvement of private sector providers in DTI services, a lack of customer focus and a low level of awareness by SMEs of most of the services that were available.[1] The review in part let to the BL initiative which can in many ways be seen as already involving commitment from the key partners who would have to implement it.

Mr Heseltine appears to have been led to see the key objectives of BL as twofold. First and foremost, there was the aim of bringing greater coherence to the provision of local support services. In all areas is was recognised that there was a wide variety of local suppliers, many supported by different central government department funding streams or initiatives. As we have discussed in chapter 2, the problem of coherence had been recognised in the field of economic development by the Audit Commission (1989) who termed local action by central government 'a patchwork quilt' of unrelated initiatives. The problem had been exacerbated with the establishment of the 82 local TECs which from 1990 had been encouraged by their central department masters (the DE, later to become the DfEE) to be independent leaders of the local enterprise supports. This had led to competition with Chambers. Local government had also developed a range of their own enterprise support services which varied considerably between areas, but was most actively developed in metropolitan districts and local boroughs, often associated with areas of high unemployment or industrial restructuring and most frequently led by Labour party controlled councils. About 90 per cent of local authorities were actively promoting SMEs advice support in one form or another by 1998.[2] In addition, enterprise agencies, which were sponsored by central government grants up to 1992, as well as TECs, local government and large firms, provided a network

---

1   Titchener, 1996, quoted in Priest, 1999.
2   Bennett and McCoshan, 1993, p. 132; Bennett and LGA, 1998.

of small advisory and counselling services to SMEs with a high emphasis on start-ups. There were over 400 enterprise agencies in Britain in 1992.[3] A further pattern of other specialist bodies existed promoting SMEs supports in different areas: UDCs in some major cities, the RDC in rural areas, New Town Development Corporations, and specialist regional bodies such as Yorkshire Enterprise and Lancashire Enterprise.

Heseltine saw the opportunity to use DTI money as a kind of 'glue' to try to draw these disparate bodies together to provide a coherent system of services. Hence, his emphasis on partnership as a means of developing, financing and managing BL. 'Firms are still faced with a welter of advice and information of variable quality from a confusing maze of local agencies whose services often appear to be in competition with each other'.[4] He also clearly recognised that one of the key problems was to sort out the role of the TEC in the enterprise field where TECs had been shown to have often 'floundered' and duplicated the services of other agents, or provided services with little or no take-up.[5] Heseltine had no doubt that the TECs should be seen as 'the "enabler" (rather than the provider), coordinating the network to achieve the greatest added value and to create coherent services.'[6] He further saw the problem as not lack of money:

> There is already a minimum of £40m each year being spent by TECs on business advice, information and counselling alone. This represents roughly £0.5m per TEC, plenty I would have thought to lever a major uplift in the quality of current support activity.[7]

One of the most crucial of Mr Heseltine's leads was, therefore, to press TECs not to fill gaps in present local support systems by their own provision, but to build a self-sustaining base in the local community:

> I should make it clear that if a Chamber, TEC or enterprise agency is weak in any particular area, this should not be an argument for turning our backs on it or to develop duplicate products or services from an alternative source. Rather it is a strong argument for taking decisive action to build the capacity of that particular organisation and with it the capacity of the network as a whole. [8]

---

3   Bennett, 1995.
4   In Hansard, 3 December 1992, col. 414.
5   Bennett et al., 1994, chapter 9.
6   Heseltine, 1992a, p. 9.
7   Heseltine, 1992b, p. 9.
8   Heseltine, 1992b, p. 10.

The second key objective sought was to increase the professionalism, customer focus and quality of service advice, to what became referred to as 'world class standards' in the One Stop Shop *Prospectus* and in later DTI Competitiveness White Papers of 1994 onwards. This objective has proved elusive so that in later developments, particularly under the Labour government, the emphasis on quality has had to be reasserted (e.g. by Barbara Roche, in her new vision of 1997).

The key means to improve the focus on quality has been developed through a new service that BL offers, of Personal Business Advisors (PBAs). Although previously developed in some limited local initiatives, the PBA was a concept that was new to the local scene, but developed in part from the experience of the former DTI Enterprise Initiative. The PBA was to become a sort of 'account manager' for client businesses. The analogy used in verbal presentations in the launch phase was of a local doctor who would meet the client, assess needs, give first-hand supports in many cases, but would refer on to specialists when required. 'It will be essential that customers can access from each centre a full range of local and remote services ... For services delivered by local partners, it will be important to maximize the extent to which these are co-located in a single set of premises.'[9] The full range of services envisaged is shown in Table 8.2.

Importantly, however, the PBA would also track the client to assess whether the service had been received and was beneficial, and would actively market other services that might benefit the business. The PBA was to maintain an active portfolio of businesses. Active marketing was particularly relevant to the use of other DTI – financial services which were decentralised to BL from the DTI or the Design Council: (i) Design Counsellors; (ii) Innovation and Technology Counsellors; and (iii) Export Development Counsellors. These three areas had a special network of their counsellors which were based in a few of the larger BL outlets. In addition, because the contracting was via TECs, TEC products such as IiP, NVQ accredited training, and contributions to work-based training also became key parts of active marketing.

A third aspect was the number of outlets and their geographical structure. This was not so much an explicit objective as the outcome of the decision to have a physical presence (a 'shop') in every major business centre. Heseltine wanted 'as close a point of contact as possible – hence the largest possible number of outlets'.[10] However, since the DTI finance was the chief 'glue'

---

9   DTI, 1992, p. 8.
10 Letter from Michael Heseltine, 30 September, 1999.

Table 8.2   Services to be provided in BLs, focused on business advisors as well as information and advice, and through BLs by referrals, networking and co-location with other partners

Information and Advice:
Provide high quality information and advice on:

Grants and support schemes	Business start-up
Exporting	Technology and innovation
Finance	Training
Late payment	Marketing
VAT, tax and non-domestic rates	Design
Licensing requirements	Product sourcing
Legislation (Health & Safety, Planning etc.)	Environmental issues (including BS7750)
Standards (including BS5750/BS7850	*Application of IT
and TQM)	*Property
BSI services	*Patents, trademarks and copyright
Single Market information (including new	*Education/Business Partnerships
legislation)	

Account Management:
Personal Business Advisers who maintain regular contact with a portfolio of companies and construct an integrated package of services to meet their needs

Counselling/Consultancy:
Provide *access* to:

Diagnostic /health check services	Investors in People
Start-up counselling	Other subsidised TEC consultancy schemes
General business counselling	Commercial consultancy
	Enterprise initiative consultancy

Business Skills and Awareness:
Provide *access* to:

Business skills seminars	Business start-up schemes
(including business planning,	Other relevant TEC activities
quality, marketing, purchasing, etc.)	*Management Charter initiative
'Managing in the 1990s'	

Other Services/Activities

*DTI clinics	*Small firms clubs
*Design Council services	*Professional clinics
*Customer/supplier events	

Facilities:

Information Centre	*Training resources
Counselling rooms	*Meeting/training rooms
Hot lines to external expertise	*Companies House
Data bases	(on-line ordering)

*   Indicates that a service is desirable, but not essential.

Source: derived from DTI, 1992, *Prospectus*, Annex 2.

holding the whole initiative together, the greater the number of outlets, the smaller would be the staff size and resources of each BL site. Various options were available to the DTI as local outlets. The Chambers were developing their own network of about 50–60 Approved Chambers, but in 1992–94 this was still not fully established and hence could not provide an automatic national coverage. Also DTI officials wanted to keep control of quality and branding and so were hesitant about using an independent legal entity such as Chambers. Local enterprise agencies provided a larger network of about 300 small bodies, but their finance had become almost entirely based on TECs[11] and so they provided less of a management network than a possible delivery system. Also the enterprise agencies were seen as highly variable in quality, of questionable viability in many cases, and too focused on start-ups. The enterprise agencies did, however, bring the benefit (and complication) of being partly sponsored by both large firms and local government. For these reasons Chambers, enterprise agencies and local government appeared to be key partners, but none provided a ready-made network on which BLs could be based.

The final structure was based on TEC areas to whom the local BLs were contracted. The TECs themselves were contracted to government, but through a different and rival department, the DfEE, and based on a local structure of 75 areas in England. The use of TECs in part reflected the reality that part of the funding stream to be used for BL was derived from TECs. It represented the interdepartmental shift of responsibility for the main governmental support for SMEs to DTI from DfEE. This occurred in 1993 as a result of the influence of Heseltine. It should be noted that this funding stream, which had supported the Small Firms Service as well as support to the unemployed to start up businesses, had previously moved to DfEE from DTI in 1985 under the influence of an earlier Secretary of State for Industry, Lord Young. This background, and Heseltine's more general concern with the quality of TEC activities in the field of enterprise, led the objective of DTI wishing to exert a stronger influence on TECs which they could only do through controlling some of the financial streams themselves. The outcome of considerable interdepartmental infighting was that the DTI won back most of the SME support budget. As a result the TECs came to have two separate contract mechanisms, one to DfEE for most of their budget, and a second to DTI for the business support elements for BL finance. This approach was criticised for leading to confusion and remoteness from direct management targeting and controls,[12] with a resulting recommendation by the House of Commons

---

11 see Bennett, 1995.
12 see e.g. Bennett, 1995; HoC, 1996a.

Trade and Industry Committee that contracting should be directly between the BL partnership and DTI, removing the TEC.[13] However, the TECs remained the contracting body throughout the BL initiative until the establishment of the SBS in 2000.

The local geographical structure for BL was left to local partners in each TEC area to decide. Given that the TEC was the contract holder it is no surprise that the result was largely based on TECs (although five TEC areas originally had more than one separate BL). However within these TEC areas, which came to be called 'hubs', an often large network of smaller 'satellite' offices is frequently present. These are based on the presence of a local enterprise agency, local government office and sometimes small (and hence non-Approved) local Chambers. The overall pattern was a network of over 80 hubs and over 200 satellites offices in total. In addition, in London, a London-wide BL has been established as an overall coordinating and service delivery body for the nine London TECs (as they were in 1994, reduced to 7 by 1997) each of which has its own hubs, and its own satellites in the 33 London Boroughs.

In the assessment which follows the discussion focuses on the negotiations at national level. This emphasis is used despite the known strong geographical variation in different BL structures between partners in different places. Our argument is that the key negotiations in the design of BL were between the national partner bodies, who were aware of the local patterns which acted as general constraints on their negotiations. There was of course a separate set of negotiations in each area between the partners, but this was set within the context agreed between the national partners. It was the national negotiations that set the agenda for the BL developments. National bodies were the focus of the launch, the coordination of initial bids, and the drafting of the *Operating Manual* and *Service Guide*. National bodies were also the agents who, in the meeting with Heseltine in May 1995, proved to be the key power in changing the shape of the initiative towards less prescription. Hence, whilst there is local variation in partnership structures, the actual partners involved, and the hub-satellite structure, the key decisions setting the general framework of finance, targets, services and viability were all made nationally.

The key mechanism for decision making was through negotiations in and between the meetings of the Implementation Strategy Group (ISG) of which David Grayson (a director of BiTC) was Chair. Where issues were of fundamental significance these were brought by partners directly to Mr

---

13 HoC, 1996a.

Heseltine. The ISG, and discussions with the President of the Board of Trade, are thus the key forum within which exchange took place. Hence our analysis chiefly seeks to simulate that process of decision making. In addition, parliamentary debates and formal parliamentary questions did influence aspects of thinking on BL at the implementation stage, whilst the Commons Trade and Industry Select Committee held an inquiry into BL which reported in 1996. The inquiry in particular had some influence on the degree of prescription and complexity of contracting which we build into our discussion as an influence primarily on ministers and DTI.

8.3   The Business Link Negotiations: Stakeholder's Perspectives 1992–95

Six Business Link issues were the focus of negotiations in the early years of BL. These were selected and checked with experts in interviews. The issues selected were, and continue to be, the chief policy issues generating debate and controversy surrounding the Business Link initiative as well as the SBS.

In Table 8.3, we list these six Business Link issues. Issues such as who would pay for the Business Link services, what kind of firms would be targeted or how the partnership could be best structured, reflect the key policy problems that the stakeholders involved were confronted with. These issues capture, in a tangible way, the fundamental differences existing between the various stakeholders involved in the Business Link negotiations. In this section we discuss each of these issues in terms of the policy preferences of the agents involved in the negotiations, their importance to the different agents and their capacity to influence the negotiations. We present in the Appendix the full list of the information used on the policy preferences, salience and capabilities of agents with respect to each policy issue. The Appendix tables also list the key agents.

In total there are 16 agents which can be grouped according to their 'formal' role in the Business Link initiative. The first two agents are the national level central government departments involved, the Department of Trade and Industry (DTI) and the Department of Education and Employment (DfEE). The next group of agents comprise the national level bodies representing the main formal and 'informal' partners, in the development of local level Business Links. In this group are included the TEC National Council, the local authorities, the Chambers of Commerce and the enterprise agencies. Other agents in this group include the Confederation of British Industry (CBI),

Table 8.3 Business Link policy issue

1 Level of self-financing possible for provision of Personal Business Advisors (PBAs).
2 Level of self financing possible for provision the full range of Business Link services (excluding PBAs).
3 Maximum range of BL services.
4 Target firms for Business Link services.
5 Appropriate local partnership structure for Business Links.
6 Appropriate use of Business Link brand name.
7 Number of local Business Link outlets across England.

Note: only issues 1 to 6 affect 1992–95; issue 7 became important in 1995–99 having been de facto imposed in 1992.

the main private business sponsors (such as the 'high street' banks), David Grayson as chair of the Implementation Strategy Group and Director of Business in the Community (BiTC). A special set of agents, developing in some locations such as Wigan, Milton Keynes or St. Helens, are pro-merger groups that sought to integrate BL with the local TEC, Chamber and local authority business support activity. Of a more peripheral nature in terms of their formal involvement in the national level negotiations, is a further group of agents, which include the trade associations (such as the British Printing Industry Federation), and small business representative groups such as the Institute of Directors (IoD), Federation of Small Businesses (FSB) and Forum of Private Business (FPB). We have also included in our analysis the newly appointed Business Link managers and the Institute of Business Advisors (representing PBA interests), since once individual local BLs began to be established in 1993, their executives and staff began to seek to exert influence on the design of the system.

Self-finance (Issues 1 and 2)

The first two BL policy issues both cover fees and self-finance and are discussed together here because they were closely inter-related in the negotiations. The first issue concerns the extent to which the services of Personal Business Advisers (PBAs) can be self-financing, whilst the second issue concerns the level of self-finance possible for the rest of the Business Link services.

The policy preferences of the different agents for the first issue have at one extreme are agents which sought all PBA costs to be self-financed, either through charging client fees or through the partners' own finances. The main supporters of this position were the trade associations, the Institute of Directors as well as the private business sponsors, such as the Banks. The trade associations argued that if the public funding was used to finance PBA services, this would constitute a form of unfair competition for the providers of these services in the private sector which included the associations themselves and their members. These fears continued after the first phase of national level Business Link negotiations reached their conclusion in 1995. In a statement to the House of Commons Trade and Industry Committee, for example, one association, the BPIF expressed concern 'at the extent of Government funding for Business Links, which allows them to offer free or subsidised consultancy in direct competition to those organisations which have traditionally provided it, thus cutting our earnings in this area by half. Additionally BPIF is being asked to provide free advice to Business Links on issues specific to the sector, which may be passed on to non-members as well as members of the Federation'[14] (HoC, 1996 p. 99).

Other agents close to this policy position included the small business bodies such as the Federation of Small Businesses (FSB) and the Forum for Private Business (FPB). These organizations provide some business services as well as representing many businesses which themselves provide various types of business advice and consultancy to small businesses. They argued that the commercial viability of the FSB or FPB, and their members, could be threatened by the operation of a Business Link service that was financed in part or wholly on a non-commercial basis. In particular, the Forum for Private Business argued that the provision of public funding distorts the efficient operation of the Business Link partnership, setting up false incentives for local providers to become partners at the local level. More recently they have continued to argue this point:

> One of the concepts of Business Link is that they would bring together all of the supply agencies within an area so that they could offer 'the concept of a One Stop Shop'. This means bringing together the chambers of commerce, enterprise agencies, TECs and in some cases local authority provision. It is well known that these are different types of organization and the only 'glue' holding them together is Government money. It is common knowledge that Business Links need to be self-financing in three years. If that is the case, what then will be the 'glue' that holds Business Links together? [15]

---

14 HoC, 1996a, p. 99.
15 FPB, 1998, p. 9.

Private sector sponsors were drawn into the BL discussion as a result of their role in local enterprise agencies, as well as their support for many of the other local partners, particularly Chambers and TECs. They sought particularly that BLs should have a commercial focus and manner of work. To achieve this their policy position was initially to seek 100 per cent self-financing. However, by the time of the Trade and Industry Committee hearings,[16] the various banks, including Barclays, Midland and NatWest presented their views more carefully. Barclays, for example, stated that 'We believe that the capacity and willingness for small enterprises, particularly start-ups and micro-businesses, to pay for these services is limited, however, and that it is not viable to assume that Business Links should be entirely self-financing. A continuing element of government support will, therefore, be required'.[17] This position is supported by the other main banks and suggests that they had moved closer to the policy position of the DTI. However, re-interviewing of sponsors by 1998 confirmed their commitment in 1992–95 to a fully self-financing ethic, though they had not then appraised whether it could ever be realistically achieved.

The DTI was also initially enthusiastic about self-financing. At the time of the launch of the Business Link initiative in 1992, Michael Heseltine demanded a full self-financing objective in the long-term, arguing that DTI support should be seen as essentially pump-priming. He claimed that gaps in local support services were not the results of 'the lack of money' but its proper application. Hence the *Prospectus*[18] sought that the BLs 'should move to self-sufficiency as rapidly as possible'. The DTI position was also supported by David Grayson, who became Chair of the DTI's ISG and also of the Assessor's Panel for BL. He was a very public advocate for self-financing. In 1995 although accepting that 'Business Links are not expected to survive on their own without public funding', he argued that businesses should 'increasingly expect to pay for it'.[19] However, by 1996 he had adopted a more cautious note that government should be 'funding services where there is market failure' and 'should be charging for some of their services' rather than all of them, with 'the percentage of the total budget that is generated from client fees' used as 'benchmark'.[20] It appears that the DTI early position was strongly influenced by the views of business sponsors to emphasise commerciality

---

16 HoC, 1996a, pp. 76–9.
17 HoC, 1996a, p. 96.
18 DTI, 1992.
19 Grayson, 1995.
20 Grayson, 1996.

and a self-financing ethic, that this fed through such occasions as lunch meetings between sponsors and Michael Heseltine, and that David Grayson adopted this view either at the behest of Heseltine, or because of his direct experience and lines of communication with the key sponsors through Business in the Community. Certainly in the 1992–93 launch period self-finance had to be built into the financial and business plans of the first BL bids, which had to demonstrate their progress in achieving this target at the end of the three-year pump-priming period. Indeed the lack of realistic capacity to raise fees was a criticism focused on by a DTI internal auditors report in March 1995. However, by the time of the full launch of the network in mid-1995 the DTI had settled for the 25 per cent target for self-financing. This continued to be the DTI position up to the launch of the SBS.

At the other end of the policy spectrum, agents such as the Business Link managers and the Institute of Business Advisors, which represents in part the interests of the PBAs, wanted either the Government or the TECs to pay the full the costs of the services provided by the PBA. There were several other agents whose policy preferences were close to this position. In particular, the enterprise agencies, the TEC National Council and the local authorities took the view that a high proportion of the costs of the PBA services would have to be, or should be, funded by public funds with it being generally unlikely that more than 10 per cent could be achieved through client fees. The enterprise agencies argued that, in order to provide the highest level of services, to attract the right type of candidates to become PBAs, but most of all to avoid distortions to decisions and in appropriate incentives to the PBAs, the PBA should be employed on a full salary basis, rather than on a commission basis. They feared that employing PBAs on a commission or part-time basis would encourage them to maintain their own commercial consultancy and advice business, which could distort their role in Business Link. The local authorities and TECs viewed their own resources as already stretched and did not see that they could meet the full extra costs proposed under the Business Link initiative for provision of PBAs. Hence they believed they should be heavily funded by DTI. They also had the experience of seeking client fees which suggested very limited possibilities. Other agents whose policy preferences were close to this position included the DfEE. It should also be remembered that the budget for small firms support had only recently been returned from DfEE to the DTI, and the DfEE resented this loss of power.

There were relatively few agents who held positions nearer to the middle ground in terms of policy options on the financial issues. The most prominent agent towards the middle was the Chambers of Commerce, whose policy preference was for the government and the TECs to pay about 70 per cent of the costs of the PBA services and for client fees to support the rest. This was based on their experience of running similar services in some Chambers and their existing practice of fee-based services for other activities.

The policy outcome by late 1995 was an acceptance by DTI that full self-financing was not possible and targets were set for 25 per cent of income to come from fees. The range of fee income between local BLs in 1996–97 was from 1 per cent to 9 per cent with a mean of 24 per cent.[21] The 25 per cent target was not expected to be achieved until 1999/2000 by all BLs, but this was always optimistic and in the development of the SBS the requirement has been reduced.

The second BL policy issue concerns the total self-financing package for Business Links services. A distinction is drawn by several agents between PBA services, which were new to the local support system, and the range of other services provided by BL. These services relate to other DTI-supported services, such as Design Counsellors, Export Development Counsellors and Innovation Technology Counsellors, as well as to other partner services delivered through BL. This range of services is generally referred to as the 'branded' services, for which branded fee income is the relevant criterion. DTI do not distinguish PBA and other branded fee income sources in their statistics, but the distinction is clear in many agent's minds. However, the policy positions of the agents is similar to those for the finance of PBAs. For example, those agents who oppose substantial public funding for the PBA services, on the grounds that it is distorting the market price for provision of these services, take the same view with respect to the public funding of other Business Link services. However, some contrasts in views arise for the local authorities and enterprise agencies, who believed that Business Links services, excluding PBA services, could be more self-financing than PBAs. On the other hand, the Business Links managers and the local partners, such as the TECs, continued to believe that close to 100 per cent public support would be required. The actual outcomes on this issue is a target that branded fee income should be 25 per cent by 1999/2000, as with PBA fee income. However, the DTI claim that they take a flexible view of this and in practice the fee expected to be raised by any one Business Link outlet will depend on the local conditions.

The salience, or importance, attached to the financial issues for the different agents, varies considerably. A small group of agents register medium to high levels of salience for the majority, if not all, of the Business Links issues

---

21 ISG Survey, 1997; DTI monitoring statistics.

examined. These include the DTI, BCC, TEC National Council and the enterprise agencies. On the other hand, agents for whom the Business Link issues are of relatively minor importance include the CBI the local authorities and the IoD. The two issues relating to income targets for most agents were the two most important issues in the negotiations. This is not surprising since BLs threatened the activities of some of these bodies (Chambers and enterprise agencies in particular) or certainly required their close cooperation as partners. Therefore the financial arrangements were in most cases 'the bottom line' for partner involvement. Finance was not one of the most central issues for DTI and this probably explains why it was able to accommodate a shift from its first position on 100 per cent self-financing very early in the negotiations. In any case, in relative terms for the DTI, the amount of money it allocates to Business Link is quite small, even if it has to fund the majority of the PBA and other Business Link services. Whereas the other issues sought as targets from BL development were the major target for Mr Heseltine and DTI officials.

Scope of Services Offered by Personal Business Advisors

The third BL policy issue concerns the maximum range of services which the Personal Business Advisors (PBA) should offer. The position at one extreme of the policy spectrum is that the PBA should directly assist the client through an 'in-house' solution to the majority of the client's problems. There were few agents close to this position but this view appears to be that promulgated by the IBA and is to some extent supported by David Grayson. At the other extreme, supported by the trade associations (such as the BPIF), the IoD, FPB, and FSB, is the view that PBAs should be limited to an essentially signposting function, referring the client on for more specialized advice. Both the FSB and the FPB argue that the main problem with the PBA service is the very low quality of the PBAs themselves. The FPB claim that 'it is generally reported that the "Head Hunters" are selecting individuals with known management performances in big businesses but without any proven ability in a small business environment'.[22] Given this scenario, they argue that it is best to limit the range of Business Link and PBA services available. The trade association view, expressed by the BPIF, is that 'the DTI sees Business Links and trade associations as complementary and working with each other, but the reality is that one, with government financial support, is usurping the role of the other'.[23]

22 FPB, 1997.
23 BPIF, 1997.

The DTI and Business Link managers have sought that the PBAs should supply consultancy on general management, financial and production matters, but aspects of detail relevant to a sector could be handled by the relevant trade association, perhaps subcontracted by the BL. The offering of 'such "crumbs" is unacceptable to trade associations …'.[24] Just as in the case of self-finance, the agents are concerned to protect the interests of their members, many of whom are in competition with the services provided by BL. However, unlike the self-finance issues, the vast majority of agents hold a midway position about the scope of the PBA. In particular, all of the key partners (the DTI, the Chambers of Commerce, TECs, local authorities, enterprise agencies), as well as the sponsors, hold very similar mid-preference positions. These agents believe that the role of the PBA is to offer a reasonably long diagnostic service, which may include a site visit, with referral where necessary. This underpins the role of the PBA as an 'account manager'. The final policy outcome with respect to this issue partly reflects the policy preferences of these main players, as well as the leverage of the DTI to have a wide range of service where the role of the PBA offers a reasonably extensive in-house diagnostic service and follow-up with active marketing.

In terms of the salience on this issue, the different partners vary considerably. For the DTI, the scope of the PBA role is a very significant issue, reflected in their high level of salience. They see the PBA as a key aspect of the unique value added by BL to previously available services. Amongst the other partners, it is of least importance to the local authorities and the CBI. The other partners attached reasonably high salience but indicated that this issue is not the most significant one on their agendas, compared particularly to the questions of finance.

The Main Target Clients for Business Links

The original DTI objective called for BL to be targeted specifically on larger growth firms of 10–200 employees. The issue of appropriate target firms for BL has at one extreme some agents that hold the view that all growth firms, irrespective of size, should be targeted with the BL services, with all other firms that are not classified as specifically growth-orientated signposted to other service providers. At the other extreme other agents were anxious to see a much broader range of firms being able to access the full range of BL services, including firms in the start-up phase or micro firms with less than ten

---

24 BPIF, in HoC, 1996a, p. 99.

employees. In between these two policy positions there is a range of agent preferences calling for more or less help to be given to micro firms and to firms in their start-up phase. The outcome of the negotiations by May 1995 was that all firms, which have between 10 and 200 employees, should be targeted with the full range of Business Link services. However, it was also conceded that the lower cut-off point of 10 employees was somewhat unrealistic. The enterprise agencies, in particular, were keen to point out that many areas had a very high proportion of small firms with less than 10 employees which would benefit from BL services. Although still small these firms had moved beyond the start-up phase and were growth companies.

The outcome of the negotiations conceded that a more flexible approach had to be adopted on the question of firm size, as long as the firm was not in its start-up phase. Moreover all firms and not just those that were growth oriented could be *proactively* targeted with the full range of BLs services. Looking at the data on the policy positions of agents for this issue (see Appendix), it is clear that the Chambers of Commerce, DTI, CBI, and the BiTC opposed extension to start-ups. This was in part a reaction against the previous policy emphasis of TECs and enterprise agencies on start-ups, chiefly as a result of the influence of the Enterprise Allowance Scheme (EAS). The DTI argued that:

> in terms of helping to lay foundations for future growth it is particularly important to extend help to those firms which are passing through the transition from the 'owner-manager' to the 'team-managed' stage of development. As a rough guide or proxy for firms passing through this transition, the Business Links *Prospectus* suggested a need to concentrate new services (e.g. PBAs) on businesses with between 10 and 200 employees.[25]

The Bank of England (1994) Small Firms Report also supported this view which had some influence on larger firm sponsors. Local authority representatives also supported this position. However, their position as represented on the ISG at that time was probably rather skewed from that of the local authority sector as a whole, which tends to favour an active focus on start-ups.

At the other extreme on this issue, the enterprise agencies and IBA were the main supporters of the view that the target firms should include much smaller firms, including start-ups and micro firms. This also found support among the Labour Party whilst in opposition[26] and has been included in the

---

25 HoC, 1996a, p. xxxvii.
26 E.g. Roche, 1996, in HoC, 1996.

wider targets of the SBS. However, the majority of agents involved in the negotiations favoured a midpoint position, indicating a preference for a more flexible approach: to allow access to services for micros, whilst retaining a focus on larger SMEs (10–200 employees) and especially growth firms. The outcome of the negotiations indicates the effective power of core partners rather than the enterprise agency or IBA view.

Looking at the salience for this issue, the most salient agents include the DTI, the enterprise agencies, and the private sponsors, FSB and FPB, reflecting their members' concerns. Agents such as the CBI, on the other-hand, register much lower levels of salience because few of their members are directly affected.

The Appropriate Partnership Structure at the Local Level

The fifth BL policy issue concerns the appropriate way in which the Business Link partnerships were organised at the local level. At one extreme agents such as BL Managers, the enterprise agencies and the IBA sought to set up BL as autonomous bodies, independent of the main partners. In effect this would provide a minimal and loose form of partnership, at least in a formal sense, since, the local partners would be involved only as part of a steering committee. This would allow the BL managers and the PBAs considerable autonomy. There was also a number of other agents, such as the FSB and the FBP, who took the view that the local BLs should be relatively independent companies (position 0). They opposed the BL forming close partnership arrangements with any of the other local key partners, such as the local authorities or the Chambers, since they were resistant to giving out public finance and power that might lead BLs and Chambers to integrate to form 'a public law chamber'.

At the other extreme there were some areas where the partners sought a very close integration of the BL with the activities of the main business support bodies in the area; normally the TEC or Chamber. This was indeed a key part of the original Heseltine vision. In fact, Heseltine appears originally to have seen BL as a means to stimulate local mergers, or at least a higher levels of service integration. Wigan provides the best example where this form of partnership has been established, but other areas have also sought to merge their BL into one or other of the main partners.

In between the two extremes a number of different forms of partnership structure were proposed by the agents involved in the negotiations. The key partners, such as the local authorities, the DTI and the Chambers of Commerce, took the view that there should be a partnership structure which included all the main partners. They felt that this should be a flexible form of partnership, where the local structure could vary from area to area to reflect the diversity of local agent development across the country. A special form of this view was represented by the TEC National Council, which wanted BL to be subsidiaries of the local TECs. From an organizational point of view this would certainly make the work of the local TECs easier since they were the contract holders of BL in any case. Other agents, such as the trade associations and the IoD preferred to see the BL move towards merger with the local Chambers of Commerce so that it was more likely that their mission would become clearer and they focused on filling a market gap rather than competing with SMEs.

The final outcome was one that allowed a reasonably flexible form of partnership between the partners at the local level, with the TEC as the legal contract holder. As regards the salience on this issue, it was very important for the DTI, important for the Chambers, and of relatively limited importance for the local authorities. This issue is rated very highly for the TECs, second only to the financial issues since BL related strongly to their strategic objectives of stimulating local enterprise.

Branding Business Link and Partner Services

The sixth BL policy issue of branding was one of the most contentious during the Business Link negotiations. At one extreme agents such as the Chambers of Commerce and the Business Link managers viewed BL as an additional brand, used flexibly by partners in different configurations in different areas. They argued that local partners should be allowed to continue to identify their services, either using their own brand or with joint-branding with Business Link. The BCC pointed out that their local Chambers relied on the fees or membership dues generated by the provision of services to finance their administrative and staff costs. Thus the loss of identity of their services within a single brand undermined their viability. At the other extreme, the DTI sought to have all services, including those of local partners, provided under the single brand name. The main sponsors also recognised the importance of single branding since this was close to their own practice. They argued that this was a key part of the BL concept of integration, to allow all services to be easily recognizable under a single banner from one source, rather than the complex range of providers that existed in most areas. The TEC National Council recognized the value of this BL brand concept but held that a more useful solution would be to use a single brand name only for DTI-financed services.

The final outcome called for the single branding of the services financed by DTI within BL outlets, but had to allow exceptions for partner services since the DTI had no control of how these services were branded. In practice the most common form of branding that has emerged at the local level would appear to be a flexible form of joint branding, such as that originally proposed by the Chambers of Commerce.

In terms of the level of importance that the various agents attach to this issue, this was one of the most salient issues for the DTI. This issue, perhaps more than any other, captures the original concept of the 'One Stop Shop'. The use of a single brand approach would at least covey the image, if not the reality, of a united and coherent local partnerships providing services to SMEs. However, it is not surprising that the Chambers of Commerce and some other agents also regarded this issue as highly important, as it was one of the severest challenges to their separate identity and the income they generated through commercial services. As noted elsewhere, the distinctive 'brand name capital' of Chambers is one of the key elements of linkage between them and their members.[27]

Organization of BL at the Local Level

The final BL policy issue we examine relates to how outlets should be organized at the local level. The DTI, along with the enterprise agencies, the BL managers and David Grayson as Chair of the ISG tended to support the view that local offices should be widely spread in every major town. This view was influenced by Heseltine's personal vision of a local 'shopfront' as the access point.[28] At the other extreme, the Chambers of Commerce, who had considerable experience of making local self-financing services work and had their own development strategy focused at a subregional level, pressed for BL hubs to be in no more than about 40 or 50 areas. Other agents, such as the TEC National Council, the trade associations, the CBI, the IoD, business sponsors, and the DfEE looked for a wider spread of smaller centres based on the TECs (i.e. 75). The local authorities pressed in local negotiations for an office in each of their districts (i.e. over 300). All these other agents accepted a concentrated approach for the contract for BL for the hub offices. But they each wanted a presence through satellites in as many local government districts as possible. However, NatWest, one of the private sector sponsor banks, suggested that 'the practice of joint location with the TEC, enterprise agency, Chamber of Commerce, local DTI office, PYBT, or local council should be

27 See Bennett, 1996.
28 Letter from Michael Heseltine, 30 September 1999.

encouraged to reduce costs. It is also questionable whether all satellite branches are required' (HoC 1996, p. 79).

The outcome was for a hub system of 80 BLs with over 220 satellites. However, the number of offices was a key issue for the overall cost of the system and its capacity to produce a critical mass of services at any location, this issue was not the most important for any agent except the enterprise agencies for whom their pattern of succession relied or a high number of outlets (there were about 200 enterprise agencies in England in 1994 prior to BLs). All of the other agents attached relatively low levels of salience to the issue even though, for TECs and Chambers in particular, they recognised its important financial implications.

The Distribution of Agent Capability/Power in the Negotiations

The Appendix presents the power ratings across the different agents. The most powerful agent is the DTI since it was their initiative and they controlled the new resources. The DfEE is the second most powerful agent since it is the general contractor for TECs, from which the budget for BLs had effectively been removed. Hence they were bound to keep a strong involvement in order to fight to maintain the TEC focus on enterprise. The next most powerful set of agents are the main partners involved in the ISG and in developing local partnership bids: the Chambers, TECs, local authorities and enterprise agencies. Also included in this group, although not a formal partner, is David Grayson as chair of the ISG. The least powerful agents in the early negotiations were the trade associations, the IoD and small firm bodies such as the FSB and FBP.

8.4   The SBS and BL Negotiations Since 1995

The discussion and analysis up to this point has focused on the early negotiations and set-up stage of BL up to mid-1995. By this date about 100 local BL outlets (hubs and satellites) were open and early feedback was being received. DTI had also begun to receive early results of commissioned research on awareness of BL as a brand, and this was followed by successive waves of other BL evaluations. Most important, however, in the discussions taking place between the partners and the DTI, a number of frustrations arose. These chiefly focused on what was seen as excessive prescription by DTI. In practice the partners attempted to re-open negotiations between themselves and the DTI, as well as seeking to confront the original objectives with the emerging reality.

An important meeting was held on 24 May 1995 between the chief partners and Mr Heseltine. As a result of this meeting the DTI agreed to modify their position on a number of points. In practice this meeting set the scene for a new framework of negotiations rather than immediately resolving all the outstanding issues. Most immediately it led to a strengthening of the partners' hand in negotiating the detail of the final drafts of the BL *Operating Manual* and *Service Guide* published in October 1995, much of which had been rejected by partners in the first drafts of April 1995. Less immediate and more progressive over time was the erosion of the DTI prescription on branding and on the nature of the local partnerships. Over time a situation of dual branding has become more routinely accepted, whilst the original structure of BL as independent companies has been overtaken by many BL hubs becoming subsidiaries on departments of the TECs (34 per cent were in this position in late 1997) or integrated into one of the other partners. Only 31 per cent of BLs were, and intended to remain, independent companies by late 1997.[29]

The period following our analysis of 1992–95 therefore saw an important evolutionary process. This is summarised in Table 8.4. During this period two high profile resignations of BL chief executives occurred over issues of financial viability and service integration. These, combined with critical reports from IoD (1996) and HoC (1996), served further to lever a freeing up in DTI financial and other prescriptive procedures. By April 1997 the whole BL system was established for every area and a group of simplified targets and financial procedures were developed. Over this period the BLNC gained a greater role and the early evaluation studies showed a levelling off of awareness as well as defects in quality and enquiry handling.

The May 1997 general election brought a new government commitment to BL but little immediate change in substance. The government initially showed a reluctance to override the agreements that had been established between local partners. Labour was committed to BL in opposition, and reaffirmed its commitment soon after the election (e.g. Roche, 1997). However, the form of commitment changed in favour of a redefined SBS approach by March 1999. These changes reflect a general view developing across a number of Labour's involvements with business, that business can well afford to pay for many supports itself, so that government finance should be focused on those firms most in need of help. This has shifted support towards start-ups and towards filling gaps where there is a genuine public purpose. However, this approach became clear only by mid-1999 and was to some extent forced

---

29 Information from TEC National Council Survey.

Table 8.4   Business Link timetable of development 1996–2001

February 1996 March 1996	IoD report criticises BLs for poor quality service from PBAs, and conflicts of interest in self-finance. Merseyside BL chief executive suspended with BL technically insolvent.
April 1996	Barbara Roche criticises haste in setting system up. DTI assure Commons Committee and BLs that DTI will continue to finance BLs after pumping priming ends.
10 July 1996	Commons Trade and Industry Select Committee Report on Business Links published.
July 1996	81 BL hubs with 228 outlets.
November 1996	Local Partners Advisory Group (LPAG) and Management Information Quality Group (MIQG) formed.
December 1996	87 BL hubs with 263 outlets. Checks on BL income projections being made by DTI accountants. Resignation of Sheffield BL Chief Executive over 'tensions between partners' and an absence of a 'holistic approach'.
March 1997	LPAG Report published: recommends greater integration of other DTI initiatives with BL.
1 April 1997	First year in which *all* BLs are operational. DTI announce 'stream-lined' BL finance with emphasis on targets of service take up, number of businesses paying fees, and self-financing ratio.
1 April 1997	Second edition of *Service Guide* published. Greater emphasis on one stop enquiry handling, counselling of PBAs, quality, and benchmarking.
April 1997	BL chief executives and partners agree to develop BLNC as a stronger independent force with its own income generating strategy and a direct access to DTI support.
July 1997	Interdepartmental Working Group on impact assessment recommends moving to output measures of BL impact on SME sales, assets, employment, profits, exports.
August 1997	BL mystery enquirer report published (survey undertaken in March 1995–Sept. 1996); leads to suggested improvements in service.
1 September 1997	1st draft of Roche *Vision* statement sent out for consultation. 25% income generation target set.
7 October 1997	Barbara Roche publishes *Enhancing Business Links – A vision for the Twenty-First Century*.
November 1997	25% self-financing target reaffirmed.
March 1999	Development of a ***Small Business Service (SBS)*** announced by Treasury and DTI.
June 1999	Detailed proposals for SBS announced for consultation by DTI.
October 1999	Areas for 45 BL franchises announced.
January 2000	Detailed guidance on SBS local franchises announced.
April 2000	Start of transition process, with BL franchises contracted within SBS.
April 2001	BL entirely within SBS with new contract structures.

by the changes of TECs. As one Senior DTI official noted:

> the change in BL contracts was largely the result of opportunism, since the DfEE was forcing a change by abolishing TECs. We were not looking for a new structure. But it has given us the opportunity to develop some important changes in the system.[30]

One of the most important changes was the removal of TECs from BL contracting altogether. Instead, BL is now contracted directly to a central government NDPB, the SBS. This alone has contributed to overcoming confusion between local agents. However, the SBS still has a key aim to overcome 'the criticism that support programmes are fragmented, of variable quality and difficult for small business to access'.[31] This echoes Heseltine's 1992 concerns.[32]

A further change has been the reduction in number of local BL hubs to 45. This was not a strong DTI concern as a department, but ministers became keen to have a stronger sub-regional focus in order to better complement the RDAs and to align BL with the 47 subregional areas developed for the LLSCs that superseded TECs (see chapter 7).[33] On other issues the DTI has become less prescriptive (DTI, 2000). This has produced less change in policy positions than a change in their salience or commitment to holding the line on their preferred outcome (as shown in the Appendix tables).

Other changes have also occurred for the other agents. Once BL was established the BL managers themselves, the PBAs, and the IBA which represents many of the PBAs employed by BL, became more influential. They could argue from experience on the ground that a particular policy was or was not working. This can carry a lot of weight. In any case the BL managers have to be consulted, informed and have to be drawn into a commitment if any developments sought by the partners are to work. The BL managers also formed a national body (BLNC) in July 1995. Although the shares in this company were held by the key national partners (the TNC and BCC) as a deliberate policy to ensure that BL, TECs, and Chambers worked in a continuing partnership, tensions began to emerge with BL chief executives seeking an

---

30 Interview comment, July 1999.
31 DTI, 1999a, p. 18, para. 5.3.
32 In *Hansard*, 3 December 1992, vol. 414.
33 The SBS BL hubs correspond to LLSC areas in 42 of the 45 areas; two LLSCs have two BL areas each (Manchester and Lancashire), whilst five LLSCs for London have one BL hub and five local delivery outlets, giving 45 BL hubs in all: Source: DfEE, 1999a, Press Release 473/99, 28 October.

independent voice for BL. These are tensions which continue. Thus a change in relative power has occurred in favour of BL management, whether or not the partners liked it.

The experiences developed by BL have also influenced some partner positions. Whilst the development of advice and support services to established businesses was already understood by the Chambers and TECs, the experiences of local BLs provided new information to them. But it also involved some of the local partners in this type of support for the first time and this inevitably modified their policy positions. This applied particularly to the CBI, sponsors and enterprise agencies.

Operational experience also opened the whole BL system to scrutiny by a wider population. This has had the effect of bringing some of the more peripheral groups to the original negotiations into a stronger position to influence. For example after 1995, the trade associations, IoD, FPB and FSB were all able to exert a greater influence through parliamentary pressure, or on the DTI directly, than was previously possible. This influences their capability and salience in our models.

Other changes occurred as a result of changes in personality or position. For example, one of the main local authority representatives on the ISG changed in 1996 to a less enthusiastic interventionist who represented probably more closely than his predecessor the more general local government position. The previous representative admitted that 'I am one of the most enthusiastic local authority representatives for BL.'[34] Also, from 1997, the former local government associations merged into one body, the LGA, which adopted a stronger oversight of its representation on the ISG which brought the local government views more in line with average local practice. This has changed some policy positions and salience.

Hence, the main shifts in the policy positions and salience recorded in between 1992–95 and 1999 are those resulting from changes in political thinking influencing the DTI, evolution in partner pressure and the effect of on-the-ground experience.

8.5 Simulations

The information on each agent's policy position, salience and power is combined in our analysis using the four models outlined in chapter 4. These

---

34 Interview comments.

are applied to the two periods of negotiation we have focused on here: 1992–95 and 1995–99.

The overall accuracy of the different models, assessed using the mean square error criterion, is shown in Table 8.5. As in earlier chapters, the exchange model performs best overall by a considerable margin in the early phase of negotiations. However, it performs less well for the negotiation in the 1995-99 period where all models perform very poorly.

Table 8.5   Comparison of predictions of Business Link negotiations using the mean square error criterion

	Negotiations 1992–95	Negotiations 1995–99
Compromise (base) model	39.2	1522
Exchange model	20.8	1738
Strategic control model	82.2	1949
Conflict model	310.8	1617

It is clear from comparison of the two periods that a very different negotiation process occurred leading up to the development of the SBS than that which led to the original establishment of BL. Recalling the earlier discussion, the 1992–95 period saw BL established as a result of a review instituted by Mr Heseltine which involved the key partners (Chambers, TECs, local authorities and enterprise agencies). Hence, it had a strong consensual approach, although driven by Heseltine's objective of significantly raising the performance of the support system for SMEs. Given its strong consensual origins, it is not surprising that the exchange model works best. It reflects the log-rolling between issues and policy objectives by which the agents sought to safeguard and improve their positions.

The establishment of the SBS, however, had very different origins. Announced by the Chancellor in the 1998 March budget, it was an initiative that was a surprise even to the DTI: 'it came out of the blue.'[35] Its key elements were then developed by the DTI. But two key aspects were very much at odds with the former consensual approach of working with partners. First, there was the reduction in number of hub areas, and second there was the imposition of a stronger central management by SBS responsible for contracting the BL as local franchisees rather than as loose partnerships. Furthermore, the DfEE's objective to abolish TECs and replace them by LLSCs also had its origins in

---

35 Comment from senior DTI official.

concerns that were almost totally independent of how BL partners saw the future. These changes were de facto imposed on BL partners and hence models based on exchange and negotiation are unlikely to reflect this reality. Rather our model predictions for evaluation reflect what might have happened had not the SBS and changes in DfEE objectives for LLSCs been developed.

The poor predictions of all the models for the SBS BL development result particularly from issue 7 (the number of outlets), where most agents wanted to remain with the status quo. Also poorly predicted are issues 3, 4 and 5 for the role of the PBA, target firms and partnership structure.

The very different performance of the exchange model between the two periods of development is very clear in the prediction-realisation diagrams in Figures 8.1 and 8.2. The way in which these diagrams are constructed is described in chapter 5. Whereas there is a close alignment on all issues for 1992–95 in Figure 8.1, only one issue (finance of PBAs) is well modelled for the SBS BL for 1995–99. Issues 7, 5, 3 and 4 are particularly badly modelled. These had become largely consensual between partners and did not fit well with the government's new priorities.

Already it is clear in our assessment of the SBS, therefore, that Labour's approach has shifted the agenda considerably for the agents on the ground concerned with implementing local and regional economic development policy.

8.6   Power Relations: Gainers and Losers

As in earlier chapters, a key part of our concerns is to assess how agent power relations have developed under Labour: who is gaining and who is losing. We can estimate this directly from our models by examining for each agent and each issues their utility loss or gain at the end of the negotiations. The utility loss of any agent for an issue is calculated by estimating the absolute distance between the agent's policy position and the actual outcome issue by issue, but allowing for the relative importance of that issue for the agent (its salience). This is derived from our discussions in chapter 4 (equation 4.1), as specified in chapter 5.

Table 8.6 compares the agent net utility losses summed across each of the BL issues. For the first phase of negotiations the main losers were the Chambers of Commerce, the trade associations and the small business associations (FSB, FPB). BL was an interventionist DTI approach that cut across and competed with business associations, self help and the suppliers already available. The main gainers were BL managers, PBAs and enterprise agencies who were

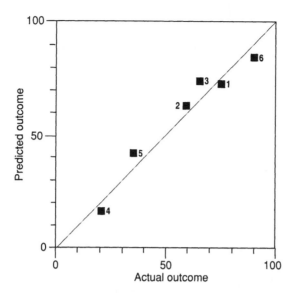

**Figure 8.1   Prediction-realisation diagram for Business Link
negotiations 1992–95 (exchange model)**

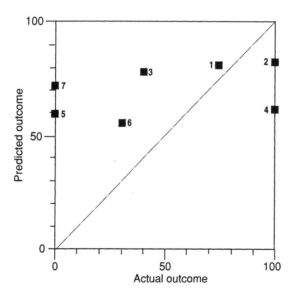

**Figure 8.2   Prediction-realisation diagram for SBS Business Link
negotiations 1995–99 (exchange model)**

directly employed or contracted by BL. The main government departments are little affected, the DTI even losing some utility as a result of not obtaining its objectives fully on prescription and branding. Local government gains modestly as a result of having a new central government support in most localities with which it is involved as a partner. The overall net utility loss reflects the increase in competition with private sector suppliers from government subsidies.

Table 8.6   Net utility loss or gain for each agent across all issues for Business Link negotiations (exchange model)

Agent	Negotiations 1992–95 on BL	Negotiations 1995–99 on SBS
DTI	-0.009	-0.014
DfEE	+0.008	-0.003
BCC	-0.014	+0.080
Enterprise agencies	+0.021	+0.044
TEC national council	-0.004	-0.327
Local authorities	+0.004	+0.008
Business sponsors	+0.007	+0.003
BiTC	+0.014	-0.064
CBI	-0.002	+0.006
BL managers	+0.034	+0.059
IBA/PBAs	+0.032	+0.008
TAs/PAs	-0.034	+0.045
IoD	+0.004	+0.004
FSB	-0.040	-0.006
FPB	-0.040	+0.050
Pro-merger local groups	+0.000	+0.000
Total	-0.343	-0.749

For the second phase of negotiations to develop the SBS, the main gainers are the BL managers, enterprise agencies and Chambers of Commerce, which each reinforce their positions independently of the TECs. The main losers are the TECs, with smaller losses also for BiTC whose original vision has largely disappeared. The overall pattern is of a greater net utility loss chiefly as a result of the major loss of control by TECs as a result of the centralisation process under the SBS.

Table 8.7 compares the net utility losses for each issue, summed for all agents. On the issues of the finance of PBAs, the range of PBA services, organisation of the BL partnership, and branding, the net utility loss is higher in the later period.

Table 8.7   Net utility losses and gains for each issue for Business Link negotiations (exchange model)

Issue	Negotiations 1992–95	Negotiations 1995–99
1 Finance of PBAs	+0.005	-0.001
2 Finance of BL	+0.000	-0.001
3 Range of PBA services	-0.0010	-0.004
4 Target firms	-0.010	+0.001
5 Organisation of BL partnership	-0.003	-0.008
6 Branding	+0.003	-0.001
7 Number of outlets	–	+0.001
Average (all issues)	-0.343	-0.749

In terms of the alternative explanatory interpretations for the outcome of negotiations the developments of the BL and SBS initiatives demonstrate even more strongly than in previous chapters that government is the prime mover of change in business support policy. Developments do not accord well with either resource dependence, social class or institutional theories. The conclusion drawn has to be that a strong state corporatist model has been followed, with greater exchange and negotiation in the earlier period, and with stronger direction in the later period. But in both cases the clear leadership of government is strongly evident.

8.7   Extent of Progress

The extent to which the initiative of SBS and its development of BL has really led to progress in SME supports is still a controversial topic. On the positive side a large number of businesses are aware of and have used BL. A number of studies show awareness of BL to reach 70 per cent within 1-2 years of local BL outlet opening.[36] Use of BL by the end of 1997 had reached 9 per cent of all firms with at least one employee and 19 per cent in the early target group of firms with 10–199 employees.[37] Impact studies have suggested

---

36 MORI, 1996 and subsequent surveys.
37 DTI, 1997a, Monitoring Statistics.

the BL advice increases average firm employment by 0.4 jobs, turnover by £76,000 and profits by £9,000.[38] DTI evaluation of satisfaction show 90-95 per cent satisfaction levels.[39] Overall, BL has become the single most used public support body by SMEs, shown to be used by 27 per cent of SMEs in a large scale sample survey in 1997,[40] with a fairly high emphasis on intensive supports involving site visits and/or contract relationships with clients.

On the more negative side, however, comparisons of BL with the earlier enterprise initiative show that use levels have not so far reached the same levels (about 33 per cent of SMEs), that impact levels are at best moderate and are exaggerated in DTI evaluations by focusing on those clients that had positive outcomes. Satisfaction levels also appear exaggerated in DTI studies compared to other assessments that show satisfaction running at 66 per cent,[41] or between 57 per cent and 86 per cent depending on the service and satisfaction criterion used.[42] There has also been particular doubt caste on the relevance of PBAs and the diagnostic assessment foci for BL which was a core part of the original vision for the system. These aspects tend to have the lowest use levels (less than 30 per cent of clients) and among the lowest and most variable satisfaction levels.[43]

There is thus considerable controversy about some key aspects of BL, although the undisputed high awareness and use levels mean that it is also clearly achieving some considerable success. In terms of evaluation it is actual SME clients who will be the ultimate arbiters who vote with their feet by making use of the service if they find it useful. However, it is also possible to compare the BL and SBS with different agent views to see if alternative scenarios for organization and targets would have achieved a structure more in line with bodies representing business and other interests. As outlined in Chapter 5 and followed in the other case chapters, we compare four scenarios where additional power is given to the views of Chambers of Commerce, the CBI, the TECs, or local government.

8.8   Alternative Scenarios

The four alternative scenarios are compared in Table 8.8. This compares the

---

38 PACEC, 1998.
39 DTI, 1996.
40 Bennett and Robson, 1999.
41 Bennett and Robson, 1999.
42 See also Priest, 1998; Tann and Lafaret, 1998; Sear and Agar, 1996.
43 Bennett and Robson, 1999.

closeness of accord of actual outcomes and scenarios based on strengthening the power of different agents. It is clear that the actual outcome in 1992–95 was best reproduced by the original exchange model prediction. This has far lower mean square error than the other scenarios, though it is close to the outcome that would have resulted from significantly increasing either the CBI or local government power. Of the scenarios assessed, therefore, it is clear that the actual outcome was quite distant from that sought by the main local business agents of Chambers and TECs. For Chambers the main differences arise from the way in which branding was treated. The early emphasis on single BL branding was a huge difference from the objectives sought by BCC. For TECs the main gaps were in the partnership structure (where they wanted greater control), and in the target firms (where they wanted a broader emphasis to include the smallest businesses).

Table 8.8   Comparison of alternative scenarios and the actual outcomes of Business Link negotiations using the mean square error criterion (exchange model)

	Negotiations 1992–95	Negotiations 1995–99
Scenario 1: Chambers of Commerce	633.3	1320
Scenario 2: CBI	36.6	1465
Scenario 3: TECs/LLSCs	178.5	1381
Scenario 4: Local government	39.3	2063
Original prediction	20.8	1738

The comparisons for the period up to the establishment of the SBS in 1999 are in marked contrast. All scenarios are now very distant from the actual outcomes, but most of these scenarios are better than the exchange model predictions. This suggests that although each of the agents loses out in the SBS development, the Chambers, TECs and the CBI lose to a relatively lesser extent than local government. The main factors leading to the major differences of agent objectives from outcomes relate to the targeting firms (where the CBI, BCC and TECs opposed the widening to include a greater proportion of micro-businesses), the partnership structure (where the franchise structure was most distant from BCC and TEC objectives), branding (which was still a problem for BCC), and the number of outlets (where local authorities in particular were unhappy about the reduced number of BL hubs and potential contraction in number of local satellites).

The different scenarios are compared in terms of prediction-realisation diagrams in Figures 8.3 and 8.4. The actual outcomes maintain the same position on the horizontal axis of these figures independently of the scenarios. The wide spread of the scenarios from the actual outcomes is particularly evidenced in Figure 8.4 for issues 4, 5 and 7 (target firms, partnership structures and number of outlets).

As in the earlier discussions, the difference between outcomes and agent views can be calculated using the net utility loss measure for each scenario. This produces much less extreme measures since now differences of outcomes from objectives are weighted by agent salience (Table 8.9). The SBS structure in general leads to higher average agent net utility loss. All the scenarios significantly reduce losses, with similar results irrespective of which agent's power is modified. Each of the scenarios would lead to a major shift in power for local agents which shows the extent to which the SBS is relatively distant from local supplier perspectives.

Table 8.9   Net utility losses and gains under different scenarios for Business Link negotiations (exchange model)

	Negotiations 1992–95 on BL	Negotiations 1995–99 on SBS
Scenario 1: Chambers of Commerce	+0.001	-0.006
Scenario 2: CBI	-0.001	-0.002
Scenario 3: TECs/LLSCs	+0.014	-0.001
Scenario 4: Local government	+0.002	-0.002
Original prediction	-0.343	-0.749

8.9   Conclusion

Business support to firms through advice, information, grants and other means is an important aspect of local and regional economic development policy. As with the other case studies examined, it is a complex and fragmented field in which many agents are involved.

The Business Link initiative sought to reduce confusion, improve professionalism and quality, and give a stronger focus on a local partnership delivery system primarily based on TECs, Chambers of Commerce, local authorities and enterprise agencies. The many tensions of this approach, particularly its variable quality and focus on provision of intensive advice

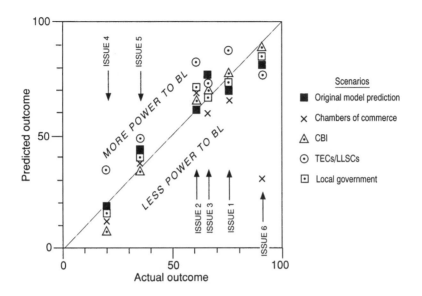

Figure 8.3   Prediction-realisation diagram for comparing scenarios for Business Link negotiations 1992–95 (exchange model)

through PBAs and diagnostic assessment, led to criticisms of its competition with the market and highly variable assessments of its client impact and satisfaction. However, it was not so much these criticisms that influenced Labour's reforms developed since 1999. The stimulus came instead from the Treasury which was concerned to influence SMEs to develop improved payroll and accounting systems to help the Chancellor implement reform of taxation and the benefits systems. Also important was the opportunity that opened up once a decision had been made to replace TECs by LLSCs. This allowed the contracting relation for BL between DTI and TECs to be modified.

The outcome has been a much more centrally managed system of small business support under an NDPB at arms length from the DTI. This was not what any of the partners sought directly, and it undermined much of the cosy consensus that had developed between partners at national and local levels which had covered the previous period of DTI policy development following Heseltine's 'review' of the department in 1992. The SBS emphasis on a single system with stronger local management where partners had less individual control was not the first priority of any agent. Where it was combined with a

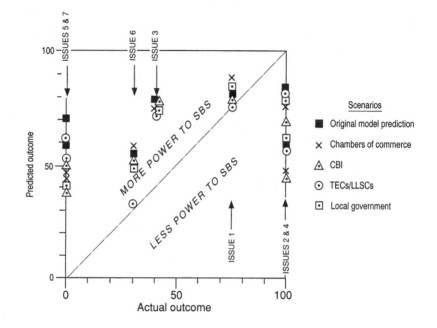

Figure 8.4   Prediction-realisation diagram comparing scenarios for SBS Business Link negotiations 1995–99 (exchange model)

strong emphasis on branding it was particularly resisted by the Chambers. Where it emphasised larger management units of 40–50 in number across England, it was strongly resisted by local authorities. The wider spread of concerns with targeting start-ups and micro-businesses as well as established firms was also out of line with CBI and BCC objectives.

Our assessment has shown that the early stage of development over the 1992-95 period was strongly consensual based primarily on an exchange or log-rolling process. The exchange model interpretation performs far better than any alternative interpretation over this period.

The development of SBS is not well interpreted as an exchange process, however. The exchange model is one of the worst models for predicting the outcomes in 1999. Instead, our analysis demonstrates the strength of government acting to impose a settlement on three of the key issues: number of outlets, targeting, and structure of local partnership management. In effect these were not negotiable. As a result an exchange process did not occur since agent objectives on many issues were not well met.

Our analysis confirms the importance of interpreting the power of government as having a level of autonomy from the resource dependence, social class and institutional frameworks argued by many academics. Indeed in both the exchange model covering 1992–95, which assigns government departments the highest power levels among agents, and particularly in the development of the SBS in 1999, the strength of central government is clearly demonstrated as a dominant force in small business support policy. The chief interpretation of both periods is that a form of state-led corporatism has been followed. This accords with both Heseltine's view of the role of the DTI and with that of Labour.

The simulation of alternative scenarios that accord some agents greater power would have shifted the BL initiative away from competing with either private sector suppliers or those local partners that are suppliers of business support services. The dangers inherent in state-led corporatism are therefore made very evident for SBS and BL: that it is easily possible to design a system in conflict with market needs and existing market suppliers. This suggests a different form of challenge to Labour's objective of joining-up policy which we assess further in the next chapters.

PART III
'UNFINISHED REVOLUTION'?

9 Power-relations under Labour

9.1 'Unfinished Revolution'

Labour's professed aim is to develop ongoing change through reform of most of the key elements that influence the performance and competitiveness of the economy. We have focused on the key local and regional economic development policy initiatives. In addition, there are reforms of company law, competition law, regulatory systems, constitutional structures, employment rights, minimum wage, citizens rights and other areas. The key criterion for evaluation that has been professed to run through the reforms is the pragmatic one of 'what matters is what works'. In this sense the ongoing project developed by Labour requires learning-by-doing and feedback to develop further change or refinement of policy. To achieve this its core needs a pluralist and consultative process, but this has been sought within a structure of leadership that keeps the general trajectory flowing in a particular direction. The difficulty with this approach is determining what is an appropriate direction. Whilst the concept of a 'third way', between state and market, may be a useful generalised political tool, it has not provided a coherent philosophy and does not offer particularly strong guidance on how to make detailed decisions on individual policies. It is more like a new form of state-led corporatism and has the same potential pitfalls.

The explicit objectives of local and regional economic development policy, however, should be easy to define. Economic development policy should be about increasing economic growth. This is achieved by improving factor conditions, encouraging endogenous growth and responding to inward investment. The tests of 'what matters is what works' in the economic development field are, therefore, whether economic growth has increased, and whether it is likely to increase in the future as a result of the policy changes.

In this chapter we summarise and develop the findings of our case studies. We first demonstrate how Labour's agenda has led to a more fragmented local and regional policy domain which may lack strategic direction. We then demonstrate that power relations have been modified in part to disfavour business interests, but have chiefly resulted in a reshuffling of responsibilities between central government departments. Labour's local and regional economic development policies are then assessed for their impact on economic growth. We conclude that the outcomes are patchy and inconsistent, better in some areas, worse in other areas. This assessment forms the basis for suggested improvements that are developed in the next chapter.

9.2   The Labour Agenda

Labour was elected with a number of key objectives for radical change in local and regional economic development policy. Central to the process was the creation of RDAs. Also a flagship was the New Deal, delivered by local partnerships contracted to the Employment Service. The reforms of TECs came later, to create a new system of local Learning and Skills Councils, and the development of a Small Business Service which would oversee Business Link. Also slow developing has been the granting of additional power and resources to local government, although reforms to council governance and a new duty for economic development were initiated in the 1999/2000 session of parliament. These developments, together with the initiation of a Scottish parliament and Welsh assembly, certainly represent major changes to the local and regional development scene.

In chapter 2 we identified five chief elements of Labour's shift in governance regime:

- a widening of the interests and agents involved in any set of policy negotiations to be as inclusive and consultative as possible. This has been underpinned by seeking to shift policy towards a more pragmatic agenda: 'what matters is what works';
- a greater emphasis on social inclusion within economic development policy, particularly to achieve employment creation rather than wealth creation;
- a search for improved 'accountability', chiefly developed at local and regional level through stronger involvement of local government in the boards or executives of development bodies. But also formalised through the Regional Chambers, London Authority, Scottish Parliament and Welsh Assembly;
- a shift from general purpose bodies to special purpose economic development bodies under individual government departments. In the case of LLSCs and the SBS this is in the form of NDPBs. This has placed more emphasis on individual programme performance and reduced the emphasis

on integration, instead emphasising the need to cooperate and 'join-up' government;

- attempts to encourage a more flexible structure that allows bottom-up initiatives to be supported within a strengthened central government control (especially by the Treasury) to encourage endogenous growth and improve productivity and competitiveness.

Our assessments and case studies have shown that this agenda is still giving rise to many tensions. A more inclusive consultative process does not necessarily help to resolve what is the best way forward for a given policy; it may just increase the range of voices and diversity of views that have to be taken into account. It may also raise expectations among agents that cannot be satisfied. More inclusiveness may lead to more frustration.

The question of 'what works' is also full of value-laden questions such as; what works for whom, to achieve what benefits, and over what time horizon are outcomes considered important? A greater emphasis or social inclusion has been one answer offered by Labour to the question of what benefits are sought. This has led to a greater emphasis on the employment created by local and regional economic development activities. But employment is only one objective of businesses, others being turnover, profit, market share, etc. Labour is yet to make explicit how the trade-offs between these different objectives are to be achieved. An overemphasis on economic initiatives to increase employment has dangers of trapping Labour into trying to manage local and regional initiatives as decentralised versions of the former Keynesian full employment policy, particularly that business decisions are encouraged not on economically sustainable grounds, but because they satisfy a government priority. Indeed, Gordon Brown as Chancellor has made explicit his aim of achieving full employment.[1]

Accountability has many attractive features to local and regional economic development policy. As we have argued strongly, that policies that do not have local commitment and do not 'win hearts and minds' have little chance of success. Accountability may be very helpful in winning commitment. But accountability to local government, so strongly emphasised by Labour, is only one interpretation of who and how those involved in, or affected by, implementation should be drawn into commitment. Moreover, local government activities can be quite perverse to the needs of the local and regional economy. Indeed our brief summary in chapter 2 demonstrates that many local authorities are developing their economic development policies

---

1   Gordon Brown, Budget Statement, March 2000.

too independently of other local partners and that central government initiatives are encouraging further increases in fragmentation of activity, a sentiment echoed by the Audit Commission's 1999 report[2] and by a Cabinet Office Report. Agents other than local government are also important to achieving commitment, and may be more important to the local economy; for example, business interests, trade unions, sectoral bodies, voluntary organisations. 'Accountability' to these appears to have been considered by Labour chiefly through appointments to boards to administer NDPBs, or participation in the boards of LLSCs, SBS, New Deal partnerships or RDAs. The danger is that membership of boards offers only a sliver of activity and may deliver no change in commitments on the ground.

A different set of tensions arises from the shift away from attempts to achieve local programme integration through TECs towards the expansion of separate central departmental initiatives and bodies such as LLSCs, the SBS BL and New Deal partnerships. The wide range of new local action zones, initiatives and development bodies developed by Labour is summarised in Table 2.1. Integration is being sought through the regional level of RDAs or through interdepartmental liaison nationally and locally. This process of integration is slow to develop. For local partners the 'patchwork quilt' seems to be increasing in complexity, not reducing. There is a danger that the broad economic agenda of encouraging bottom-up development and endogenous growth is lost among disparate and separated department objectives with increased difficulty of binding together the expanding number of separate agents on the ground. The broad central government commitment to the economy could be in danger of being dissipated among a myriad of initiatives without a coherent vision. Certainly Labour's more fragmentary approach has put a lot of pressure on the main national, regional and local agents: for them to be able to keep up with the pace of initiative creation, to resource adequately their information needs and the consultation demands by government, and to be able to communicate with and engage effectively with their constituents or members. The CBI, BCC and other business bodies have all complained about the number of new initiatives and the pressures on individual businesses being able to participate nationally or locally. Similar concerns have been expressed by the LGA, TUC and voluntary bodies.

Our case studies have demonstrated the tensions for each agent in this change process, and the gains and losses that are resulting. We summarise these findings below.

---

2   Audit Commission, 1999; Cabinet Office, Performance and Innovation Unit, March 2000.

9.3   Negotiations as Exchange or Control?

The approach we have developed in this book has emphasised an analysis of the negotiation process which has assessed the outcomes of the interactions between the objectives, commitment and power of each agent. It is an encompassing approach which seeks to interpret how outcomes have been determined rather than how policy networks operate.

Our case studies have demonstrated that two different sets of processes are at work. First, for the cases of the development of RDAs, TECs and Business Link, we have found that the exchange model is by far the best predictor of outcomes. We use this evidence, together with the information gained from our extensive process of interviews, to conclude that a genuine log-rolling and exchange process occurred between the chief agents involved. This log-rolling occurred in the early years of Labour government, despite the fact that for the RDAs much of the policy development had occurred chiefly within the political party whilst Labour was in opposition. The actual implementation required strong involvement and commitment from the participating agents which necessitated considerable adjustments to the detail and some aspects of the general strategy. For the RDA initiative a reduction in the breadth of powers originally envisaged occurred to keep happy the local authorities, other central departments and interests in higher education. In the case of TECs and BL, developed under the Conservatives, implementation again required commitment from the main partners involved. By the time we focus on these two initiatives, in 1995, both had achieved a strong level of support and commitment from partners (even for TECs for which there had been considerable hostility at the outset) but only at the expense of significant concessions being made by central government.

A second set of processes appears to be at work for the development of negotiations to establish New Deal local partnerships, LLSCs and the SBS BL, however. The exchange model is a poor predictor of the form of these policy changes in many cases. For New Deal too little attention was paid to employers in the design stage, particularly on the form of gateway and flexibility of contracts needed. For LLSCs and the SBS their design appears strongly to be the result not of a negotiation process at all but of conflict. The outcomes are more the result of an imposition by central government of their own specific approach. The actual form of LLSCs is particularly distant from the outcome that would have been achieved by an exchange process of negotiations for the role of LLSCs in economic development policy and business support (where almost all the former roles of the TECs have been lost), for the training targets of programmes (where the employer involvement in the work-based route has been eroded), and for the relation between LLSCs and Chambers of Commerce (where the former model of merged TECs and chambers to form CCTEs has been de facto abandoned). For the SBS BL structure, the main differences of the actual and predicted exchange-based outcomes is the lesser role of partners, the changed role of Personal Business Advisors, and a shift in the chief target firms for support.

The imposition of a central government solution appears strongly to have been the result of government frustration at the exchange process. Two years of exchanges and negotiations between the chief agents and government, two internal reviews of TECs, and deep disputes between the different government departments involved, prevented an outcome being developed that was satisfactory to meet government's needs. Hence instead of accepting an outcome based on log-rolling and exchange, the prime minister and cabinet imposed a settlement which de facto reflect victories for the Treasury, DfEE and DTI. Many aspects of this were a surprise to the partners. They were certainly not outcomes in line with the status quo or preferences of many agents. The results in these cases, therefore, reflect the strong autonomy of central government to decide on its policy approach, but also demonstrate the dilemma for achieving a commitment from the agents needed to implement the policy.

The results from our case studies provides some important insights into the performance of the academic interpretations we introduced in chapter 3. An important general conclusion is that each of the five interpretations offers some element of explanation of the policy negotiations we examine. The negotiations of each of the case studies certainly exhibits many aspects of pluralism, whereby each interest group interacts to influence outcomes. There is also clear evidence for the operation of resource-dependent interpretations as government and other agents use their different resources to develop support for their different objectives. To some extent this also gives some indication of the influence of countervailing power. The superior performance of the exchange model in the case of the RDA, TEC and BL negotiations suggests support for both pluralist and resource-dependent interpretations. But in these cases, and even more strongly in the case of LLSCs and SBS BL, the state-led corporatist model emphasising the leadership, coercion and attempted incorporation of agents by government seems more appropriate to describing the power and control exerted by government departments. They are the most powerful agents, as estimated by our experts in interviews, and our models demonstrate that it is they who finally determine the outcomes. However, the effectiveness of the outcomes, and hence their long-term sustainability, depends on having the commitment of other agents to implementation. As we argued at the outset, economic development is not the monopoly of central government and its departments, but is a multi-agent process where many of the key agents can freely walk away from implementation. The outcomes of the RDA and New Deal discussions suggest that the agent commitment will exist, even though the power of RDAs is less than desired. In the case of LLSCs and SBS BL, however, the distance of the imposed solution from the exchange model outcome demonstrates how hard the government will have to work to win hearts and minds and 'incorporate' agents into its agenda. The predominantly state-led corporatist approach that has been adopted looks particularly uncertain to provide the employer commitment needed for the development of work-based training through LLSCs or the work-readiness required of New Deal participants.

The role of social class relations between the key negotiators representing each agent, and institutional forces of cohesion and embeddedness may also play a role in those cases where the exchange model has superior performance. Where agents have a similarity of leadership viewpoints, or are formally or informally embedded in similar approaches, this will facilitate exchange and make agreement more likely. We have no direct evidence of this. However, the two cases of LLSCs and SBS BL, where they exchange model works particularly badly, indicate that social and institutional models do not apply; or if they do apply, the government has been able to act relatively autonomously of these forces in order to develop a solution that is not embedded at the outset. Despite this, Labour will be using its shift in governance regime to try and embed its policies within the response of the different agents. The extent to which this is being achieved, or is likely to occur, is assessed further below.

For the present, we note that none of the single academic interpretations of how policy networks operate, introduced in Chapter 3, offers a full explanation of how developments have occurred in the field of local and regional economic development policy under Labour. Elements of each approach seem to apply in differing proportions to each of our case studies. This confirms the importance of taking a broader, multifaceted and encompassing approach as we have done through our negotiations model.

9.4 Winners and Losers under Labour

Labour's agenda does not specifically set out to create winners and losers from its policies of local and regional economic development. However, a greater emphasis on social inclusion and accountability has been judged by many to work in favour of voluntary groups and local government, whilst a broader emphasis on open consultation may reduce the influence of business and economic interests that were perceived to have been given too strong an emphasis in the Conservative period. Hence, despite an explicit policy of not favouring or disfavouring specific agents, Labour has created winners and losers. No policy change is neutral in its consequences.

The negotiations model we have applied in chapters 5 to 8 has allowed us in each case study to evaluate the utility gains and losses of each agent, as well as the total utility gain/loss over all agents involved. The chief agent gains and losses for each case study are summarised in Table 9.1. This table only lists the chief shifts in power in order to simplify the discussion.

A major feature to note is that the agents that experience most change in almost all cases are government departments, or the agents funded directly by government departments. This leads to the important conclusion that much of what government is achieving through its changes of local and regional economic development policy is a shuffling of departmental power and responsibility. This may have important consequences, but it often does not affect the overall balance of gains and losses of most other agents to any very large extent.

A second feature is the relatively small extent to which business agents are affected, except insofar that they are represented through the local or regional boards of the government agents involved. Hence, although the whole field of policy development is aimed at improving business and economic performance, representative business bodies are not usually the main recipients of benefits. This reinforces the view that most change has focused on reshuffling the government furniture, and is not strongly embedded in change by other agents and has at best marginal impact on the economy.

A third feature is that where there are more significant gains for some business bodies, other business bodies often experience losses. This occurs particularly for the cases of TECs, LLSCs, BL and SBS BL. Hence, government policy whilst having generally lower impact on business bodies than government departments, does have some impact on redistributing power between business bodies. Some agents have won more power or resources and others have lost in the reshuffling process. Generally, Chambers of Commerce and the CBI have been chief gainers among business interests, with sector associations, FSB amd FPB having smaller losses than previously.

Fourth, where a change of policy is evident in our case studies from the former Conservative approach to that of Labour, the main losers of power

Table 9.1   Chief agents making large utility gains and losses in each local and regional economic development policy field: summary of results from the case studies in chapters 5 to 8

Policy Field		Successful agents receiving large utility gains	Unsuccessful agents receiving large utility losses
RDAs	Phase 1	GOR	Local Partnerships
		Local government	English Partnerships
		RDA Boards	TUC
	Phase 2	RDA Boards	DfEE
		CBI	GOR
		BCC	
		DETR	
	Phase 3	Other government departments	Local government
		RDA Boards	
		DETR	
New Deal		Employment Service	TECs
		Specialist Counsellors	FE
		Business Leaders (NDTF)	Other government departments
TECs		Training Agency Areas Offices/	TEC Boards/TNC
		GORs	BiTC
		BCC	LEAs
		CBI	DETR
LLSCs		BCC	TEC Boards
		Business leaders	DETR
		Local partnerships	Local government
		DTI	FE colleges
			LEAs
			Employment Service
BL		BL Managers	BCC
		PBAs	Trade associations
		Enterprise agencies	FSB
			FPB
SBS BL		DTI	TECs
		Treasury	BiTC
		BCC	
		Enterprise agencies	

have been the boards and staff of the former local agents (TECs, BL), and to a lesser extent local government. Business-led bodies funded by government have lost influence in comparison with non-departmental public bodies or leadership by other agents.

An interesting aspect of the pattern of utility losses and gains is the evidence it gives of the centrality of different agents within networks of negotiations. Although linkages between agents are not directly measured in our analysis, it is clear that it is the lead government department that acts as the 'hub' of the negotiation and hence of networks of exchange. Since it is departmental expenditures and priorities which are being negotiated, this is not surprising. Those agents that work most closely with the lead departments obtain a 'derived' centrality in the negotiations.[3] These are the key partners in each of our case studies. However, aspects of the state-led corporatist process of incorporation of these partner agents mean that they come to reflect some of the main viewpoints as the lead government department. This is particularly the case for Business Link which was set up as a very explicit partnership structure from the outset with the objective of encouraging a new local structure, including mergers between local agents. Overall the pattern of major utility changes shown in Table 9.1 suggests that business agents have not usually been allowed to be central to the gains or losses, even though it is an economic development process that depends on businesses that is sought.

The overall utility gain or loss from each case study policy initiative is summarised in Table 9.2. This is the average change for all agents across all issues. Since the agents involved form a closed set determined by those included in or relevant to the negotiations, these utility values give a measure of gains or losses to the whole system. But since agent power is unequally distributed and not all interests may be influential in the discussions or be represented, the utility estimates are not a total welfare estimate for the economy. Indeed, economic interests tend to be under-represented in the discussions with the main power and the largest group of agents being those of central government departments and other public sector interests.

Even within these constraints, the results shown in Table 9.2 demonstrate that the total utility changes from most of the policy initiatives examined is fairly modest. This reinforces the conclusion that the main change that have so far taken place is a reshuffling of the furniture among central government departments. The cases of RDAs, New Deal and TECs result in overall utility gains. The cases of LLSCs, BL and SBS result in overall welfare losses.

Tables 9.1 and 9.2 together suggest a general impression of utility losses and gains under Labour to be one of modest shifts away from leadership by business and economic agents, but with the main changes being an increased focus on individual government department performance. The general utility changes that result are, however generally modest with the exception of New Deal. There is thus some indication that Labour's first three years have mainly

---

3   See chapter 3 and discussions by Laumann and Pappi, 1976, Mizruchi and Galaskiewicz, 1994.

Table 9.2   Total utility gains and losses in each local and regional economic development policy field: summary of results from the case studies in chapters 5 to 8

Policy field		Total utility gain/loss
RDAs	Phase 1	+0.084
	Phase 2	+0.083
	Phase 3	+0.036
New Deal		+1.120
TECs		+0.700
LLSCs		-0.370
BL		-0.343
SBS BL		-0.749

reshuffled the furniture of central departmental responsibilities as far as local and regional economic development policy is concerned. We turn below to assessing how far our analysis is supported by other evaluations.

9.5   The Extent of Economic Improvement

We noted in chapter 3 that the outcomes of policy negotiation are not 'optimal' in the sense of inevitably improving the economic parameters they set out to improve, even when the objectives are as clearly focused on economic targets as they are in the fields of local and regional economic development policy that we have been examining. Our negotiation model approach has focused on how outcomes are influenced by each agent, and how each agent's objectives, salience and power combine to produce a given outcome. The outcome is not 'optimal' in an economic sense because:

- there is an *inequality of opportunity*, resources and power of different interests to influence outcomes. We have demonstrated that economic interests may be minor in policy decisions compared to the interests of central departments;
- there is *path dependence* on the previous power positions and policy outcomes that constrain future developments;
- there is *imperfect arbitrage* between policy objectives because of imperfect information, the constraints of administrative procedure, and the influence of political and other objectives.

As noted by Douglass North, 'democracy is not to be equated with competitive markets'. Hence, there is no reason to believe that the outcome of policy negotiations that is 'politically efficient', through log-rolling and exchange, is also 'economically efficient'.[4]

Our analysis has shown that the pluralist idea that all interests combine and 'concert' to produce an agreed outcome may well describe key elements of the process by which the policies in RDAs has developed. This is well modelled by an exchange process. But elements of a state-led corporatist interpretation appear more appropriate for the way in which policy was decided on New Deal, LLSCs and the SBS BL: for these developments central government took a strong lead against key partner interests and has then sought to incorporate their interactions effectively.

Thus in some of our case studies we may have outcomes that are in some sense 'politically efficient'. In the other case studies we have outcomes that demonstrate government leadership that is attempting to rise above outcomes derived purely from inter-agent exchange and negotiation. Has either approach worked well? Although it is early days to evaluate fully the outcomes of many of the changes that have occurred, some indications are clear.

(i)   RDAs

For the case of RDAs there is strong support from the business community to make them work. They are offering an opportunity to bring together a strong business view with that of local government and other regional interests to develop strategies for each region. This may be improving the sensitivity and focus of allocation decisions on regeneration, and it may be encompassing different local interests to bind together to reduce local competition and improve the effectiveness of infrastructure investments and promotional activity. This improved focus may be particularly effective in encouraging more effective local authority economic development activity.

However, despite some improvements in coordination and the continued strong support from the business community and regional partners, RDAs fall a long way short of what most agents desire. First, the government regional offices still maintain a strong control of many DETR decisions and, because the main DfEE and DTI funding streams for economic development have stayed outside the RDAs, there remain major difficulties of interdepartmental coordination which the RDAs cannot overcome.

---

4   North, 1990, p. 56; see also our discussion in chapter 3.

Second, the range of power and resources of the RDAs is too restricted. With respect to central government activity, the separation from strong business involvement of the LLSC funding of FE and work-based training generates an important fracture between the major streams of economic development activity, whilst the SBS BL leaves business supports in a further separated agency with particular tensions for how Investors in People (IiP) is developed. With respect to local government activity, the lack of RDA power in transport, SSA funding allocations and environmental policy leaves it as a coordinating body with little power. The RDA is thus given a difficult, and probably impossible task, of acting as a coordinator of agents rather than as a leader. It is in real danger of writing strategies that no one takes account of, other than by genuflection: a 'wallpaper job' in the words of one regional business leader interviewed. This would be similar to Labour's 1960s regional planning bodies.

Third, is the question of flexibility of funding and the balance with central government pragmatic objectives. The powers of virement sought by RDA leaders have so far been highly restricted. Whilst an RDA can draw on multiple funding sources and apply these to a single project, each funding stream still requires separate auditing and accounting, and each reflects different external targets (for central government departments, EU programmes etc.) which frequently constrain the structure of the projects on the ground. This flexibility is further constrained by central government, EU and other funding requirements to meet highly specific and sometimes conflicting objectives. The result is often a 'tick list' approach whereby RDAs and their project managers have to spend much management resource checking off a project on externally defined criteria that are locally of low relevance. The experience of TECs appears to be being reproduced in RDAs, in being over-audited, over-constrained in vertical budget lines, and over-prescribed in terms of multiple external targets.

Fourth, and as a result of these constraints, RDAs have a real danger of becoming just another agent in an already complex scene. Too weak to exert a counter-force to government departments to really join-up policy at the regional level, and swimming in a pool already highly populated by other agents, the RDAs look like just another voice in the pluralist clamour for attention. Their origin, from what we have shown is predominately an exchange process, therefore is also their weakness. They are in many ways the lowest common denominator possible, given the constraints of other central government departmental targets and power, and the reluctance to strengthen regional oversights of central or local government.

(ii)   New Deal

The New Deal has also achieved remarkably strong support from the business community and most other agents, including most voluntary sector bodies that were initially critical of it. Its key strengths have been the high volumes of young people and 25-plus that it has processed with a large number entering jobs. The number entering unsubsidised jobs has exceeded planning targets. The local partnership delivery process has generally worked well and has achieved a high level of employer involvement in both preparedness to recruit New Dealers and actually to recruit them. There has also been effective marshalling of employer leadership through the New Deal Task Force which has been able to interface with government at the highest level. This has allowed particularly strong development of coordination by the Treasury of the employment job centres and the benefit office systems, effectively joining-up three government departments: DfEE, DSS and Treasury.

But despite the undoubted benefits of the New Deal, significant problems remain. Most important has been the failure of the design to cope with the large number of participants who should be in an option but remain on benefits or have 'unknown' destinations. This constitutes over 40 per cent of young people and 17 per cent of 25-plus. New Deal has a very high proportion of participants that are difficult to attach to the labour force, so difficulties were to be expected. However, there is considerable concern at this stage that the programme is working best chiefly for those in least need of support, who quickly find unsubsidised jobs. Those remaining on benefits or 'unknown' show how far joining-up between DSS, DfEE and Treasury approaches has yet to go. Government is clearly aware of this problem and the ONE Service and increased use of sanctions are attempts to develop further integration.

A second difficulty is the need to improve the Gateway process. Too many participants going into both subsidised and unsubsidised jobs have been found by employers to lack the necessary 'work-readiness skills'. This leads to either higher costs as a result of recruitment of New Dealers (through more extensive in-house training, mentoring, etc.) or to an employer refusing the recruit, who then re-enters unemployment, thus undermining the achievement of the target of obtaining sustainable jobs (with 42 per cent of unsubsidised and 19 per cent of subsidised job placements terminated in less than 13 weeks). Although some employers can be criticised for being unwilling to offer long-term commitments, it is clear in the 1999 NDTF report that too many participants are inadequately prepared by the Gateway, by advisers, or by their education and training options.

Improving the Gateway has become a key part of the focus of future development. And it is here that the greatest tensions of local partners and employers with the Employment Service has arisen. New Deal effectively removed many local partners from the counselling and job-matching roles; of seeking to evaluate, pre-train, and link participants to known or expected vacancies. Instead, the ES has taken on these roles in most areas, with the ES also acting as a contract manager of delivery. At the outset its staff had none of the requisite skills, as the ES had never previously performed these roles on a large scale. The key local partners had the skills in TECs, private sector training providers, Chambers of Commerce and a range of industry and voluntary training organisations. The shift in partnership structure and rigidity of contracts in the face of the needs of local partners required to ensure delivery have caused numerous tensions.

Our finding, that New Deal negotiations are best described as a 'conflict' process, demonstrates how government has sought to impose an approach through public sector leadership by the ES. The deficiencies in outcomes, chiefly of those participants still on benefits, unknown or follow- through, shows how far the programme has to go to incorporate not only local partners but the participants it is seeking to serve.

(iii) LLSCs

The development of local Learning and Skills Councils was not an outcome that was negotiated through an exchange process. Our analysis shows that an exchange process would have led to more mergers of TECs and Chambers of Commerce, a stronger focus on employer-led work-based training, greater flexibility of funding, stronger control by the RDA over strategic funding allocation, and an interrelation between LLSC business support and economic development policies instead of removal of these fields from LLSCs altogether. Despite disquiet about TECs, the partners had overall found an accommodation from which they chiefly wanted adjustments not radical reform. The development of LLSCs to replace TECs therefore demonstrates central government's leadership, or ministerial imposition of a political objective, following a state-led corporatist approach for which they have had to work hard to achieve incorporation of other agent's support.

There has been some strong support for the reforms. In many ways the key aspect of LLSCs, which is the combination of the TEC training expenditure with FE funding streams, was presaged by the Skills Task Force.[5] This task

---

5   See Skills Task Force reports, 1998, 1999.

force has a majority of business members and is chaired by Chris Humphrey, the Director General of the BCC and former chief executive of the TEC National Council. In one sense, then, the Skills Task Force should have brought with it the support of some of the main business interests. The reforms also won over FEFC and most local government interests since they saw this as an enhancement of their power through the removal of a more independent business-led TEC system. Labour party activists also saw victory in the removal of the TECs which they had always identified as a Thatcherite initiative which removed accountability from the grass roots and local government.[6]

Despite the clear benefits of combining the FE and work-based funding streams from TECs, however, the development of LLSCs have raised a number of concerns. First, has been concern about the erosion of employer involvement. Although LLSCs have employers as the single largest group (40 per cent) on their executives, they are no longer a majority and their role is not enshrined in the Act, but depends on continued support by the Secretary of State. The mere act of abolishing TECs by ministerial fiat alienated much local employer support. Given the frustrations of business leaders working with TECs, the challenge of working in a minority position within a NDPB structure for LLSCs was seen as too great by many. Hence, there has been considerable erosion of employer membership on the Boards of TECs in their dying phase, with only small continuing membership on LLSCs. A new group of employers has had to become involved, with concerns in some cases about the extent of their ambition and their overall strength of influence.

Second, has been the perceived effect of what is seen by many as the FE takeover of the work-based training route. With many former TEC programmes and most TEC funds routed via the Employment Service to New Deal, the main funding for LLSCs derives from the former FEFC. The FEFC had developed a sophisticated funding model for FE colleges based on student course registrations, participation and outcomes. A complex tariff was associated with each stage of student progress. This system has been transferred to all work-based funding through LLSCs. Whilst having many advantages, it has more difficulty for employer-based than college-based training.

The problems for employer participation and the supply-side emphasis of LLSC membership and funding therefore suggests that as time progress the already fragile commitment of employers to participation in government-funded work-based training will be further eroded. This may not be important if the view is taken that college-based training is more appropriate for young

6   See e.g. *Working Brief*, 106, July 1999.

people, or that if employees want their own specific training then they should pay for it themselves. But the emphasis on the FE supply-side flies in the face of the rather mixed quality of FE found in employer evaluations, the low level of performance of FE in placing unemployed New Dealers into work, and also contradicts the main priorities sought by the Skills Task Force.

Third, the development of LLSCs has removed any government ambition to join-up at the local level the strategy for economic development, business supports and workforce skills. An integrated agenda was the chief mission of TECs, although it was never fully achieved. With the shift to individual departmental bodies of LLSCs and SBS BL, joining-up will now be fashioned either by inter-agent cooperation or by the strategic oversight of RDAs. Because, as we have seen, RDAs do not have sufficient power or responsibility, joining-up policies at the regional level is proving to be highly imperfect. Inter-agent cooperation is being facilitated by the retention of coterminous areas for LLSCs and BL, but the shift to larger units at sub-regional level has created further liaison and coordination problems.

The overall conclusion at this stage of development in that the increased fragmentation of the local level economic development agents between different departments has created confusion, raised administrative and partnership transaction costs and hence reduced the likelihood of inter-agent coordination, and significantly eroded employer motivation and hence involvement. The strong state leadership exerted by government to establish LLSCs, therefore, appears to have had the outcome of reducing the tuning of government policy decisions to economic needs.

(iv)   SBS BL

The development of the SBS and its business support arm of Business Link is rather different from that of LLSCs. Although again evidencing strong government leadership acting through ministerial fiat but seeking in a corporatist way to incorporate other agents within the public policy framework, many elements of the former BL systems have remained in place. In many ways, therefore, the SBS reflects more of a jump in evolution rather than an entirely new system. Nevertheless, the jump in evolution involved was significantly beyond what many of the partners were seeking through a pluralist exchange process. Our analysis shows that an exchange process would have led to a considerable number of mergers of TECs, BL and Chambers of Commerce, a continued emphasis on small geographical areas with many satellite offices, a much wider range of PBA services with continued emphasis on the PBA as the 'core' service of BL, and a lesser emphasis on start-up businesses.

The development of the SBS is most radical in introducing a small business voice into central government policy making and developing a new service for BL to assist SMEs with complying with government regulations. These were not generally issues mooted as major concerns by any of the agents in our expert interviews. Interestingly, however, the regulation issue had been raised by most SME representation bodies, particularly the FSB, FPB, IoD and other commentators, as a major concern for SMEs where enhanced business support could provide considerable help to SMEs.[7] But these suggestions had never been part of the policy negotiations on BL. In the sense we have developed in our analysis, they were not feasible and lay outside of the current decision set. It is a tribute to Labour's shift in governance regime, therefore, that help for SMEs with regulation came onto the agenda. However, because it was not identified as a key issue by the chief agents involved in the negotiations until a very late stage, it did not figure in the main negotiation between agents.

There has been much support for the development of the SBS, including the specifically new initiative of helping SMEs with regulatory compliance and representing the SME view to government. The general principles underlying the policies have gained almost universal acceptance from business bodies and most other interests. The restructuring of BL has also received considerable support. The increase in size of areas is welcome in reducing management costs and allowing a more strategic approach. The broader targeting to include micro-businesses has been generally welcomed, although it is recognised that more pressure is placed on the front end of the service to handle high volumes of enquiries, as a call centre and information enquiry help-line that can sift and reroute enquiries as appropriate. The repackaging of the PBA as a specific service for those clients to whom it is most appropriate had de facto already occurred within most local BLs. But its formal repackaging by DTI has helped local franchisees to better focus their marketing on what is delivered rather than having to play lip-service to an inappropriate DTI target. In general, the refocusing of the SBS BL as an information service first, with specific advice and PBA back-up when required, has allowed BL much better to fill a genuine market gap of imperfect information and has reduced attempts by BL managers to compete with the general market for business advice. Because referral is now the chief design focus of service delivery, outside as

---

7 See e.g. Bannock, 1989 ; IoD, 1996.

well as inside the SBS system, much of the tension over branding has also been removed.

Where there are criticisms of the SBS BL these mainly derive from how the detail of the new service will evolve. One concern is to keep the process of referral as open as possible against pressures from government, the Treasury and the DTI to take on more and more 'services' as initiatives from government. There is a danger that SBS looks like a 'tick list', similar to the role that TECs were forced to play. A second concern has been the separation of IiP activity from the rest of business support. IiP was the most important specific advice service of the former BL system, used by 40 per cent of clients and having one of the highest impact and satisfaction levels.[8] The high use levels were in part the result of the contracting structure of the former BL though TECs, who passed on their DfEE targets for IiP accreditation in their contracts for performance of BL. Hence, IiP was a strongly incentivised activity for BL managers and carried with it a significant level of grant subsidies. The separation of DfEE funding for IiP into LLSCs, with SBS BL still responsible for delivery of much actual IiP advice has left a very awkward future. The government statement on how this is to be resolved is largely impractical and leaves much to be desired:

> The local LSCs will contract with SBS franchisees to provide advice to SMEs on workforce development, including Investors in People (although the LSC will remain accountable for meeting National Learning Targets for Investors in People). Organisations wishing to pursue IiP through supply chains or through their sector may wish to seek advice and support from LSC direct. The DfEE is also ... looking at ways in which NTOs may support sectoral approaches to IiP.[9]

A third set of concerns over SBS BL has been the shift in trajectory it has given to the evolution of the local business support system. Formerly the merger of TECs, Chambers of Commerce and BL was developing a strong momentum. A single business support body had already been established through these mergers in Wigan, and to some extent in Sussex, Milton Keynes and other areas. The SBS is an NDPB with crown servants and a delimited public purpose. It is separate from the TECs, which have been abolished and replaced by LLSCs, with significantly less employer involvement and no remit for business support. The Chambers of Commerce have been left somewhat

---

8   Bennett and Robson, 1999, and DTI Evaluations.
9   DfEE, 1996b, para. 4.23.

in the cold, though many of the large chambers as well as some CCTEs have become the leading partners in local SBS franchises. As with the development of RDAs, New Deal and LLSCs, therefore, the SBS demonstrates Labour's focus on individual government departments with a resulting fragmentation at the local level.

A fourth concern is how far the SBS will actually operate as a strong independent voice. An NDPB staffed by crown servants has tensions over how the business skills and knowledge will be recruited and maintained. A commitment to SME consultation panels, or focus groups, may be able to fulfil some of these needs. But the SBS is not likely ever to develop as a system that is regarded as fully owned and managed in the business interest. It contains a particularly strong ambiguity that it is to help SMEs comply with regulations and yet to offer advice that, if it were most appropriate, might cause an SME to avoid regulations altogether. It is very difficult in practice for a government-financed public body to fulfil its brief of being both 'a strong voice for small businesses at the heart of government' and 'helping small firms on regulation ... working closely with regulators to ensure that regulations are enforced in a way which recognises particular problems of small businesses'.[10] In the case of the parent department of SBS, the DTI, the regulatory function is developed within the DTI at arms length and independently of the sponsorship and business support role of the DTI. The same separation needs to be developed for the SBS. At present the development of the SBS is assumed to have ready-made and painless synergy between regulatory compliance and business support: this is not usually the case.

(v)   Barometer of General Change

The overall pattern of change can be summarised for each of our case studies, as shown in Figure 9.1. This uses four axes to compare Labour's position on each policy initiative. The four axes depict: (i) the balance of interests among the decision makers on the executive of local and regional agents; (ii) the extent of coordination between governmental department programmes; (iii) the extent of flexibility for local partners and executive boards; and (iv) the size of geographical areas covered by the agents concerned. The aim of the figure is to present a 'barometer' measuring Labour's shift in policy stance.

Labour's policies have generally shifted the balance of interests significantly away from business, reduced coordination and increased departmental

---

10 DTI, 1999a, paras. 2 and 7.

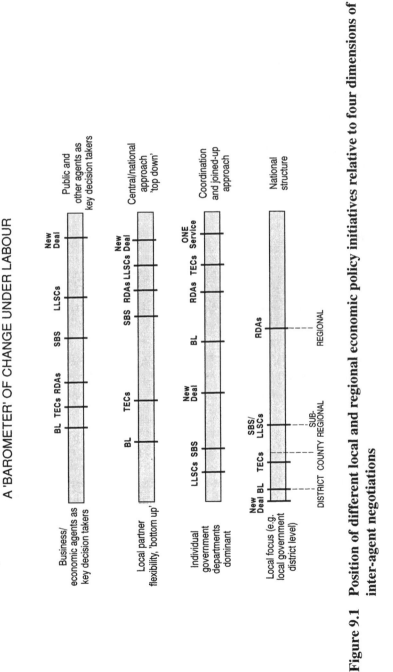

A 'BAROMETER' OF CHANGE UNDER LABOUR

Figure 9.1 Position of different local and regional economic policy initiatives relative to four dimensions of inter-agent negotiations

Note: the positions on each scale are schematic, derived from the discussions in chapters 5 to 8. The position of the New Deal on the third chart shows its current position; the potential position if the ONE Service is fully developed is also indicated.

separation, reduced local partner flexibility within stronger centralised structures, and focused on a mixture of larger sized regional and subregional areas as well as smaller sized Employment Service Districts. The combination of these changes in general shows a relatively systematic pattern. The only counterpoints are the development of RDAs and the possible impact of the ONE Service on New Deal. The RDAs are the only present systematic structure offering the possibility of increased coordination and are an initiative with a business led-board. Much, therefore, rests on RDAs if joined-up government is to be achieved and business interests are to be engaged and involved in local and regional economic development initiatives. However, our assessment suggests that unless RDAs are given much greater flexibility and powers, they will fail to be able to achieve this joining-up.

9.5   Conclusion

This chapter has sought to give an overview of how power relations between agents in the field of local and regional economic development policy have been modified under Labour. Also, mindful of our observations in Chapter 3, that neither pluralist negotiation between agents nor state corporatist leadership necessarily lead to 'optimal' outcomes for the economy (that 'political efficiency is not economic efficiency'), we have also sought to evaluate how far Labour's local and regional economic development policies are likely to contribute to improved economic performance. Evaluation against this criterion is particularly appropriate given Labour's avowed aim that 'what matters is what works'.

Our analysis shows that the Labour agenda has widened the interests involved in policy negotiations, has given greater emphasis to employment over wealth creation as an output of economic development, has sought to improve 'accountability' chiefly through stronger involvement of local government and supplier interests in the executive bodies of local and regional agencies, has shifted towards individual departmental approaches and away from local integrative bodies, and encouraged a more flexible framework of local responses within a strong central control by the Treasury.

The results of these changes have been chiefly a shift of power between government departments. Whilst business interests gained some power, except for New Deal, the changes have been relatively modest. Similarly any losses or gains by other agents have also usually been very small. The overwhelming impression is of changes within government, a reshuffling of the furniture of government departmental responsibilities. A similar conclusion was drawn by the assessment of the government's venture capital policies by the *Financial Times*.[11] Labelling these a 'patchwork of promises and performance', the conclusions drawn are that there is little new money, the new agents of the RDAs are likely to waste resources and be incapable of competing in quality of decision with private sector managers, that the whole initiative is hedged with constraints, and that the overall change is modest.

We have identified two different processes of change that have occurred. For the case of RDAs a negotiated outcome within Labour's manifesto commitments has resulted in an exchange process whereby the policies have been determined. The process has been a largely pluralistic trading off between the different interests involved. Since the major resources and responsibilities involved have been those exercised by central government departments, it is no surprise that it is they that have most fundamentally constrained developments. In the case of New Deal there are some indicators of positive developments for greater coordination, chiefly because of the control exercised by the Treasury to drive coordination between DfEE and DSS into a single unemployment and benefits system, being developed through the single gateway of the ONE Service. In the case of the RDAs, the resistance of the main government departments affected has prevented a coordination between DETR, DfEE and DTI activities and funding streams. This outcome undoubtedly derives from the resistance of the Treasury, prime minister and cabinet to a loss of control to the regional level. The result is similar to that of the 1960s previous Labour initiative to create Regional Economic Planning Councils and Regional Planning Boards, which was again defeated by Treasury resistance. The result is an absence of significant coordinative power at the regional level.

In the case of LLSCs and the SBS a different process of policy development has been evident. Frustrated by two years of inconclusive negotiations between government departments and partners, and after two abortive reviews of TECs, the government decided to abolish TECs and replace them with separate systems of LLSCs for skills and training and SBS BL for local business support. This has demonstrated the capacity for government to act autonomously of major interest groups and impose a solution through ministerial fiat, but it has required a corporatist process of incorporation to be developed to ensure that these interests can be subsequently involved in order to ensure policy delivery.

---

11 *Financial Times*, 'Patchwork of promises and performance', supplement on private equity p. VIII, 17 September 1999.

In the case of LLSCs the evidence suggests that at present the extent of incorporation of employers is too weak and the strength of the supplier interests too strong to yield the major uplift in training-led economic performance sought. In the case of the SBS the government leadership was more sympathetic to what had been learnt on the ground. Thus whilst ruffling the feathers of some interests and leading to some concerns about its organisation, in general the SBS structure for BL offers a significant improvement of how business supports will contribute to economic growth, but its capacity to act as a strong 'voice' for SMEs looks likely to fail.

In the case of New Deal government has given a strong lead following its manifesto and opposition development of policy. But implementaton has demonstrated the major gap that has opened up between public sector provision through ES advisors and the Gateway, and employer needs for work-ready recruits. The state-led approach is now exhibiting severe constraints that have to be overcome by greater pressure on the groups that return to benefits or are 'unknown'. There is a real danger that New Deal is a 'revolving door', or even worse a 'closed door', for many of the participants that are most difficult to attach to the labour market.

Our analysis shows the strengths and weaknesses of both pluralist and state-led corporatist approaches by government to policy negotiations. In one set of cases the outcomes depend on how different agents operate and their relative power positions. In the other set of cases the outcomes depend on the quality of government's leadership and ability to make the best decision possible in the circumstances. The general 'barometer' of change under Labour which is depicted in Figure 9.1 shows inconsistencies, a patchwork of change, but a general shift against executive involvement by economic interests.

The fact that we find the outcomes inconsistent in terms of their political contribution to economic growth is, therefore, not surprising: 'political efficiency is not economic efficiency'. However, against the government's professed criterion of 'what matters is what works' we turn in the next chapter to suggest how the policies in each of our case study areas could be improved.

10 Unblocking Change: A Future Agenda

10.1 Getting Beyond Reshuffling the Furniture

We have found that the main thrust of Labour's reform of local and regional development policy has focused on reshuffling the furniture of central government departmental responsibilities. Or in the words of the *Financial Times*, relatively modest effects with a 'patchwork' of promises and performance. Where changes in the interests of different agents have occurred these have tended to reduce the opportunities for business inputs to help the management of government programmes and to undermine economic objectives, although the extent of change for any non-public sector agent has been relatively small. We are left with the difficult policy question. Assuming government really wants to develop a governance regime that increases endogenous economic growth, how can the blockages to change be removed that have prevented more positive economic progress? It is the same dilemma facing other aspects of Labour's economic policy: how can a government that professes so much concern to decrease regulations and red tape be helped to overcome the blockages that have resulted in Labour increasing regulatory burdens at a faster rate than any government for the last 30 years?

In this chapter we first remind the reader that improving endogenous economic growth is fundamentally about improving the exchange process of information and objectives between the key agents. We then set out the criteria that have to be met for effective exchange processes to occur. Four key elements are then expanded in detail to show how Labour needs to improve the departmental consultation process, develop stronger credibility of commitment, offer stronger leadership and strategic focus to unblock change, and develop policy innovations to fill gaps in the current processes of exchange.

Exchange is the fundamental process by which information flows to government from those agents that are important to the economy. The design of government policies which seek to support economic agents through local and regional economic policy initiatives has to rely on that flow of information.

Our whole thrust of argument focuses on how these information exchanges can be improved and made more valuable to those that design policy.

10.2 The Endogenous Growth Objective

Local and regional economic development is a multi-agent arena. The agents involved are diverse, fragmented, unequal in resources and power, and highly variable in objectives. Yet to achieve successful local and regional economic development requires these agents to operate in concert. Generally the greater that concert, the greater will be the potential for the local economy. It is this concert or cooperation process that we refer to as capacity building.

As we set out in chapter 1, there are five key elements of economic development: human resources and social opportunities; land, infrastructure and site provision; capital formation and investment; innovation, entrepreneurship and technological change; and a supportive institutional context. Each of these elements constitutes a factor of production that must be brought together for each firm, and for all firms, if an economy is to develop. But the supply of these factors is fragmented between many agents: diverse businesses, social and support institutions, and government and its agents. The overall context, as Porter and Kanter recognise, is the way in which factors combine, between supply and demand, related and supporting industries, and the structure of institutions.

Our emphasis in this book is on institutions and public policy: on how the government contributions to economic development can be improved. We have focused on the exchange process that leads to policy issues being framed and their outcomes determined. This policy development process is a key element in economic development. As recognised in the 1998 report of the McKinsey Global Institute, a key factor underlying Britain's low long-term productivity has been deficiencies in regulation and the business-government interface. This interface is also crucial to the development of endogenous growth theory, prominently espoused by Gordon Brown, the Chancellor of the Exchequer. As we set out in chapter 1, endogenous growth is not solely the result of technological drivers of change. It is also strongly influenced by how government sets the structure of institutions and property rights, how it influences the climate of priorities, and how far it encourages supportive services such as educational and training programmes.

The central government approach to endogenous growth sets the scene for how its ministers, departments and agencies operate, and how other public and private agents respond at the regional and local level. The counterpart of Kanter's thinkers, makers and traders in endogenous growth are those agents and individuals who focus and improve the networks of exchange that lead change and 'glue' it together at the local and regional level. The field of economic development policy, because it is dominated by a complex multi-agent environment, demonstrates better than any other the way in which endogenous growth depends on what Kanter calls the 'skills for collaborative advantage'.

10.3   The Criteria to be Met

Our focus on endogenous growth as fundamentally an exchange process leads us to establish a set of key criteria required if improvements are to result from policy changes. There are eight key aspects. These may at first seem rather abstract. We demonstrate their relevance to unblocking change.

First, an exchange process must exist. Agents with different information must be able to give voice to those that need that information. Crucial is that the policy designers in government departments, and ministers that must make final decisions, are open to exchange.

Second, agents must be prepared to give voice. This requires a predisposition on both sides not only to voice, but to listen. For a channel of communication to be open, both ends have to operate. This is a challenge for some agents to resource and organise themselves to improve their presentation of information to government. It is also a challenge for government to be more receptive.

Third, exchange must be proactive and prescriptive, not just responsive. This is a particular challenge for government. Exchange is much less effective if a policy is announced and then only the detail can be negotiated and improved, as occurred with LLSCs and SBS, and also characterises many annual Budget announcements. To be effective the objectives and design of the policy also needed to be open to exchange to ensure that they are appropriately specified.

Fourth, exchange must also contain commitment: that if government responds to the concerns of a given agent, that agent will then act; conversely if government asks for involvement from an agent, it must be committed to backing that agent if its views are valid. It is this area where many tensions have emerged between government and both individual businesses and business bodies.

Fifth, not only must there be commitment, it must be credible. Credibility is based on a level of trust and experience of past performance. But, as emphasised in management economics, commitment is most credible when it is demonstrated that the resources devoted to a given initiative are sufficient and sustained, and it is impossible or very expensive not to go ahead. We have emphasised throughout our case studies the crucial importance of 'winning hearts and minds' if local and regional economic development initiatives are to be successful. This is not possible if government's commitment is seen as weak, short term, internally ridden with contradictions, purely self-serving or unsustainable. The contradictions between claiming joined-up approach and continually fragmenting the economic development scene are particularly damaging to Labour's credibility of commitment.

Sixth, the focus of whom and where to exchange information must be clear. For government this is particularly a challenge since many departments and agencies are involved. For a credible commitment to exist, there has to be a focus of exchange. That focus has to be clear and it has to be able to marshal information, respond and offer commitment.

Seventh, the exchange process has to have leadership. There has to be intelligence and strategy among the key agents that must respond. For government this means that although the exchange process must be open in order to maximize information, a shifting and weighting of information must be applied. But for this sifting to occur, whilst maintaining credible commitment, it must demonstrate rationality and strategic capacity. It must be particularly free from detailed political interference. This is, of course, a virtually impossible challenge for government, but it is what is required if a commitment to 'what matters is what works' is to be delivered. For supporting endogenous economic growth this means that a greater weight to business and economic information must normally be given than to other sources. We have seen clearly in our case studies the strong influence exerted by public sector bodies, and central government departments in particular, as a result of their large number, high salience and high power on most issues. They are the 'insiders' to the policy process and some means to be found of keeping their interests in check, in order to be properly balanced with those of economic concerns who are always the 'outsiders' to the policy process. We have demonstrated in our case studies the ability of government to lead, as in the case of New Deal, LLSCs and SBS. But if it leads it must do so in the right direction by carefully weighting the information it receives. But even if this can be achieved, because of the many different sources of economic information received, strategic leadership by government is needed because of the unequal power and resources of the different economic agents involved. The challenge of delivering strategic leadership is perhaps the greatest of all the criteria outlined here, and is where Labour appears to have shifted against economic growth as measured by our 'barometer' of change.

Eighth, there must be an alertness to gaps or holes in information where no agent exists so that no effective flow of information and exchange can occur. And alertness to gaps must be complemented by efforts to fill them. These gaps may relate to a clearly recognisable field; for example some business sectors are very poorly represented by business organisations. Or gaps may relate to an absence of a viewpoint or expertise; for example the improvement of participation in economic initiatives by education institutions, trade unions and professional associations is often blocked by their lack of existing expertise, or the mere voicing of change is prevented by the pressures from existing interests to maintain the status quo.

These eight criteria can be collapsed into four key objectives: assuring information exchange, developing credible commitment, offering leadership and strategic focus, and filling gaps. We show how these objectives can be met in the next section.

10.4 Meeting Economic Growth Objectives through Improved Exchange

We have demonstrated in chapter 9 the gaps emerging in the structure of Labour's local and regional economic development policies. The key difficulties are:

- a wider process of consultation has generated difficulties of weighing the information received. The development of more pluralist concertation has exposed a gap in strategic leadership;
- a stronger emphasis on social inclusion has often raised unrealistic expectations, in some cases it has become a 'tick list' of targets, and has distracted some agents from their primary purpose of supporting economic growth;
- local accountability has been too normally interpreted as focusing on local government and supplier interests;
- broadening of the involvement of other interests in the boards of local and regional economic development agents has downgraded the role of economic interests;
- the decisions so far on most local and regional economic development policy issues has generally eroded the business role compared to central

government and other agents, as shown by our 'barometer' of change in Figure 9.2;

- individual government departmental initiatives have multiplied, with increased complexity on the ground resulting in a significantly increased fragmentation and greater burdens of participation, exchange and coordination among all agents;
- structural changes, particularly the replacement of TECs by LLSCs and SBS have reinforced fragmented and independent departmental agendas;
- the coordination sought to join-up initiatives largely relies on the RDAs, but these are too weak in power and resources to perform the role required.

These difficulties in Labour's policies derive from various deficiencies or confusions in approach that undermine the criteria outlined in the previous pages. We discuss below how improvements can be achieved by increasing information exchange, improving the credibility of commitment, offering stronger leadership and focus, and filling gaps.

(i)   Improved Information Exchange

This is one of the easier objectives to satisfy. Labour is already committed to a more open and consultative government process, so that no change of principle or political commitment is required.

Our case studies have demonstrated how a relatively open exchange process between the agents involved has led to a broad consensus in the development of RDAs. This demonstrates, that although the initiative was launched by government with a clear leadership intent based on concepts developed in opposition, nevertheless openness of consultation and exchange on detail significantly improved the fit of RDAs to agent needs which then contributed to winning commitment. In both cases leadership, plus open exchange, has opened the way to implementing an improved set of policies.

In contrast, New Deal, LLSCs and SBS were launched in haste, respectively by DfEE and Treasury, with very little consultation. Subsequently more open exchanges have occurred. In the case of the SBS BL this has led to significant improvements, closely associated with its transfer of leadership from Treasury to DTI, which has allowed closer tailoring of the initiative to real market gaps and removing some of the earlier concepts of a payroll and Inland Revenue regulatory compliance services. In the case of LLSCs, however, DfEE have been much more impervious to information exchange, probably either as a result of the influence of education interests within the department, or as a result of an ideological commitment to downplay business involvement. Whatever the reason, the LLSCs remain an initiative somewhat isolated from the business interests they are attempting to serve through the supply of skilled people. For New Deal considerable practical success has been achieved, but there remain formidable challenges to developing the work-readiness of the participants who are the most difficult to attach to the workforce. The key elements of redesign required lie with improving Employment Service skills of advice and managing local contracts, particularly for the Gateway stage of New Deal.

The greatest problems for government often focus around the timing and content of exchanges with other agents. Most important is an opening up of the policy design process at an early stage. Once a policy is announced it is far more difficult for ministers to modify their positions or back down. Also a policy announcement automatically engenders the setting up of a departmental group that works on designing the policy implementation which will usually be unable to change significantly the targets and objectives. The government machine once started is usually difficult to deflect and improve.

Interrelated with an earlier opening of governmental policy discussions to outsiders is improving the quality of the receptors and users of information. The skills of many in government departments are not well tuned to economic needs, yet it is these civil servants who have to design policy, understand the strengths and weaknesses of different approaches, weigh the different representations and information they received, and make judgements on many aspects of the final drafting required. Labour has recognised the need to develop a broader range of staff skills within government departments and has begun setting up a new training process to achieve this. But much still needs to be done. Perhaps most crucial is the need to recognise that a stronger alignment of civil service processes to the external market of skills available would allow a more ready recruitment and interchange with businesses and other agents. Too often, in the field of local and regional economic development, as in other fields, it is recognised that 'public sector skills' need specially to be developed in order for external agents to perform properly. Why should external agents have to expend time and resources adjusting to a system with inferior capacity to understand and act on the information exchanges offered? The gap seems to be one that could be best filled if the skills of public sector personnel were better aligned with the general market of external skills.

Improved information exchange also relies on agent commitment and activities external to government. Government departments can do a lot to help facilitate their development through opening opportunities, identifying gaps and helping to fill them. For example, greater support and recognition could be given to sector and area-based business associations such as trade associations, professional associations and chambers of commerce. Greater openness to small businesses is needed, which SBS may be able to achieve. There is a challenge for developing supports that help these bodies to operate in a way that helps government. They will not do this entirely independently, chiefly because of their well evidenced lack of resources to do so.[1] Government support is the only escape from the 'low services-low capacity equilibrium' offered by many business associations.[2] For government to get better inputs, therefore, it will have to find a way to pay for them.

(ii)   Developing Credible Commitment

Credible commitment requires various conditions to be met. First, the pledge of support must be sustained for the lifetime of the exchanges sought. For economic development policy the lifetimes required for policies are often very long. A piece of physical infrastructure or a planning decision will influence decades of subsequent development; changes in education policy will take 10–15 years to see their first outcomes as that age cohort leaves from their schools or colleges. This means that government must undertake to ensure a level of stability of its own activities. The commitment by the DfEE not to review the national curriculum again for several years, for example, is the sort of statement that could be developed in other areas. The granting of budget commitments to departments by the Treasury for three years as a result of the Comprehensive Spending Review is also a positive development, although it also appears to have been undermined by the form of the Budget process in March and July 2000.

A second element of credible commitment is that the resources offered for a given initiative must be sustained. The early phases of the development of Business Link for example, were undermined by the launch concept of DTI support as being chiefly for pump-priming not for supporting long-term recurrent costs. Similarly, the early stages of the RDA launch as an explicitly evolutionary process has offered encouragement to some agents to continue to lobby for change in a wide variety of conflicting directions. It would have been preferable to have given a firm commitment to no change for a period of years.

---

1   See Bennett, 1998a, 1998b.
2   Bennett, 1998b.

Third, resources must be sufficient. The agenda of TECs was continually undermined by totally inadequate resources to meet their stated mission for economic development and business support objectives. Their mission set by government was not capable of being fully delivered. The credibility of the TECs was undermined and the commitment of government was judged flimsy. Similarly, the breadth of the agenda for RDAs is far beyond their current resources and responsibilities. This undermines the credibility of all their guidance statements to the other agents on the scene. Agents either pay lip-service to RDA strategies that are impossible to achieve, or they ignore them altogether. There is growing evidence that RDAs, like TECs, are not sufficiently credible with businesses so that most just ignore their activity. The confusion of messages would be clarified by focusing on what RDAs really can do – they can help allocate and structure the framework of some government regeneration expenditures within their region. They are not all-purpose economic development bodies.

Fourth, statements of support for any agent must be backed up by real support. The development of LLSCs, for example, is recognised explicitly as needing a strong employer input, yet the DfEE would only initially give a commitment to businesses being the single largest group of representatives on the board of LLSCs. Only later this was modified to 40 per cent of the members and this may be fragile. Again for New Deal, the boisterous launch claimed that the ready supply of New Deal participants would help employers solve their recruitment problems. This has not been backed up by sufficient attention to adviser or Gateway focuses to ensure the work-readiness of participants, with the consequence that government claims have become non-credible. Similarly for RDAs, the DETR spin has been that these are business-led, yet the power of these boards is meagre and the business majority on RDA boards is only just achieved in most regions (only by counting as business agents such bodies as universities, development bodies and retired business directors). Credibility is achieved where claims match reality. The commitment of the hearts and minds of partner agents will not be won by government spin or deception.

(iii)   Improved Leadership and Strategic Focus

This is the area where perhaps greatest difficulties beset any government, but where information exchange is most vital. We have demonstrated in our case studies the ability of government to lead through ministerial fiat, particularly in the cases of LLSCs and SBS. But leadership can only work if it is based on accurate and appropriate information. The continuing tensions in LLSCs suggest many deficiencies in how the information was obtained to launch this initiative. The much improved structure of SBS over BL reflects the converse, how government strategic leadership can break out of logjams and 'turf wars' that are created by being totally influenced by the interests and information exchange received from the key agents.

A major problem for developing leadership in the field of local and regional economic development policy is the number of agents and issues involved which span so many government departments. As we set out in chapter 2, there are three main departments involved (DETR, DTI and DfEE) as well many other departments affected. The overall structural diagram, shown in Figure 2.1, is complex. It is easy to criticise this structure and argue that all elements should be integrated in a single central department, or should flow through an integrated structure at regional or local level. However, a full integration will never be realistic. This would involve the coordination of the total impact of government on the economy: getting the government's mainstream services right in terms economic responsiveness. This task is not possible by coordination alone, except in a command-and-control structure that would be too sluggish and costly to be effective.

Nevertheless, the leadership focus in the case of any specific policy should be clearer. And different policies should pull in the same direction with sufficient flexibility to allow coordination on the ground, or at the project level. It is in these areas where Labour has sent some highly confused messages, generally increasing fragmentation whilst professing to increase joining-up.

The leadership of the main initiatives we have examined has been highly confused for the cases of the RDAs, LLSCs and SBS BL. The RDAs, whilst certainly led from the DETR, have involved attempts by DETR or its ministers to lead in other fields. The DfEE and DTI have been resistant to change and loss of power to RDAs and have offered alternative leadership. Rather than strategic vision and leadership, the outcome has been demonstrable departmental rivalry with uncertainty for economic agents as to who is in the lead.

This conflictual experience has extended to how intelligence and strategy is applied by government. Different departments have put different emphasis on the information they have received. In simple terms the DETR and DfEE has generally been less receptive to developing the economic relevance of their initiatives, tending to rely heavily on 'supplier' advice – from planning and local government in the case of DETR, and from educational specialists in the case of DfEE. Somewhat in contrast has been the DTI which has been closer to business concerns on issues such as RDAs, although with problems of its own in unravelling an overly prescriptive and somewhat perverse architecture of the earlier structure of Business Link. Both conflict between departments, and differences in emphasis, need to be removed.

If it is difficult to coordinate at the centre of government, then the coordination has to be achieved elsewhere. Whilst the regional level offers some opportunities, the key coordination has to occur on the ground, initiative by initiative, project by project. Local agents can cope with diverse funding streams and different departmental priorities (provided that they are not in total conflict with each other), provided there is the flexibility in the targets and budgetary control of programmes to allow projects to be adapted properly to fit local needs. This bottom-up integration offers an effective alternative to central coordination. It is in this area where Labour has done least to reform the departmental resource allocation systems to expand the flexibility possible on the ground and has instead increased fragmented and centrally directed initiatives.

The chief problems, which are the same as those suffered under previous governments, in most explicit form by the TECs which were the main agents that previously sought to join-up central initiatives until they were abolished, are:

- multiple, centrally-defined, detailed and independently defined performance criteria for each programme, usually in excess of the breadth of policy leverage available;
- performance criteria that include many areas over which the policy initiative has little or no influence e.g. increasing the profits, employment or turnover of SMEs helped by BL; increasing the GNP of the region through RDA activity;
- over-burdensome and multiple audits for each separate funding stream, even when funding comes through the same department;
- conflicting performance targets and audit processes for similar initiatives from different departments, with rigid restrictions on whether or not funding streams can be combined;
- inflexibility of virement between specific programme funds, and insufficient general budget, to allow a focus on local definitions of needs and priorities.

A key reform by Labour has been the Comprehensive Spending Review which, as well as making a positive contribution of offering three year budget commitments to departments, has required each department to produce public service agreements as performance targets. This has had some positive benefits, but it has also had the negative consequence of giving further support to multiple centrally-defined targets often outside of the responsibility of the department involved: for the DTI, for example, to increase national GNP. Ironically, the Treasury's emphasis on stimulating endogenous growth has not been matched by recognition that endogenous change comes from supporting the flexibility of endogenous agents to respond from the bottom-up, not from meeting targets set at the top-down.

(iv)   Filling Gaps

Gap-filling and strategic leadership are strongly interconnected. Effective leaders understand when the information signals they receive are pulling too much in one direction. The overwhelming weight we have found in our case studies for the influence of public sector voices, especially central departments, is completely out of line with their importance to the economy. It is also a negative counterweight limiting the economic and businesses information that is brought to bear on government economic policies. Our simulation of alternative scenarios shows distance from current structures that would develop if greater weight were given to business points of view. Strategic leadership by Labour needs to recognise these gaps in information, or how it is used, and fill them.

Our analysis shows the key gap is the insufficient weight given to business and economic interests in final decisions. This is partly because business interests are poorly resourced, fragmented and sometimes conflicting, particularly between sectors, and between SME and larger or dominant firms. But it is chiefly because insufficient weight is given by government to the economic point of view when decisions are made. Thus, whilst there may be some gaps in the strength of business interest representation in some sectors, location or fields, the primary problem is a failure by government departments administers to use and weigh information strategically.

One way to improve how information is weighted is to construct a new voice as advocate. Mark Casson has referred to this also as developing specialist intermediaries[3] that marshal and handle information, acting as a 'trader' to introduce agents to each other, or to transfer information between them. This approach has been evaluated by the DTI as a framework for restructuring its sector sponsorship division.

The development of the SBS as 'a voice for SMEs at the heart of

---

3   Casson, 1997; see also Ebers, 1997.

government' can also be interpreted as an attempt to overcome gaps in information by setting up an intermediary body. But to achieve these objectives, the intermediary must be independent, trusted, business-owned and managed, and it must have access to all key policy developments before they are launched as well as advising on regulation and policy once a government commitment to them has been made. There are clear tensions in the design of both SBS and the DTI's sponsorship divisions that will make achieving all of these goals difficult.

Even if the SBS and DTI sponsorship divisions prove to be successful, it leaves open the question of how business interests outside of the 'inner circle' of those closely consulted exchange information. SMEs and the DTI sectors are only one group of business concerns, even though they are very diverse. Large firms, other sectors and local economic issues are also important. At present there are gaps in how some groups of businesses can access and exchange information with government:

- the sectoral aspects that are developed through DTI sponsorship divisions in conjunction with trade associations, are relatively low key exchanges and do not fully spillover from DTI to influence other government departments, policies and regulatory regimes. They are particularly isolated from DfEE and DETR. Also many professional association sectors are not well represented. Many other government departments also deal with sectoral issues as well as the DTI, which results in a highly fragmented and varied approach between one sector and another;
- a general force for business inputs has been present through the Better Regulation Task Force. Some elements of this have moved into the SBS. But the more general concerns developed by the Task Force remain its responsibility. Whilst the Task Force has enjoyed considerable influence, its effectiveness in limiting regulations has been marginal and its continued influence primarily depends on the personal relation between its chair (Chris Haskins) and the prime minister. This is a benefit built on personality rather than formal standing. A better position would be an established agency like the SBS, or a body with standing responsibility, that could act as an intermediary for information exchange with business on a longer term, more formalised and a wider scale;
- the local level is still a mess. Whilst the business support aspect of the SBS franchising has involved many of the larger and Approved Chambers of Commerce, this has not solved the problem of information flows and business representation at a local level. If anything it has confused matters

by creating a public agency to represent business views in competition with chambers. LLSCs fragment the training mission from the broader agenda. Local government has still to develop many of the strategic economic roles needed.[4] And the RDAs are too weak to provide the coordination required.

10.5 Specific Developments Needed

We have assessed above some of the key general developments needed to improve exchanges so that endogenous growth can be improved. We summarize here the main specific developments needed.

1 Continued openness and consultation *before* as well as after the announcement of policy initiatives.

2 Recognising defects in structures to strengthen the economic view: Increase further the proportion of business members on LLSCs, strengthen their quality on RDAs, embed the Better Regulation Task Force, maintain the strength of business leadership on the New Deal Task Force and improve it in local New Deal partnerships, and give all of these bodies greater financial flexibility.

3 Improve civil service private sector skills, align civil service training more closely with the general market for skills, radically reduce the need for specialist 'public sector' skills that are low in tradeability and isolate government from the economy.

4 Develop credible commitment. Match rhetoric to reality in resourcing. Align objectives, guidance and targets with the resources available. Offer sustained commitment. Focus on the public purpose of government initiatives, and leave the rest to the economic agents. Do not attempt to claim indirect effects of government on increasing GNP when the contributions cannot be measured and chiefly depend on business not government. Adjust the framework and targets of the Treasury's public service agreements for departments to focus on managerial effectiveness not immeasurable impacts.

---

4 Audit Commission, 1999.

5 Improve the opportunities for specialist exchange of economic information and give it greater weight. Ensure that consultations on design of policy involve a strong presence of economic and other interests, not merely departmental representatives. Be led by 'what really matters' outside of Whitehall in the economy and society. Key elements of this are the development of improved information gateways through enhanced intermediaries.

   • Develop further the DTI's sectoral sponsorship model. Give it greater independence, higher profile staff and status, greater private sector leadership, and stronger access to senior level government policy making.
   • Develop sponsorship into a standing brief independent of ministerial initiatives.
   • Apply the sponsorship model across *all* departments.
   • Resource, staff and support the SBS as a strong independent intermediary.
   • Give all of these intermediaries full access, across government, to the policy development stage as well as consulting on implementation.
   • Ensure that intermediaries use the input and resources of private and voluntary bodies, not compete with them. Trade and professional associations, chambers of commerce and other SME bodies should be built strongly into the networks of information exchange of sponsorship divisions and the SBS. This requires urgent simplification of the role of SBS: *not* to 'represent SME interests at the heart of government', but to ensure that the most accurate information on SME issues is provided at the heart of government and that it is fully weighed.
   • Help external intermediaries develop their role for government by overcoming their 'low services-low capacity equilibrium'. This needs greater governmental financial support as well as recognition and openness to their inputs.

6 Realign the needs of 'accountability' with the stronger economic representation.

   • A thrust of responsibility back to the local level reinforces the key element of accountability in the field of local economic development to local government.
   • Accepting that the scope for RDA activity will remain limited reduces the need to consider extensive or expensive representation at this level, reducing the need for directly elected regional assemblies and

strengthening the local government level of responsibility at the expense of regional Chambers.

7   Provide more flexibility in funding streams to allow greater flexibility on the ground, at the level of the individual initiative or project. Encourage the agents at the grass roots to identify and respond, not command or constrain what they can do:
   • reduce centrally-defined detailed performance criteria and targets; replace them by broader strategic goals.
   • align audit and monitoring paper trails into a single stream across all funders so that any agent or initiative has only one set of reports to prepare.
   • replace central auditing by local performance appraisal and project assessment: to assess whether strategic objectives been achieved within reasonable value for money criteria.
   • where direct client benefits can be assessed, focus on measurable aspects of customer appraisal rather than immeasurable economic impacts.
   • allow virement between departmental programmatic funding, subject only to satisfying the strategic goals set in each case.

8   Recognise RDAs for what they are and align the 'spin' accordingly. They have the capacity to offer business leadership and partnership working at the regional level that can give a broad context and can shape strategic priorities at the local level. This can be an important supplement to the suggested framework of broad strategic goals of departments and the increased flexibility of local agents. But their scope for specific action should not be exaggerated. Also clarify the issue of 'accountability' at regional level: recognise that the modest role of RDAs does not need a complex architecture of elected assemblies, streamline existing regional Chambers.

9   Clarify the trails of responsibility at regional level by abolishing the functions of Government Regional Offices and transfer their responsibilities either back to Whitehall or to local agents. Within broader governmental performance targets and increased local flexibility the supervisory roles of government office staff disappear – they are part of a command-and-control architecture that is no longer necessary. Rely on the strength of the local agents to respond to endogenous requirements, remove all the residual architecture that seeks to 'direct' change.

10.6 Conclusion

The agenda we have outlined is a major challenge for any government. It focuses on giving endogenous agents the freedom to act: *placing responsibility in the hands of those that are closest to the problem*, backing them with resources and support to help them develop, offering guidance and leadership in terms of strategic goals, but accepting that the best outcomes will derive from variable local practice and flexibility case-by-case, initiative-by-initiative, project-by-project. This is the key requirement if support for endogenous growth objectives is to be effective. The challenge is – will the Treasury and central government departments be able to adjust to such an operating environment, where expertise and responsibility is transferred to the bottom, and removed from the top. Our assessments have shown Labour so far to have achieved chiefly a shuffling of the furniture between central departmental responsibilities. What we propose is a more fundamental change requiring greater strategic leadership from government and stronger weighting of economic interests against the pressures of the lowest common denominator of an unweighted pluralistic process.

Our second key challenge is the greatest one in terms of a real shift to an improved government response: to fill gaps in information exchange by *developing new information gateways* through an enhanced structure of intermediaries. This focuses on developing the SBS model to the full, letting it have its head of freedom, encouraging its strong linkage directly with business and with business associations not competing with them. We have also suggested developing the model as an enhanced sector sponsorship structure for *all* central departments, putting this on a standing footing, and allowing each element to develop further the inputs of the Better Regulation Task Force at an early stage in the policy process, not just being consulted on implementation. This is a major challenge to Labour since it means giving economic interests a much stronger and more appropriate weight. Without stronger weight for business needs the future offers continual erosion appropriateness of economic policies, as indicated in our analysis by the pattern of utility losses and our 'barometer' of changes under Labour shown in Figure 9.1. Without such changes the so-called endogenous growth policies for local and regional economic development followed by Labour are likely, on balance, to continue to be chiefly about shuffling the furniture and are likely over time to make matters worse rather than better.

APPENDIX

Definition of Policy Issues

The following tables present the information used in the simulation models developed in Chapters 5-8. The issues, policy positions, salience and power ratings are all derived from the structured interview process with experts and agents.

List of Appendix Tables

Table A1   RDA policy issues

Issue A.1: DTI versus RDA with respect to Regional Selective Assistance (RSA)

The DTI continues to assess all bids, with interdepartmental input via GOR   0

The RDA assesses all bids and recommends level of support, which is then referred to the DTI, to adjudicate between regions (concordat)   10

(low maximum) The RDA assesses all bids and allocates RSA funds up to a maximum of £200,000 independently of DTI

(high maximum) The RDA assesses all bids and allocates RSA funds up to a maximum of £5m independently of DTI   60

The RDA assesses all bids for its region and allocates support completely independently of the DTI (with RSA funds allocated by formula to regions) 100

Issue A.2: DETR's responsibility and RDA with respect to SRB

The DETR continues to allocate SRB funding separately, as a national bidding process with regional coordination and advice from the GOR   0

As above, but with coordination and advice from the GOR and RDA   10

The GOR receives all of the SRB funding, which it allocates according
to its own procedures and advice from the RDA   30

The RDA receives all of the SRB funding, which it allocates according to
advice from the GOR.   60

The RDA receives all SRB funding, which it allocates according to its own
criteria, with freedom to vire within programmes   80

The RDA receives all of the SRB funding, which it is free to vire between
programmes   100

Issue A.3: RDA versus English Partnerships

English Partnerships retain all former powers   0

English Partnerships retain all former powers but must take account of the
RDA strategy   10

The RDA receives all former powers of the English Partnerships, but there
is also a national advisory body established for English Partnerships   80

RDA receives all former powers of English Partnerships   100

Issue A.4 RDA versus Rural Development Commission (RDC)

The Rural Development Commission retains all former powers   0

The Rural Development Commission retains all former powers but must take
account of the RDA strategy   10

The RDA receives all former powers of the RDC but there is also a national
advisory body established for the RDC   80

RDA receives all former powers of the Rural Development Commission   100

Issue A.5: RDA versus Commission for New Towns (CNT)

The Commission for New Towns retains all former powers   0

The Commission for New Towns retains all former powers but must take
account of the RDA strategy   10

The RDA receives all former powers of the CNT, but there is also a national
advisory body established for the CNT   80

RDA receives all former powers of the Commission for New Towns   100

Issue A.6: Board composition: private led or public led?

The Board has 100% private sector employers and representatives	100
The Board has at least 66% private sector employers and representatives	80
The Board has at least 51% private sector employers and representatives	70
The Board has at least 50% private sector employers and representatives	50
The Board has not more than 40% private sector employers and representatives	20
The Board has not more than 33% private sector employers and representatives	10
The Board has not more than 10% private sector employers and representatives	0

Issue A.7: Chamber composition: private led or public led?

The Regional Chamber has 90% local authority representatives	100
The Regional Chamber has 80% local authority representatives	80
The Regional Chamber has 70% local authority representatives	70
The Regional Chamber has 60% local authority representatives	60
The Regional Chamber has 50% local authority representatives	50
The Regional Chamber has 40% local authority representatives	20
The Regional Chamber is comprised of 30% local authority representatives	0

Issue A.8: Accountability of the RDA Board to Regional Chamber

The RDA Board is an implementation authority largely working with programmes and targets set by central departments, GOR and the Chamber	0
The RDA Board is an implementation authority largely working with programmes and targets set by GOR and the Chamber	30
The RDA Board is an implementation authority largely working with programmes and targets set by the Chamber	35
The RDA is an executive body, working within the strategy set by the Chamber, but with executive autonomy only for projects of less than £200,000	50

The RDA is an executive body, working within the strategy set by the Chamber, but with autonomy for all projects below £5 million	60
The RDA is an executive body, working mainly within the broad strategy set by the Chamber, but makes its decisions independently	80
The RDA is an executive body accountable only to minister(s) and Parliament	100

Issue B.1: TECs, LLSCs versus RDA with respect to training policy

The DfEE allocates funding separately, with interdepartmental coordination via GOR	0
The DfEE allocates funding via GOR to LLSCs, taking account of the relevant RDA strategy	10
The DfEE allocates funding via GOR to LLSCs, but taking account of the RDA strategy (e.g. skills agenda), which is monitored by the RDA	20
The DfEE allocates funding via GOR to TEC, but takes account of the RDA strategy for that region. The RDA also has responsibility for a Development Fund	30
RDA has full executive responsibility for funding allocations (e.g. allocation to LLSCs in region) with ability to vire within TEC budgets	55
As above but with ability to vire with other funds in the RDA budget	75
RDA has full responsibility for training and LLSC training responsibility is abolished	100

Issue B.2: TECs /LLSCs versus RDA with respect to LED policy

The DfEE continues to allocate funding separately, with interdepartmental coordination via GOR	0
The DfEE allocates funding via GOR to LLSCs, taking into account the relevant RDA strategy for that region	10
The DfEE allocates funding via GOR to LLSCs, but takes into account the RDA strategy for LED, which is monitored by the RDA	20
The DfEE allocates funding via GOR to LLSCs, but takes into account the RDA strategy for LED. The RDA also has responsibility for a Development Fund	30
RDA has full executive responsibility for funding allocations (e.g. allocation to LLSCs) with ability to vire within LLSC budgets	50

As above, but with ability to vire across policy programmes	75
RDA has full responsibility for LED policy, and LLSC responsibility for LED is abolished	100

Issue B.3: TECs/LLSCs versus RDA with respect to enterprise policy, including Business Links

The DTI and DFEE continue to allocate funding separately via LLSCs to Business Links	0
With interdepartmental coordination via GOR	
As above, but taking into account the relevant RDA strategy	10
As above, but take into account the RDA strategy, which is monitored by the RDA	20
As above, but in addition, the RDA would have responsibility for a Development Fund	30
RDA has full executive responsibility for funding allocations (e.g. allocation to Business Links in the region) with ability to vire within enterprise policy block	50
RDA has full executive responsibility for funding allocations (e.g. allocation to Business Links in the region) including ability to vire across policy programmes	75
RDA has full responsibility for enterprise policy, with its own local structure	100

Issue B.4: RDA versus local authorities with respect to transport policy

The local authority remains the chief agent for local transport policy decisions	0
As above, but local authority must take account of the relevant RDA strategy for the region, with decisions monitored by the RDA	20
The RDA is the chief agent for transport policy decisions, but is mandated to take account of the relevant local authority strategies	80
The RDA has independent power with regard to making transport policy decisions for a defined range of economic development purposes (as UDC model)	100

Issue B.5: RDA versus local authorities with respect to planning policy

The local authority remains the chief agent for physical planning decisions   0

As above, but the local authority must take account of the relevant RDA
strategy for the region, with decisions monitored by the RDA   10

The RDA is the chief agent for physical planning decisions, but must take
account of the relevant local authority strategies   80

The RDA has independent planning powers for a defined range of economic
development purposes   100

Issue C.1: DfEE versus RDA with respect to HE

The DfEE continues to allocate funding via HEFCE etc.   0

The DfEE allocates funding to HEFCE which takes account of RDA
strategy   10

The DfEE allocates funding to HEFCE which must take account of RDA
strategy for that region, which is monitored by the RDA   20

As above, but the RDA has responsibility for a Development Fund   30

RDA has full executive responsibility for HEFCE funding including ability
to vire within policy programmes   80

As above, but with RDA ability to vire between policy programmes   100

Issue C.2: DfEE versus RDA with respect to FE

The DfEE continues to allocate funding via FEFC   0

The DfEE allocates funding to FEFC which takes account of RDA strategy   10

The DfEE allocates funding to FEFC, which must take account RDA
strategy for that region, which is monitored by the RDA   20

As above, but with RDA has responsibility for a FE Development Fund   30

RDA has full executive responsibility for FEFC funding, including ability
to vire within policy programmes   80

As above, but with RDA ability to view between policy programmes   100

Issue C.3 DETR versus RDA with respect to Standard Spending Assessment (SSA)

DETR allocates money to the local authorities using England-wide
SSA formula   0

DETR allocates money to local authorities using England-wide SSA formula
with additional factors to take account of RDA priorities   10

RDA receives a block grant from DETR, which the RDA allocates to local
authorities, according to its own SSA formula   60

As above, but RDA is free to vire between programmes   100

Issue C.4: RDA versus local authorities with respect to use of compulsory purchase power

The local authority remains the chief agent with respect to use of compulsory
purchase power   0

As above, but local authorities must take account of the RDA strategy for the
region, with decisions monitored by the RDA   10

The RDA is the chief agent with respect to use of compulsory purchase
power for a narrow range of economic development purposes, but must
take account of the relevant local authority strategies   50

As above, but RDA has a compulsory purchase power for a relatively
wide range of economic development purposes   80

The RDA has independent use of compulsory purchase power for a defined
range of economic development purposes (as UDC model)   100

Issue C. 5: RDA versus local authorities with respect to environment and sustainability policy

The local authority remains the chief agent for environment and
sustainability policy   0

As above, but local authority must take account of RDA strategy, with
decisions monitored by the RDA   10

The RDA is the chief agent for environment and sustainability policy
decisions, but must take account of the relevant local authority strategies   80

The RDA has independent environment and sustainability policy powers
for a defined range of economic development purposes (as UDC model)   100

Table A2   New Deal policy issues

Issue 1: Length of time in the Gateway

Up to four month period in Gateway and then enter one of four options   0

As above, but guidance given to some clients requiring additional costs
and/or training to advisors or specialist providers   30

Up to four month period and then enter options, but flexibility for
special clients of extra one/two months before sanctions imposed   60

Time in Gateway flexible, dependent on particular client' needs.
Sanctions optional   100

Issue 2: Proportion of jobs subsidized and extent of public or private employer involvement

No more than 45% of jobs should be subsidized in any ES district.
No clear ratio of public/private supply established   0

As above, but it is recognised that in some areas both types of employers
need more encouragement through greater publicity   30

As above, but because of extreme difficulties in local labour markets the
public sector needs to offer a substantial proportion of total places and the
overall proportion of subsidised places should be at least 50%   100

Issue 3: Size of subsidy to employer wage and training costs

The subsidy for subsidised jobs needs to be increased and additional training
costs, specialist advice and costs should be assigned to the Gateway   0

The wage subsidy for subsidised jobs is appropriate at £60 plus £750 for
training, but Gateway costs should be increased   40

The existing subsidy at £60 for wages and £750 training costs is appropriate   50

The payment of £60 for wages and £750 for training should be reduced to
remove competition with other schemes, or the subsidy for other schemes
should be increased   100

Issue 4: Partnership and contracting structure

The national ES should be the primary contract decision maker for suppliers
of New Deal   0

The national ES in cooperation with the ES District manager makes all
strategic and contract decisions   10

The national ES makes all contract decisions with large employers, but the
ES District Manager handles all other contracts   20

The national ES makes decisions only for large employer contracts. The ES
District manager makes all other contracts but in consultation with the
main local partners   50

As above, but with the ES District Manager the chief decisions maker,
within the context of local partnership plans: 'strategic partnerships' 70

As above, but delivery is placed under the responsibility of a partnership
for the ES district, which can include the ES as the contractor: 'delivery
partnerships'   95

As above, but the local partnership also includes all large employer contracts 100

Issue 5: Flexibility of contracts

The contracting process should be similar to the process of commercial
competitive tendering   0

As above, but the ES should provide specialised advice (i.e. workshops,
interviews) to encourage applicants from smaller private sector and/or
voluntary sector providers   10

The contracting process should have a more flexible timetable to enable
providers to prepare a proposal and to identify potential extra/hidden costs
before the contract is signed   20

As above, but where the potential for partnership does emerge, the
contracting process should be flexible enough to cater for this   30

Potential applicants from smaller, particularly, voluntary sector providers
should be able to access sufficient funds to enable them to prepare their
proposal and/or to develop consortia with other agents for the provision of
New Deal services   70

In addition to capacity building funds there should be some safeguards
(financial or otherwise) to insure smaller voluntary/community sector
providers against financial risk of non-take-up   100

Table A3   TEC policy issues

Issues 1: Breadth of responsibility for training, enterprise and LED policy

TECs should be confined to unemployment Training (YT, ET) plus role in vocational education   0

All of the above plus support for training through Investors in People (IiP)   15

All of the above plus business advice/enterprise role   40

All of the above plus LED role (catalyst role)   50

All of the above plus LED specific budget from the DfEE   70

All of the above plus LED specific budget funded through transfer of funds from other government departments   100

Issue 2: Scale of TEC budget for publicly financed training and vocational education

All finance for unemployment programmes goes to FE colleges, no TEC budget   0

TECs get DfEE unemployment training budget only   25

All of above plus Careers Service   30

All of above plus mandated joint planning with FE colleges   50

All of above plus FE budget hold back to TECs of 25% allocated in collaboration with LEA's   60

All of above, plus FE budget hold back to TECs of 25% with TEC autonomy of allocation   100

Issue 3: Targets for training programmes

TECs targets are completely focused on unemployed. No employed persons are targeted   0

All of above, except range of 5–10% of budget for employed persons training   20

All of above, with main emphasis on unemployed training, plus modern apprenticeships and adult IiP   50

TEC contracts support broad range of training programmes which unemployed may participate in. However, the unemployed have no special status/access or guarantee of entitlement   100

Issue 4: Number of areas

49–50 TEC areas	0
Approximately 80 TEC areas	40
More than 100 TEC areas	70
More than 100 TEC areas (with a TEC in every local authority which has education responsibilities)	100

Issue 5: Flexibility of use of funds

Funding blocks are based on Treasury and Parliamentary budgetary lines. There is no virement allowed and audits follow all programmes to the final recipient, through the TEC	0
All of above, but initiatives fund (flexible) and flexible use of surpluses	20
All of above, but with limited virement (5–10% budget is flexible)	40
More general virement across all programmes within corporate plan and programme targets (license model)	60
lock grant with general performance targets (single audit stopping at level of TEC)	100

Table A4   LLSC policy issues

Issue 1: LLSCs: versus RDA with respect to training policy

The DfEE continues to allocate funding separately, with interdepartmental coordination via GOR	0
The DfEE allocates funding via GOR to LLSC, taking account of RDA strategy	10
As above, but LLSC has to take account of the RDA strategy (e.g. skills agenda), which is monitored by the RDA	20
As above, but also the RDA has responsibility for a Development Fund	30
RDA has full executive responsibility for funding allocations (e.g. allocation to LLSCs in region) with ability to vire within training budgets	50
RDA has full executive responsibility for funding allocations with ability to vire across policy programmes	75

RDA has full responsibility for training and the LLSC specific autonomy is
abolished   100

Issue 2: LLSCs versus RDA with respect to LED policy

The DfEE continues to allocate funding separately, with interdepartmental
coordination via GOR   0

The DfEE allocates funding via GOR to LLSC, taking into account the
relevant RDA strategy   10

As above, but LLSC has to take account of the RDA strategy for LED,
which is monitored by the RDA   20

As above, but also the RDA has responsibility for a Development Fund   30

RDA has full executive responsibility for funding allocations (e.g. allocation
to LLSCs in region) with ability to vire within LED budgets   50

RDA has full executive responsibility for funding allocations with ability
to vire across policy programmes   75

RDA has full responsibility for LED policy and LLSC autonomy is
abolished   100

Issue 3: LLSCs versus RDA with respect to enterprise policy, including Business Link

The DTI to allocate funding separately to Business Link, with interdepartmental coordination via GOR   0

The DTI and DfEE allocate funding separately via LLSCs to Business Link,
taking account of the RDA strategy   10

As above, but LLSC has to take account of the RDA strategy, which is
monitored by the RDA   20

As above, but also the RDA has responsibility for a Development Fund   30

RDA has full executive responsibility for funding allocations with ability
to vire within enterprise policy block   50

RDA has full executive responsibility for funding allocations including
ability to vire across policy programmes   75

RDA has full responsibility for enterprise policy, with its own local
structure   100

Issue 4: Scale/scope of LLSC budget for publicly financed training and vocational education

LLSCs have an enlarged budget responsibility for work-based training (taking FE or ES budget)	0
LLSCs maintain the TEC budget and responsibility for work-based training	30
LLSCs lose some budget and responsibility for work-based training	50
LLSCs lose most elements of work-based training budget to FE/ES	75
LLSCs lose all elements of work-based training budget to FE/ES	100

Issue 5: Targets for unemployment training programmes

As TEC Issue 3

Issue 6: Scale/scope of LLSC budget for publicly financed training and vocational education

As TEC Issue 4

Issue 7: Flexibility of use of funds

As TEC Issue 4

Issue 8: TECs and Chambers merge: the future for CCTEs

All TECs merge with Chambers of Commerce so that LLSC system is a structure of CCTEs	100
Most TECs merge with Chambers of Commerce but separate TECs and Chambers remain in a few areas	80
TECs, and hence LLSCs, and Chambers of Commerce are separate entities	0

Table A5   SBS and Business Link policy issues

Issue 1: The finance of Business Link Personal Business Advisors (PBAs)

The government pays all costs	100
The government pays about 90% of costs, the rest paid through client fees	85
The government pays about 80% of costs, the rest paid through client fees	75
The government pays about 70% of costs, the rest paid through client fees	65
The Ggovernment pays about 50% of costs, the rest paid through client fees	50
The government pays less than 50% of the costs	35
All costs are self-financed by partners and fees	25
All costs are self-financed through client fees	0

Issue 2: The finance of Business Links as a whole (excluding PBA services)

The government pay for all costs	100
The government pays about 90% of costs, the rest paid through client fees	85
The government pays about 80% of costs, the rest paid through client fees	75
The government pays about 70% of costs, the rest paid through client fees	65
The government pays about 50% of costs, the rest paid through client fees	50
The government pays less than 50% of costs	35
All costs are self-financed by partners and fees	25
All costs are self-financed through client fees	0

Issue 3: The maximum range of a Personal Business Advisor Services

The role of the PBA is to signpost /refer the client to more specialist advice	0
The PBA should offer a short diagnostic service, and then refer the client to specialists	15
The PBA should offer a longer diagnostic service, perhaps involving a site visit, and then refer to specialists	40
The PBA should offer a comprehensive service, lasting up to one week where a total business plan is assessed and other consultants may be used	75

The role of the PBA should be to provide an 'in-house' solution to the
majority of the client problems   100

Issue 4: Target firms for Business Link services

Only growth oriented businesses of between 10 and 200 employees.
All other firms signposted   0

All growth oriented firms of between 10 and 200 employees. Other firms
signposted   10

All firms, of between 10 and 200 employees. All other firms signposted   20

All firms, of between 10 and 200 employees, but a *short* diagnostic service
available for *start-up firms*. Other firms signposted   50

All firms, from small start-ups firms to 200 employees firms, with a *substantial*
diagnostic service available for start-ups. Other types of firms signposted   100

Issue 5: The organisation of Local Business Link partnerships

Business Links are independent companies with partners providing only a
Steering Committee   0

A partnership structure contracts for Business Link   30

Business Link is a subsidiary of the TEC/LLSC   50

The local Chamber of Commerce contracts as a merged body with Business
Link   65

The local Chamber of Commerce, the TEC and Business Link contracts as a
merged body, with Business Link as a subsidiary   75

The local Chamber of Commerce, the TEC and Business Link contracts as a
merged body   100

Issue 6: How the Business Link brand name should be applied at the local level

The Business Link is an additional brand, used flexibly by partners in
different configurations in different areas   0

A joint branding approach (e.g. 'Chamber of Commerce and Business Link') 30

A single brand name used to identify *all* Business Link financed services   75

A single brand name used for all *main* partner servicers   100

Issue 7: How Business Link outlets should be organised at the local level

Sub-regional groups of Business Link hubs in about 40–50 areas   0

Business Link hub offices in 75 areas (same as TECs)   30

Business Link offices should widely spread as hubs, satellites and access points, resulting in about 200 plus Business Link outlets   100

Bibliography

Aghiou, P. and Howitt, P. (1998), *Endogenous Growth Theory*, MIT Press, Cambridge, Mass.

Alden, J. and Morgan, R. (1974), *Regional Planning: A comprehensive view*, L. Hill, Leighton Buzzard.

Aldrich, H.E. (1976), 'Resource Dependence and Interorganizational Relations: Relations between local employment service offices and social service sector organizations', *Administration and Society*, 7, 419–54.

Aldrich, H. and Whetten, S. (1981), 'Organisation Sets, Action Sets and Networks: Making the most of simplicity', pp. 385–408 in P.C. Nystrom and W.H. Starbuck (eds), *Handbook of Organisational Design, Vol. 1 Adapting Organisations to Their Environments*, Oxford University Press, Oxford.

Anderson, P. and Mann, N. (1997), *Safety First: The making of New Labour*, Granta Books, London.

Atkinson, M.M. and Coleman, W.D. (1992), 'Policy Networks, Policy Communities and the Problems of Governance', *Governance: An International Journal of Policy and Administration*, 5(2), 154–80.

Audit Commission (1989), *Urban Regeneration and Economic Development: The local government dimension*, Audit Commission, London.

Audit Commission (1990), *Urban Regeneration and Economic Development: Audit guide*, Audit Commission, London.

Audit Commission (1999), *A Life's Work: Local authorities, economic development and economic regeneration*, Audit Commission, London.

Audretsch, D.B. (1989), *The Market and the State: Government policy towards business in Europe, Japan and theUnited States*, Harvester Wheatsheaf, London.

Banham, G. (1992), 'Taking Forward the Skills Revolution', *Policy Studies* 13(1), 5–12.

Bank of England (1994), *Finance for Small Firms, First Report*, London.

Bannock, G. (1989), *Government and Small Business*, Paul Chapman, London.

BCC (1997), *Making Local and Regional Economies Work: A report on England's regions*, British Chambers of Commerce, London.

BCC (1998), *Skills for Competitiveness: A report on skills for business,* Alex Lowrie for British Chambers of Commerce, London.

Beaumont, G. (1995), *Review of 100 NVQs and SVQs*, a report submitted to the Department for Education and Employment, London.

Becker, G.S. (1983), 'A Theory of Competition Among Pressure Groups', *Quarterly Journal of Economics*, 98, 372–99.

Bennett, R.J. (1979), *Spatial Time Series: Analysis, forecasting and control*, Pion, London.

Bennett, R.J. (1994), *Enterprise Agencies: A survey of organization and services*, Research Paper, Department of Geography, London School of Economics.

Bennett, R.J. (1995), 'The Refocussing of Small Business Services in Enterprise Agencies: The influence of TECs and LECs', *International Journal of Small Businesses*,

Bennett, R.J. (1996), 'Can Transaction Cost Economics Explain Voluntary Chambers of Commerce?', *Journal of Institutional and Theoretical Economics*.

Bennett, R.J. (1997), 'The Relation Between Government and Business Associations in Britain: An evaluation of recent developments', *Policy Studies*, 18(1), 5–33.

Bennett, R.J. (1998a), 'Business Associations and their Potential to Contribute to Economic Development: Re-exploring an interface between the state and market', *Environment and Planning A*, 30, 1367–87.

Bennett, R.J. (1998b), 'Business Associations and their Potential Contribution to the Competitiveness of SMEs', *Entrepreneurship and Regional Development*, 10, 243–60.

Bennett, R.J. (1998c), 'Explaining the Membership of Voluntary Local Business Associations: The example of British Chambers of Commerce', *Regional Studies*, 32, 503–14.

Bennett, R.J. (1998d), *Survey of ITOs and NTOs*, Department of Geography, University of Cambridge.

Bennett, R.J. (1999), 'Business Routes of Influence in Brussels: Explaining the choice of direct representation', *Political Studies*, 67, 240–57.

Bennett, R.J. and Krebs, G. (1991), *Local economic development: public-private partnerships initiatives in Britain and Germany*, Belhaven, London.

Bennett, R.J. and L.G.A. (1998), *Survey of Local Economic Development (LED), Activity in Local Government*, Department of Geography, University of Cambridge. Shortened version in *Journal of the Institution of Economic Development*, 062, March 1999, 1–3.

Bennett, R.J. and McCoshan, A. (1993), *Enterprise and Human Resource Development: Local capacity building*, Paul Chapman Publishing, London.

Bennett, R.J. and TEC National Council (1998), *Survey of Local Economic Development Activity in TECs and LECs*, Department of Geography, University of Cambridge, summary version published by TEC National Council.

Bennett, R.J. and Robson, P.J.A. (1999), 'Business Link: Use, satisfaction and comparison with Business Shop and Business Connect', *Policy Studies*, 20(2), 107–31.

Bennett, R.J., Wicks, P. and McCoshan, A. (1994), *Local Empowerment and Business Services*, UCL Press Limited, London.

Benson, J.K. (1975), 'The Interorganizational Network as a Political Economy', *Administrative Science Quarterly*, 20, 229–49.

Benson, J.K. (1982), 'A Framework for Policy Analysis', pp. 137–76 in D.L. Rogers and D.A. Whitten (eds), *Interorganisational coordination: theory, research and implementation*, Iowa State University Press, America.

Best, M. (1990), *The New Competition: Institutions of industrial restructuring*, Polity Press, Cambridge.

Blank, S. (1978), *Industry and Government in Britain: The Federation of British Industries and Politics 1945–65*, Saxon House, Farnborough.

British Printing Industry Federation (BPIF), (1997), *A Strategy to Promote Effective Working Relationships between the Business Links and the British Printing Industries Federation*, London.

Bueno de Mesquita, B., Newman, D. and Rabushka, A. (1985), *Forecasting political events: the future of Hong Kong*, Yale University Press, New Haven, Conn.

Bueno de Mesquita, B. and Stokman, F.N.N. (eds) (1994), *European Community Decision Making. Models, Applications and Comparisons*, Yale University Press, London.

Bueno de Mesquita, B. (1994), 'Political Forecasting: An expected utility method', pp. 71–104 in B. Bueno de Mesquita and F.N.N. Stokman (eds), *European Community Decision Making. Models, Applications and Comparisons*, Yale University Press, New Haven.

Burt, R.S. (1980), 'On the Functional Form of Corporate Cooption', *Social Science Research*, 9, 146–77.

Casson, M. (1997), *Information and Organization: A new perspective on the theory of the firm*, Clarendon Press, Oxford.

Cawson, A. (ed.) (1985), *Organized Interests and the State*, Sage, London.

CBI (1997a), *Regions for Business: Improving policy design and delivery*, Confederation of British Industry, London.

CBI (1997b), *Regional Development Agencies – Issues for Discussion. CBI Response to DETR Paper*, Confederation of British Industry, London.

Coleman, J. (1990), *Foundations of Social Theory*, Belknap Press, Harvard University Press, Cambridge, Mass.

Coleman, W.D. (1988), *Business and Politics: A study of collective action*, McGill-Queen's University Press, Kingston and Montreal.

Committee on Trusts (1918), *Report*, Parliamentary Papers Cd 9236, HMSO, London.

Convery, P. (1997), 'The New Deal gets real', *Working Brief*, October, pp. 7–14.

Cook, K.S. (1977), 'Exchange and Power in Networks of Interorganizational Relations', *Sociological Quarterly*, 18, 62–82.

Crafts, N.R.F. (1997), 'Economic History and Endogenous Growth', pp. 43–78 in D.M. Kreps and K.F. Wallis (eds), *Advances in Economics and Econometrics: Theory and applications*, Vol. II, Cambridge University Press, Cambridge.

Crozier, M. and Friedberg, E. (1977), *L'acteur et le Système*, Edition du Seuil, Paris.

Davis, Sir Peter (1997), 'Providing a Windfall for the Jobless: Sir Peter Davis explains the task ahead for welfare-to-work', *Financial Times*, 6 June.

Davis, Sir Peter (1998), *New Deal: Importance for Business*, text of presentation to Conference for Trade Associations, DTI, London, 26 March, 1998.

DE (1988), *Employment in the 1990s*, Cm 540 Department of Employment, London.

DE (1989), *Training and Enterprise Councils: A prospectus for the 1990s*, Department of Employment, Training Agency, Sheffield.

DE (1992), *People, Jobs and Opportunity*, Cm 1810, HMSO, London.

DETR (1997), *Building Partnerships for Prosperity: Sustainable growth, competitiveness and employment in the English regions*, Department of Environment Transport and the Regions, Cm 3814, HMSO, London.

DETR (1998), *Evaluation of the Single Regeneration Challenge Fund Budget, A partnership for regeneration: An interim evaluation*, Department of Environment, Transport and the Regions.

DETR (1999), *Supplementary Guidance to Regional Development Agencies*, Department of Environment Transport and the Regions, London.

Devlin Committee (1972), *Report of the Commission of Inquiry into Industrial and Commercial Representation*, ABCC/CBI, London.

DfEE (1995), *Efficiency Scrutiny: The TEC contract and management fee*, Department for Education and Employment, London.

DfEE (1999a), *Learning to Succeed: A new framework for post-16 learning*, Cm 4392, Department for Education and Employment, London.

DfEE (1999b), *The Learning and Skills Council Prospectus: Learning to succeed*, Department for Education and Employment, London.

DiMaggio, P.J. and Powell, W.W. (1990), *The New Institutionalism in Organizational Analysis*, University of Chicago Press, Chicago.

Donnelly, C., Nimmo, M. and Convery, P. (1998), *The New Deal Handbook*, Unemployment Unit and Youth Aid, London.

Downs, A. (1957), *An Economic Theory of Democracy*, Harper and Row, New York.

DSS/DfEE (1998), *A New Contract for Welfare: The gateway to work*, Cm 4102, Department for Education and Employment, Department of Social Security, HMSO, London.

DTI (1992), *A Prospectus for One-Stop Shops for Business*, Department of Trade and Industry, London.

DTI (1995), *Business Links Service Manual*, Department of Trade and Industry, London.

DTI (1996), *Evaluation of DTI Funded TEC services*, Report by PA Cambridge, Department of Trade and Industry, London.

DTI (1998), *Our Competitive Future: Building the knowledge driven economy*, Competitiveness White Paper, Department of Trade and Industry, London.

DTI (1999a), *The Small Business Service: A public consultation*, URN 99/815, Department of Trade and Industry, London.

DTI (2000), *Guidance for Proposals to Deliver Local Services on Behalf of the Small Business Service*, Department of Trade and Industry, London.

Dunford, M. (1990), 'The Aims of Regulation', *Environment and Planning D: Society and Space*, 8, 297–332.

Ebers, M. (ed.) (1997), *The Formation of Inter-organizational Networks*, Oxford University Press, Oxford.

Elkin, S. (1985), 'Twentieth Century Urban Regimes', *Journal of Urban Affairs*, 7(2), 11–28.

FEFC (1997), *The FEFC's Response to the Department of Environment's consultation on Regional Development Agencies*, Further Education Funding Council, London.

Finn, D. (1997), 'Labour's New Deal for the Unemployed: Making it work locally', *Local Economy*, November, 247–58.

Fletcher, D.R. (1999), 'Ex-offenders and the Labour Market: A review of the discourse of social exclusion and consequences for crime and the New Deal', *Environment and Planning C: Government and Policy,* 17, 431–41.

FPB (1997), *The Fundamental Flaws in Business Links,* Forum of Private Business, Cheshire.

Galaskiewicz, J. (1979), *Exchange Networks and Community Politics*, Sage, London.

Gibbs, D. (1998), 'Regional Development Agencies and Sustainable Development', *Regional Studies*, 32 (4), 365–68.

Goddard, J.B. and Chatterton, P. (1999), 'Regional Development Agencies and the Knowledge Economy: Harnessing the potential of universities', *Environment and Planning C: Government and Policy*, 17, 685–700.

Goldthorpe, J.H. (ed.) (1984), *Order and Conflict in Contemporary Capitalism*, Oxford University Press, Oxford.

Goodin, R.E. (ed.) (1996), *The Theory of Institutional Design*, Cambridge University Press, Cambridge.

Gould, P. (1998), *The Unfinished Revolution. How the modernisers saved the Labour Party*, Abacus, London.

Granovetter, M. (1985), 'Economic Action of Social Structure: The problem of embeddedness', *American Journal of Sociology*, 91(3), 481–510.

Grant, W. (1993), *Business and Politics in Britain,* 2nd edn, Macmillan, London.

Grant W. (2000), *Pressure Groups*, Cambridge University Press, Cambridge.

Grant, W. and Marsh, D., (1977), *The Confederation of British Industry*, Hodder and Stoughton, London.

Grayson, D. (1995), 'Business links no myth', letter to *Financial Times*, 22 March.

Grayson, D. (1996), 'Building a Network for Business Cooperation', in *Financial Times,* Mastering Enterprise, reprinted in S. Birley and D.F. Muzylea (eds), *Mastering Enterprise,* F.T. Pitman, London, pp. 131–5.

Greenwood, J. (1997), *Representing Interests in the European Union*, Macmillan, London.

Greenwood, J., Grote, J. and Ronit, K. (eds) (1992), *Organised Interests and the European Community*, Sage, London.

Griffiths, J. (1999), 'A New Deal for Employers?', *Working Brief,* 104, May, 18–19.

Grote, J.R. (1997), *Interorganisational Networks and Social Capital Formation in the South of the South*, European University Institute, RSC 97/38, Florence.

Hales, J. and Collins, D. (1999), 'New Deal for Young People: Leavers with unknown destinations', *Labour Market Trends,* November, 605–6.

Hall, S. and Nevin, B. (1999), 'Continuity and Change: A review of English regeneration policy in the 1990s', *Regional Studies*, 35, 477–82.

Hanf, K.H. and Sharpf, F.W. (eds) (1978), *Interorganisational Policy Making: Limits to coordination and central control*, Sage, London.

Harding, A., Wilks-Heeg, S. and Hutchins, M. (1999), 'Regional Development Agencies and English Regionalisation: The question of accountability', *Environment and Planning C: Government and Policy*, 17, 669–84.

Heclo, H. (1978), 'Issue Networks and the Executive Establishment', pp. 87–124 in A. King (ed.), *The New American Political System*, American Enterprise Institute, Washington DC.

Heinelt, H. and Smith, R. (1996), *Policy Networks and European Structural Funds*, Avebury, Aldershot.

Heseltine, M. (1989), *The Challenge of Europe*, Weidenfeld and Nicholson, London.

Heseltine, M. (1992a), 'Forging Partnerships for World Class Support', *TEC Director*, No. 15, Sept./Oct. 1992, pp. 8–9.

Heseltine, M. (1992b), *Text of Speech to TEC's Conference*, 10 July.

Heseltine, M. (1993), *Speech on Trade Associations*, CBI, 17 June, Department of Trade and Industry, London.

Hilferding, R. (1910), *Finance Capital*, Routledge and Kegan Paul, London (1981 English edn).

HoC (1996a), *Business Links*, House of Commons, Trade and Industry Committee, Fifth Report, Session 1995–96, HC302, HMSO, London.

HoC (1996b), *First Special Report. Government's Response to the First Report from the Employment Committee, Session 1995–96: The Work of the TECs,* London: HMSO.

HoC (1996c), *The Work of TECs*, House of Commons, Employment Committee, First Report, Session, 1995–96, HC 99, HMSO, London.

HoC (1997), *Regional Development Agencies*, House of Commons Environment, Transport and Regional Affairs Committee, First Report, Session 1997–98, HC 415, HMSO, London.

HoC (1998a), *The Relationship between TECs and the Proposed Regional Development Agencies*, House of Commons Education and Employment Committee, Session 1997–98, Fourth Report, HC 265, HMSO London.

HoC (1998b), *The New Deal/The New Deal Pathfinders*, House of Commons Education and Employment Committee, Eighth Report, Session 1997–98, HC 263–III, HMSO, London.

HoC (1998c), *Government's Response to the Fourth Report of the Committee: The relationship between TECs and the proposed Regional Development Agencies,*

House of Commons Education and Employment Committee, Session 1997–98, Fourth Report, HC 752, HMSO London.

HoC (1998d), *Government's Response to the Eighth Report: The New Deal Pathfinders*, House of Commons Education and Employment Committee, Session 1997–98, HC 1123, HMSO, London.

HoC (1999a), *The Performance and Future Role of the Employment Service*, HC 197, House of Commons Education and Employment Committee, session 1998–99, Seventh Report, The Statutory Office, London.

HoC (1999b), *The ONE Service Pilots*, HC412, House of Commons Education and Employment Committee, Session 1998–99, Sixth Report, The Statutory Office, London.

Hogarth, T., Hasluck, C., Pitcher, J., Shackleton, R. and Briscoe, G. (1998), *Employers' Net Costs of Training to NVQ level 2*, Report RP57, Department for Education and Employment, London.

Hollingsworth, J.R. and Boyer, R. (eds) (1997), *Contemporary Capitalism: The embeddedness of institutions*, Cambridge University Press, Cambridge.

Hughes, J.T. (1998), 'The Role of Development Agencies in Regional Policy: An academic and practitioner approach', *Urban Studies*, 35(4), 615–26.

IoD (1996), *Your Business Matters: Report from the regional conferences*, Institute of Directors, London, on behalf of IoD, CBI, BCC, TNC, FSB and FPB.

Kanter R.M. (1995), *World Class: Thriving locally in the global economy*, Simon and Schuster, New York.

Kantor, P., Savitch, H, and Haddock, S.V. (1997), 'The Political Economy of Urban Regimes: A comparative perspective', *Urban Affairs Review*, 32(3), 348–77.

Katzenstein, P.J. (1978), 'Conclusion: Domestic structures and strategies of foreign economic policy', in P.J. Katzenstein (ed.), *Between Power and Plenty*, London.

Knoke, D. (1983), 'Organisation Sponsorship and Influence Representation of Social Influence Associations', *Social Forces*, 61, 1065–87.

Koenig, T. and Pappi, F. (1993), *Political Decisions and Private–Public Influences in Policy Domain Networks: Or access model for the analysis of collective decisions in the American and German Labour Policy domain*, paper presented at International Sunbelt Conference, Tampa, Florida.

KPMG (1997), *Interim Report on New Deal Partnerships within Pathfinder Districts*, KPMG, London.

Kreps, D. (1990), *A Course in Microeconomic Theory*, Princeton University Press, Princeton, New Jersey.

Labour Party (1995), *A Choice for England*, Consultation Paper, Labour Party, London.

Labour Party (1996), *Getting Welfare to Work: A new vision for social security*, Labour Party, London.

Laumann, E.O. and Knoke, D. (1987), *The Organizational State: Social change in national policy domains*, University of Wisconsin Press, Madison.

Laumann, E.O. and Pappi, F.U. (1976), *Networks of Collective Action: A perspective on community influence systems*, Academic Press, New York.

Layard, R. (1998), 'Personal View: Will the New Deal Work?', *Financial Times*, 8 January.

Layard, R. and Nickell, S. (1987), 'The Labour Market', pp. 131–79 in R. Dornbusch and R. Layard (eds), *The Performance of the British Economy*, Oxford University Press, Oxford.

Lehmbruch, L. (1984), 'Concertation and the Structure of Corporatist Networks', pp. 60–80 in J.H. Goldthorpe (ed.), *Order and Conflict in Contemporary Capitalism*, Clarendon Press, Oxford.

Lindberg, L.N., Campbell, J.L. and Hollingsworth, J.R. (1991), 'Economic Governance and the Analysis of Structural Change in the American Economy', in J.L. Campbell, J.R. Hollingsworth, and Lindberg, L.N. (eds), *Governance of the American Economy*, Cambridge University Press, Cambridge.

Lindenberg, S. (1990), 'Homo Socio-economicus: The emergence of a general model of man in the social sciences', *Journal of Institutional and Theoretical Economics*, 146, 727–48.

Lively, J. (1978), 'Pluralism and Consensus', in P. Birnbaum, J. Lively and G. Parry (eds), *Democracy, Consensus and Social Contract*, Sage, London.

Marin, B. (1987), *Contracting Without Contracts: Economic policy concertation by autopoietic regimes beyond law?*, European University Institute, WP87/278, Florence.

Marin, B. and Mayntz, R., (eds) (1991), *Policy Networks: Empirical evidence and theoretical considerations*, Campus, Frankfurt am Main.

Mawson, J. (1997), 'New Labour and the English Regions: A missed opportunity?', *Local Economy*, November, 194–203.

Mawson, J. and Hall, S. (2000), 'Joining it up Locally? Area regeneration and holistic government in England', *Regional Studies*, 34, 67–74.

McKinsey Global Institute (1998), *Driving Productivity Growth in the UK Economy*, McKinsey and Co., London.

Middlemas, K. (1983), *Industry, Unions and Government: Twenty one years of NEDC*, Macmillan, London.

Middlemas, K. (1990), *Power, Competition and the State, Vol 1 Britain in Search of Balance 1940–61; Vol 2 Threats to Postwar Settlement in Britain 1961–74; Vol 3 The End of the Postwar Era: Britain since 1974*, Macmillan, London.

Miller, J. (1980), 'Access to Interorganizational Networks as a Professional Resource', *American Sociological Review*, 45, 474–96.

Mills, C.W. (1956), *The Power Elite*, Oxford University Press, London.

Mills, L. and Young, K. (1986), 'Local Authorities and Economic Development: A preliminary analysis', in V.A. Hauser (ed.), *Critical issues in Urban Economic Development*, Clarendon Press, Oxford.

Mincer, J. (ed.) (1969), *Economic Forecasts and Expectation: Analyses of forecasting behaviour and performance*, National Bureau of Economic Research, New York.

Mintz, B. and Schwartz, M. (1985), *The Power Structure of American Businesses*, University of Chicago Press, Chicago.

Mizruchi, M.S. (1982), *The American Corporate Network, 1904–1974*, Sage, London.

Mizruchi, M.S. and Galaskiewicz, J. (1994), 'Networks of Interorganizational Relations', in S. Wasserman and J. Galaskiewicz (eds), *Advances in Social Network Analysis*, Sage, London.

Mizruchi, M.S., Mariolis, P., Schwartz, M. and Mintz, B. (1986), 'Techniques for Disaggregating Centrality Scores in Social Networks', pp. 26–48 in N.B. Tuma (ed.), *Sociological Methodology*, American Sociological Association, Washington DC.

Mokken, R.J. and Stokman, F.N.N. (1976), 'Power and Influence as Political Phenomena', in B. Barry (ed.), *Power and Political Theory. Some European Perspectives*, John Wiley, London.

Mokyr, J. (1990), *The Lever of Riches, Technological Creativity and Economic Progress*, Oxford University Press, Oxford.

Mokyr, J. (1992), 'Is Economic Change Optimal?', *Australian Historical Review*, 32, 3–23.

Morgan, K. (1999), 'England's Unstable Equilibrium: The challenge of RDAs', *Environment and Planning C: Government and Policy,* 17, 663–8.

MORI (1996), *Business Links: Baseline tracking study. Business advice among small and medium-sized enterprises and the Business Link campaign – wave 4*, MORI, London.

Murdoch, J. and Tewdwr-Jones, M. (1999), 'Planning and the English Regions: Conflict and convergence amongst the institutions of regional governance', *Environment and Planning C: Government and Policy,* 17, 715–30.

Murphy, P. and Caborn, R. (1995), 'Regional Government for England: An economic imperative', pp. 184–221 in S. Tindale (ed.), *The State and the Nations: The politics of devolution*, Institute for Public Policy Research, London.

NCRS (1999), *New Deal Monitoring*, National Centre for Social Research, London, for the Employment Services.

NDD (1997), *Design of the New Deal for 18–24 Year Olds*, Department of Education and Employment London, October.

NDD2 (1998), *New Deal for Long-term Unemployed People Aged 25 Plus*, Department of Education and Employment, London.

NDL (1998), *What is New Deal for Young People?*, NDL6, Employment Service, London.

NDL1 (1998), *New Deal for Employers,* Employment Service, London.

NDTF (1999), *Jobs Retention and the New Deal: Recommendations*, New Deal Task Force, Department of Education and Employment, London.

Nelson, R. and Winter, S.G. (1982), *An Evolutionary Theory of Economic Change,* Harvard University Press, Cambridge, Mass.

Nickell, S.J., Nicolitsas, D. and Dryden, N. (1997), 'What Makes Firms Perform Well?', *European Economic Review*, 41, (3–5), 783–96.

North of England Assembly (1995), *Regional Government: Consultation Paper*, North of England Assembly of Local Authorities.

North of England Assembly (1996), *Regional Government for the North of England: Prospectus*, North of England Assembly of Local Authorities.

North, D.C. (1990), *Institutions, Institutional Change and Economic Performance*, Cambridge University Press, Cambridge.

Offee, C. (ed.) (1985), *Disorganized Capitalism*, Polity Press, Cambridge.

Offee, C. (1996), *Modernity and the State*, Polity Press, Cambridge.

Offee, C. and Wissenthal, H. (1985), 'Two Logics of Collective Action', in C. Offee (ed.), *Disorganized Capitalism*, Polity Press, Cambridge.

PACEC (1998), *Business Links – Value for Money Evaluation: Final Report*, Public and Corporate Economic Consultants, Cambridge.

Payne, D. (1999), *Policy Making in the European Union: An analysis of the impact of the reform of the structural funds in Ireland*, Interuniversity Centre for Social Science Theory and Methodology, Groningen, The Netherlands.

Payne, D., Mokken, R. and Stokman, F.N.N. (1997), 'European Union Power of Regional Involvement: A case study of the political implications of the reform of structural funds for Ireland', *Aussenwirtschaft*, 52, 2/3.

Peck, J. (1999), 'New Labourers? Making a New Deal for the "workless class"', *Environment and Planning C: Government and Policy*, 17, 345–72.

Peck, J. and Tickell, A. (1992), 'Local Modes of Social Regulation? Regulation Theory, Thatcherism and Uneven Development', *Geoforum*, 23, 347–63.

Pelzman, S. (1976), 'Toward a More General Theory of Regulation', *Journal of Law and Economics*, 19, 211–40.

PEP (1957), *Industrial Trade Associations: Activities and organization*, Political and Economic Planning, London.

Pfeffer, J., and Salancik, G.R. (1978), *The External Control of Organizations: A resource dependence perspective*, Harper and Row, London.

Pierce, R. (1994), 'Introduction: Fresh perspectives on a developing institution', pp. 1–14 in B. Bueno de Mesquita and F.N.N. Stokman (eds), *European Community Decision Making. Models, Applications and Comparisons*, Yale University Press, New Haven.

Porter, M.E. (1990), *The Competitive Advantage of Nations*, Macmillan, London.

Porter, M.E. (1998), *On Competition*, Harvard Business Review Press, Cambridge, Mass.

Posner (1976), *Antitrust Law: An economic perspective*, University of Chicago Press, Chicago.

Priest, S.P. (1998), *Stimulating the Performance of SMEs through Business Link: An assessment of customer satisfaction, dissatisfaction and complaining behaviour*, unpublished PhD, University of Cambridge.

Priest, S.P. (1999), 'Business Link SME Services: Targeting, innovation and charging', *Environment and Planning C: Government and Policy*, 17, 177–94.

Ramsdale, P. and Capon, S. (1986), *Small Factories and Economic Development*, Gower, Aldershot.

Regional Policy Commission (1996), *Renewing the Regions: Strategies for Regional Economic Development*, Labour Party Report, Sheffield Hallam University.

Rhodes, R.A.W. (1986), *The National World of Local Government*, Allen and Unwin, London.

Rhodes, R.A.W. (1992), *Beyond Westminster and Whitehall*, 2nd edn, Routledge, London.

Richardson, J. and Jordon, G. (1979), *Governing under Pressure,* Martin Robertson, Oxford.

Roche, B. (1997), *Enhanced Business Links: A vision from the 21st Century*, Department of Trade and Industry, London.

Schmitter, P.C., and Lehmbruch, G. (eds) (1979), *Trends towards Corporatist Intermediation,* Sage, New York.

Sear, L. and Agar, J. (1996), 'Business Link and Personal Business Advisors: Selling services irrespective of client's needs?', *Proceedings,* 19th ISBA Conference, University of Central England Business School, Birmingham.

Scott, J. (1985), 'Theoretical Framework and Research Design', ch. 1, in F.N.N. Stokman, R. Ziegler and J. Scott (eds), *Networks of Corporate Power: A comparative analysis of ten countries*, Polity Press, Cambridge.

Scott, J.P. (1979), *Corporations, Classes and Capitalism,* Hutchinson, London.

Scott, J.P. (1987), 'Intercorporate Structures in Western Europe: A comparative historical analysis', pp. 208–32, in M.S. Mizruchi and M. Schwartz (eds), *Intercorporate Relations*, Cambridge University Press, London.

SCPR (1999), *The New Deal for Young Unemployed People: A good deal for employers?*, Social and Community Planning Research, for Employment Service, London ESR6.

Sellgren, J. (1987), 'Local Economic Development and LocalInitiatives in the Mid-1980s: An analysis of the Local Economic Development Information Service', *Local Government Studies*, 13, 6, 51–68.

Sellgren, J. (1989), *Local Economic Development in Great Britain: An evolving local government role*, unpublished PhD, London, School of Economics.

Selznick, P. (1949), *TVA and the Grass Roots*, Harper and Row, New York.

STF (1998), *Towards a National Skills Agenda*, First Report, Skills Task Force, Sheffield.

STF (1999), *Delivering Skills for All*, Second Report, Skills Task Force, Sheffield.

Stigler, G.J. (1971), 'The Theory of Economic Regulation', *Bell Journal of Economics and Mangement Science* 2, 3–21.

Stokman, F.N.N. (1995), 'Modelling Conflict and Exchange in Collective Decision Making', *Bulletin de Methodologie Sociologie* No. 49, pp. 7–22.

Stokman, F.N.N. and Van den Bos, J.M.M. (1992), 'A Two-Stage Model of Policy Making with an Empirical Test in the U.S. Energy Policy Domain', in G. Moore and J.A. Whitt (eds), *The Political Consequences of Social Networks. Research in Politics and Society*, Vol. 4, JAI Press, Greenwich, Conn.

Stokman, F.N.N. and Van Oosten, R. (1994), 'The Exchange of Voting Positions: An Object-Oriented Model of Policy Networks', pp. 105-130 in B. Bueno de Mesquita and F.N.N. Stokman (eds), *European Community Decision Making. Models, Applications and Comparisons*, Yale University Press, New Haven.

Stokman, F.N.N. and Stokman, J. (1995), 'Strategic Control and Interests, its Wffects on Decision Outcomes', *Journal of Mathematical Sociology*, Vol. 20 (4), 289–317.

Stokman, F.N.N. Ziegler, R. and Scott, J. (eds) (1985), *Networks of Corporate Power: A comparative analysis of ten countries*, Polity Press, Cambridge.

Stone, C. and Sanders H. (eds) (1987), *The Politics of Urban Development*, University of Kansas Press, Lawrence.

Stratton, C.N. (1989), 'TECs and PICs: The key issues which lie ahead', *Regional Studies,* 24, 70–4.

Sweezy, P.M. (1939), 'Interest Groups in the American Economy', in P.M. Sweezy (ed.), *The Present as History*, Monthly Review Press, New York.

Tann, J. and Lafaret, S. (1998), 'Assessing Consultant Quality for SMEs – The Role of Business Links', *Journal of Small Business and Enterprise Development*, 5(1), 7–18.

TEC National Council (1997a), *Memorandum to the Employment Sub Committee from the TEC National Council. RDAs: The mplications for TECs,* TEC National Council, London.

TEC National Council (1997b), *Regional Development Principles*, TEC National Council, London.

Theil, H. (1966), *Applied Economic Forecasting,* North Holland, Amsterdam.

Treasury (1998), *Comprehensive Spending Review: Public Service Agreements 1999-2002*, Cm 4181, Chief Secretary to the Treasury, London.

Truman, D. (1951), *The Governmental Process*, Knopf, New York.

TSC (1999), *First Report*, Training Standards Council, Sheffield.

Walsh, K., Atkinson, J. and Barry, J. (1999), *The New Deal Gateway: A labour market assessment*, Employment Service, Report ESR24, Sheffield.

Williamson, O.E. (1985), *The Economic Institutions of Capitalism,* Free Press, New York.

Wright, M. (1988), 'Policy Community, Policy Network and Comparative Industrial Policies', *Political Studies*, 36, 593–612.

Zeitlin, M. (1974), 'Corporate Ownership and Control: The large corporation and the capitalist class', *American Journal of Sociology*, 79, 1073–119.

Zald, M.N. (ed.) (1970), *Power in Organisations*, Vanderbilt University Press, Nashville, Tenn.

Index

287